Psychology FOR AS-LEVEL

Student Workbook

Hugh Hillyard-Parker
Mike Cardwell

An imprint of
HarperCollinsPublishers

Contents >> Psychology for AS-level: Student Workbook

Introduction

USING THE BOOK

This book is designed to be used alongside *Psychology for AS-level Third Edition*, by Cardwell, Clark and Meldrum, published by Collins. That book – which we refer to throughout this workbook as 'the textbook' – provides a detailed coverage of all aspects of the AS psychology course offered by the Assessment and Qualifications Alliance (AQA), Specification A.

This workbook will help you prepare for the AS examination by providing a wealth of additional resources:

- structured activities to help with understanding, note-taking and summarizing the large volume of information in the textbook
- sheets to help with planning your work and revising – see 'Keeping track' below and on p. iv
- hundreds of example exam questions
- example worked answers to AO1+AO2-type exam questions
- detailed guidance on answering all types of exam questions.

How this workbook relates to the textbook

This workbook is divided into seven units, each corresponding to the unit in the textbook with same number. There is no workbook unit relating to Unit 8 of the textbook ('Preparing for the AS examination'); this is because the whole of this workbook is about preparing for the AS exam. However, you will often be asked to look at parts of Unit 8 as you work through the seven main units.

Key features

- Like the textbook, each unit is divided into *topics*. Each topic covers a distinct part of the AQA (A) specification.
- A *Preview* at the start of each unit enables you to check quickly the topics covered and the pages of the textbook you'll need to use.
- The *Introduction* at the start of each unit includes a diagram showing where the unit fits into the AS qualification.
- *Understanding the specification* at the start of each topic provides an extract from the AQA specification and a related activity with feedback. These will help you really get to grips with what the AQA (A) expects of you. More advice about understanding the specification is given on p. iv.
- A *topic map* gives you a visual picture of the content of each topic.
- *Keeping track* is a table that enables you to assess your progress in each topic. See p. iv for guidance on using this feature.
- *Activities*, within each topic, are designed to help you understand and absorb all the information in the workbook. Some activities are simple question-and-answer type exercises, but many of them will help you with note-taking and summarizing of key points. This will be very useful both for initial understanding and later revision.

  For most of the activities, space is left for you to write your answers in the book. Sometimes, though, you will be asked to use separate paper. Where relevant, *answers to activities* are included at the end of each topic.
- Each topic contains dozens of *example examination questions* to give you a clear idea of the kinds of questions you can expect in the exam. This includes all types of exam questions:

- AO1-type (including APFCC questions – see below)
- AO1+AO2-type
- AO3-type (as found in Research Methods questions).

- For the AO1+AO2-type questions, there is at least one *sample answer* per topic, with commentary, showing you clearly how to tackle these kinds of questions. You will also find *one for you to try ...*, together with advice on tackling the question.
- The *Check your understanding* section at the end of each topic corresponds to the feature of the same name in the textbook. This workbook provides feedback to the questions in the textbook.
- *Hints* are scattered through the topics, explaining difficult terms or giving useful bits of exam advice.

Keeping track

Planning and progress-checking are important parts of work. The *Keeping track* feature is designed to help you with these aspects of your work:

- In the 'Where is it?' column, you note down the relevant page numbers of the textbook.
- When you have finished your work on the topic, go through the checklist and tick the appropriate column according to how well you have mastered the subject matter. This will highlight any areas you need to go back over or do more work on.
- Alternatively (or in addition), use the checklist as a revision guide, ticking the final column only when you have revised the topic and are sure that you are completely on top of the subject matter.

Understanding the specification

A summary of the requirements of the AQA (A) specification is included in the textbook – see the Introduction pp. vii–viii and Unit 8 pp. 247–50.

Words are used quite precisely in the specification and it is important to understand what they tell you.

- Where you see the word '*including*' in the specification, it means that questions can be set specifically on the items mentioned. For example, the paragraph on Stress includes the following: 'The body's response to stressors, including the General Adaptation Syndrome (Selye)'. This means that there could be an exam question asking you to define, describe or criticize the General Adaptation Syndrome (see, for example, p. 60 of this book).
- Where items are preceded by '*e.g.*', that means those items are only examples of appropriate subject matter. Exam questions *cannot* ask you specifically about those items.
- Wherever you see the word '*research*', it means that there may be questions asking specifically about research studies in that area. These can be tested by a particular type of AO1 question: the APFCC question (standing for Aim, Procedures, Findings, Conclusions, Criticisms). Typically, such questions ask you to describe any two of these aspects of the research (e.g. Aims and Conclusions, Findings and Criticisms). See, for example, the questions in the panel on p. 6 of this book.

  Wherever the specification mentions 'research', you will find a 'Key study' in the textbook describing all five aspects (APFCC) of the research. In this workbook, there is an activity relating to every Key study designed to help you memorize all the relevant details. On the inside back cover is a complete list of Key studies showing the relevant page numbers of the textbook and this workbook.

Do, please, let us know what you think of the book. Feedback from users is enormously helpful and we shall pay close attention to it when we come to update this *Student Workbook*.

Hugh Hillyard-Parker, Mike Cardwell

AQA address

AQA
Stag Hill House
Guildford
GU2 5XJ
www.aqa.org.uk

1

HUMAN Memory

PREVIEW

There are three topics in this unit. You should read them alongside the following pages in the Collins *Psychology for AS-level* textbook:

INTRODUCTION

This unit covers the AS Cognitive Psychology part of Module 1 (AQA Specification A). The diagram below shows where it fits in to the overall AS qualification.

Read the Preview and Introduction on p. 2 of the textbook now. This will give you an overview of what's in the unit.

Where this unit fits in to the AS qualification

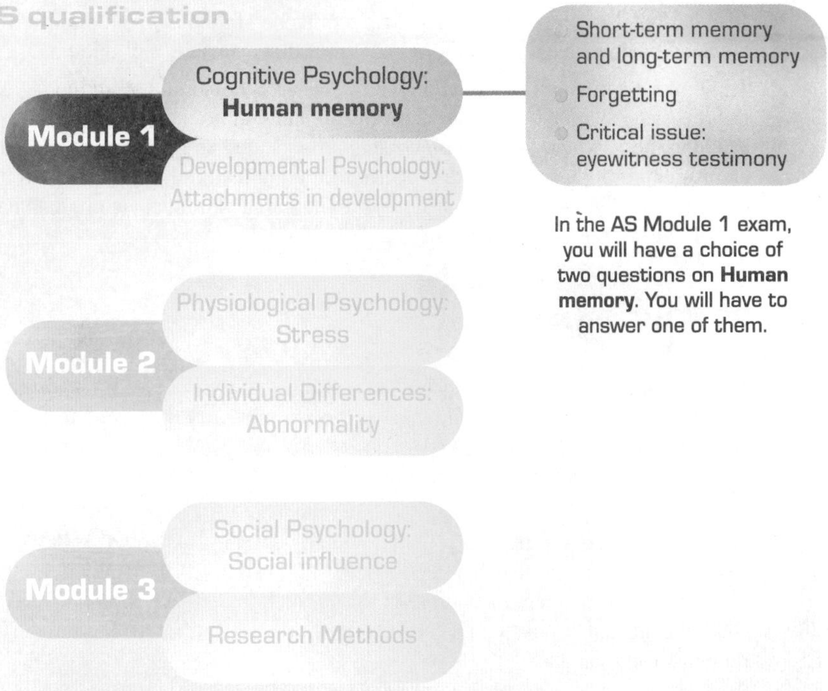

Module 1
- Cognitive Psychology: **Human memory**
  - Short-term memory and long-term memory
  - Forgetting
  - Critical issue: eyewitness testimony
- Developmental Psychology: Attachments in development

Module 2
- Physiological Psychology: Stress
- Individual Differences: Abnormality

Module 3
- Social Psychology: Social influence
- Research Methods

In the AS Module 1 exam, you will have a choice of two questions on **Human memory**. You will have to answer one of them.

Topic 1 >> Short-term and long-term memory

In this topic, we look at the structure of memory and the way that it is divided into short-term memory (STM) and long-term memory (LTM) stores. STM and LTM differ in three important ways – encoding (how the material is stored), capacity (how much data can be held in the store) and duration (how long the memory lasts).

We also investigate some important models of memory, i.e. explanations of how memory works.

UNDERSTANDING THE SPECIFICATION

Here is what the AQA (A) specification says about this topic. It forms part of AS Module 1, Cognitive and Developmental Psychology.

Read it and then try the activity on the right. You'll find answers to the activity on p. 11.

Human memory

a. Short-term memory and long-term memory

Research into the nature and structure of memory, including encoding, capacity and duration of short-term memory (STM) and long-term memory (LTM). The multi-store model of memory (Atkinson & Shiffrin) and at least one alternative to this (e.g. working memory: Baddeley & Hitch, levels of processing: Craik & Lockhart).

ACTIVITY

Understanding the specification

1 What is compulsory and what are examples? *Clue*: Look for the key words 'including' and 'e.g.' (see Introduction, p. iv).

-
-

2 Does this bit of the specification involve Key studies (APFCCs)? *Clue*: Look for the word 'research'.

-

You should be able to define the terms 'short-term memory' and 'long-term memory', and to describe (and evaluate) research that explores each of types of memory. You are also required to distinguish between these memory stores in terms of encoding, capacity and duration.

Three models of memory are named in the specification: multi-store model, working memory and levels of processing, although only one of these (the multi-store model) is specified, i.e. is 'compulsory'. Working memory and levels of processing are included as examples of alternative models. You can choose either of these as your alternative to the multi-store model. For each one you must be able to describe it and demonstrate your understanding of it; you must also be familiar with appropriate research evidence as well as criticisms of the model.

TOPIC MAP

The diagram at the top of p. 3 gives you a visual 'map' of the content of this topic. Seeing the content laid out like this will give you an overview of what you are about to study.

Seeing it as a picture (or 'visually encoding' the information – see p. 8 of the textbook!) should also help you to remember the key aspects. That's very relevant here as one of the things you'll be studying in this topic is how we remember information.

ACTIVITY

Topic map

Look through pp. 3–19 of the textbook to see where the items shown in the topic map are covered. Note down the relevant page numbers in the spaces left on the topic map. For example, sensory memory is covered on p. 5 (that has already been written in).

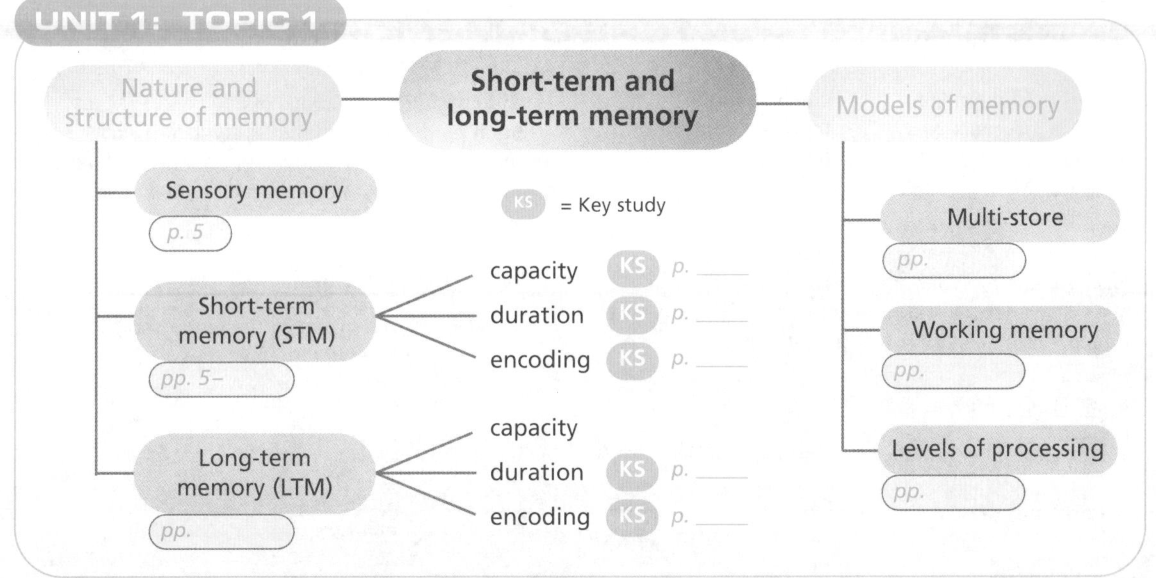

KEEPING TRACK

Use the table below to keep track of your work on this topic and plan your revision. See p. iv (Introduction) for guidance on filling it in.

What I need to learn		Tick if you ...		
Nature and structure of memory	Where is it?	could make a basic attempt	could make a good attempt	have complete mastery of this
Definition of 'short-term memory' (STM)				
Definition of 'long-term memory' (LTM)				
Definition of 'capacity'				
Factors affecting capacity in STM and LTM				
Definition of 'duration'				
Factors affecting duration in STM and LTM				
Description of 'encoding'				
Factors affecting encoding in STM and LTM				
Description of the differences between STM and LTM				
Description of research into aspects of STM and LTM				
Evaluation of research into aspects of STM and LTM				
Description of APFCC for a Key study of duration in STM				
Description of APFCC for a Key study of duration in LTM				
Description of APFCC for a Key study of capacity in STM				
Description of APFCC for a Key study of encoding in STM				
Description of APFCC for a Key study of encoding in LTM				
Models of memory				
Description of the multi-store model of memory				
Précis of the multi-store model of memory				
Evaluation of the multi-store model of memory				
Description of the working memory model				
Précis of the working memory model of memory				
Evaluation of the working memory model				
Description of the levels of processing model of memory				
Précis of the levels of processing model of memory				
Evaluation of the levels of processing model of memory				

NATURE AND STRUCTURE OF MEMORY

Memory is the storing of information over time. It involves the processes of registering information, storing it and retrieving it when needed.

Pages 5 to 12 of the textbook look at the assumption that there are different types of memory – that memory is divided into different structures. The first of these is sensory memory (covered briefly on p. 5), but most space is given to short-term memory (STM) (pp. 5–10) and long-term memory (LTM) (pp. 10–12).

STM, LTM and the differences between them

In the exam you may be asked to explain STM and/or LTM, or to summarize the differences between them (see example questions on the right).

Definitions and explanations of STM and LTM are given on pp. 5 and 10 of the textbook. For such questions, you can structure your answers by referring to the three factors of capacity, duration and encoding.

AO1 questions

- Explain what is meant by the terms 'short-term memory' and 'long-term memory'. (3 + 3 marks)
- Give three differences between STM and LTM.* (2 + 2 + 2 marks)

**Sample answers to this question are discussed on p. 251 of the textbook.*

ACTIVITY

Differences between STM and LTM

Read pages 5 to 12 of the textbook. Draw up a table listing the main differences between STM and LTM in terms of the following three factors: capacity, duration and encoding.

	STM	LTM
Capacity	• 7 ± 1 chunks	• unlimited.
Duration	• 30 seconds	• unlimited.
Encoding	• auditory	• semantical.

Check your answers by looking at Answer 2 to part (a) on p. 251 of the textbook. The table above gives you the information you need to answer AO1-type questions about capacity, duration and encoding (see panel below).

Factors influencing capacity, duration and encoding in STM and LTM

The exam may have questions that focus on capacity, duration and encoding, such as those in the panel on the right. They may refer to either STM or LTM, to both, or to neither.

It will be useful to memorize a summary of the key factors influencing capacity, duration and encoding. The activity on p. 5 will help you to do this.

AO1 questions

- What is meant by the terms 'capacity', 'duration' and 'encoding'? (2 + 2 + 2 marks)
- Outline two factors that influence the capacity of memory in STM. (3 + 3 marks)
- Outline two factors that influence the duration of memory in LTM. (3 + 3 marks)
- Describe findings of research into capacity in STM. (6 marks)
- Describe conclusions of research into duration in STM. (6 marks)

ACTIVITY

Factors affecting capacity, duration and encoding

Complete the table below to summarize the key factors affecting capacity, duration and encoding in both STM and LTM. These factors are discussed in the workbook on pp. 6–11. Against each factor write in what effect it can have (e.g. does it increase or decrease capacity?), and when or why it might have that effect. We have filled in a few of the spaces to get you started.

Factor	What effect does it have?	When or why does it have this effect?
Capacity of STM		
Long-term memory	Can increase capacity	When information is repeated, e.g. digit strings
Reading aloud	may lead to storage	After rehearsal.
Rhythmic grouping	may lead to storage	When trying to remember phone numbers easier to remember + rehearse.
Pronunciation time	English speakers have greater digit span than Arabic speakers	Shorter words easier to remember.
Duration of STM		
Rehearsal	lead to storage for 30s.	info is repeated, so can be remembered longer.
Deliberate intention to recall	longer storage	remembered as it is needed in future.
Amount of info to be retained	7±2 chunks, so more info can be remembered.	easier in chunks than individual digits.
Encoding in STM		
Sound of words		
Other ways of encoding		
Capacity of LTM		
Upper limit	none.	there is no limit.
Duration of LTM		
Childhood amnesia		
How duration is measured		
Thorough learning		
Encoding in LTM		
How material can be represented		

Key studies: capacity, duration and encoding in STM and LTM

Look again at the Topic map on p. 3. The 'KS' symbol shows which parts of this topic involve key research studies. There are five Key studies in this topic. It looks as if there ought to be six, but you can see there is no Key study for 'capacity in LTM'. Do the activity on the right to understand the reason behind this.

The panel below right shows some typical questions you might be asked about the Key studies. One of the hardest tasks in your AS psychology is to learn all the information in the Key studies – and then recall the relevant bits in the exam. One way of doing this is by creating easy-to-remember summaries, as in the example below. It has been filled in with short, memorable summaries of the information in the Key study on p. 7 of the textbook. For example, under 'Procedures', we use the trigger phrases 'XYZ – 9,6,3 – 3,6,9' to summarize three key procedures:

- **XYZ** – is a trigram of consonants, such as participants were shown (note, it's better to say XYZ than ABC, which contains a vowel)
- **9,6,3** – refers to the counting backwards in threes that participants were asked to do, so as to stop them rehearsing the trigram
- **3,6,9** – refers to the increasing intervals of time before participants were asked to recall the trigram.

Then, under 'Findings', **3 = 80%, 18 = 10%** briefly describes the findings, also summarized below.

So, in a few short prompts, you have the essential information about the main aspects of the Key study.

ACTIVITY

Key studies

Why do you think there is no Key study for capacity in LTM? *Clue:* Read 'Capacity of long-term memory' at the bottom of p. 10 of the textbook.

-

Compare your answer with the explanation on p. 11.

AO1 questions (APFCC-type)

Key study questions ask for **any two** of the aims, procedures, findings, conclusions and criticisms of a study, such as in the examples below:

- Describe the aims and procedures of one study investigating encoding in STM/LTM. (6 marks)
- Describe the findings and conclusions of one study investigating capacity in STM. (6 marks)
- Describe the procedures and findings of one study of duration in LTM. (6 marks)
- Describe the aims and conclusions of one study of LTM. (6 marks)
- Describe the findings and give one criticism of one study of duration in STM. (6 marks)

KEY STUDY textbook p. 7

Subject	DURATION OF STM
Researchers	Peterson and Peterson (1959)
Title	Trigram test – preventing rehearsal
Aims	To test how long STM lasts when rehearsal is prevented

Procedures

XYZ – Ps shown consonant trigrams.
9,6,3 – Ps count backwards in 3s (delaying task).
3,6,9 – Ps recall trigrams after X secs (gaps increase)
Test repeated with different trigrams.

Findings 3 = 80%, 18 = 10%

After 3 seconds, 80% of trigrams were recalled.
After 18 seconds, only 10% were recalled.
Longer interval = fewer trigrams recalled.

Conclusions

1 Info. vanishes rapidly from STM if rehearsal is prevented.
2 Decay is important in forgetting from STM.

Criticisms +

1 Showed cause-and-effect link between duration and rehearsal.
2 Developed technique used by other researchers (Brown-Peterson technique).

Criticisms –

1 Trigrams are artificial – not real life, hence poor ecological validity (see textbook p. 175).
2 Effect of interference – earlier trigrams may interfere with later ones (see textbook p. 21).

ACTIVITY

KEY STUDIES: Short-term memory

Write your own summaries of the Key studies on pp. 6 and 9 of the textbook, using trigger phrases, mnemonics or whatever will help you to memorize the important details. Under 'Criticisms' use the + and – columns to separate those arguments that support the study's conclusions from those that disagree with them. Don't forget to include the points mentioned in the 'AO2 checks' at the end of each study.

KEY STUDY textbook p. 6

Subject CAPACITY OF STM

Researchers Baddeley et al. (1975)

Title Immediate memory span, short words, long words

Aims to find out if length of words affects immediate memory span.

Procedures long + short words used in lists. asked to recall lists.

Findings short words easier to remember.

Conclusions smaller chunks easier to remember.

Criticisms + is supported by millers 7 magic no.

Criticisms – random words not realistic in everyday use.

KEY STUDY textbook p. 9

Subject ENCODING IN STM

Researchers Conrad (1964)

Title Acoustic confusion – 6 consonants

Aims to find out if acoustically similar not dissimilar letters are recalled better.

Procedures

Findings

Conclusions

Criticisms +

Criticisms –

ACTIVITY

KEY STUDIES: Long-term memory

Write your own summaries of the Key studies on pp. 11 and 12 of the textbook, using trigger phrases, mnemonics or whatever will help you to memorize the important details. Under 'Criticisms' use the + and − columns to separate those arguments that support the study's conclusions from those that disagree with them.

KEY STUDY textbook p. 11

Subject DURATION OF LTM

Researchers Bahrick et al. (1975)

Title Very long-term memory (VLTM), yearbook tests

Aims

Procedures

Findings 90% of schoolmates remembered

Conclusions no limits on duration of LTM.

Criticisms +

Criticisms −

KEY STUDY textbook p. 12

Subject ENCODING IN STM and LTM

Researchers Baddeley (1966)

Title Acoustic and semantic coding in STM/LTM

Aims

Procedures

Findings

Conclusions

Criticisms +

Criticisms −

MODELS OF MEMORY

Models of memory attempt to explain either how information passes from STM to LTM, or why it is that some information is retained for only a short time, while other information is remembered for a lifetime.

Pages 13–18 of the textbook look at three models:

- the multi-store model, pp. 13–14, 18
- the working memory model, pp. 15–16, 18
- levels of processing, pp. 16–17.

ACTIVITY

Models of memory

Using a separate sheet of A4 paper, draw up a table summarizing the key features of each of the three models of memory discussed in the textbook. Use the column headings shown in the tables below.

The questions and prompts will help you to fill in your tables. The relevant information for each model can be found in the textbook on the pages listed above. These tables should provide you with plenty of material to tackle AO1 questions such as those in the panel at the top of p. 10.

Multi-store model

Key feature	Arguments/evidence in favour	Arguments/evidence against
• How many memory stores are there? • How does information enter LTM from (a) sensory memory (b) STM? • How long can information stay in (a) sensory memory (b) STM? • How can information be lost at each of the various stages? • What role does rehearsal play in the process?	• How does research into people with brain damage support the model? • What evidence is provided by laboratory studies, such as that of Glanzer and Cunitz (1966)?	Use the following trigger terms to summarize possible weaknesses of this model: • simple vs complex • amounts of information vs types of information • structures vs processes • unitary stores vs multi-component stores.

Working memory model

Key feature	Arguments/evidence in favour	Arguments/evidence against
• According to the model, what are the three main components of STM? • What roles does the central executive play? • What are the main 'slave systems' and how do they work?	• What is main advantage of this model over the multi-store model? (*Clue*: look at what you wrote in the table above.) • Which studies have supported the existence of slave systems?	• Which elements of the model have not been investigated in depth? • What aspect of the central executive is the main weakness of the model?

Levels of processing model

Key feature	Arguments/evidence in favour	Arguments/evidence against
• Does this model focus on structures or processing? • What types of processing are involved, according to the model? • What happens to material that is processed in these different ways?	• Which aspects of the model have been welcomed by researchers in the field? • What studies have supported the model's basic assumptions?	• In what way is the model built on a 'circular argument'? • Where does the notion of processing effort fit into the model? • And what about other factors such as elaboration and distinctiveness?

AO1 questions

- Describe the main features of the multi-store model. (6 marks)
- Outline the main features of the multi-store model and one other model of memory. (3 + 3 marks)
- Give two criticisms of the multi-store model of memory. (3 + 3 marks)

AO1 + AO2 QUESTIONS ON MODELS OF SHORT-TERM AND LONG-TERM MEMORY

AO1+AO2 questions

- To what extent does research evidence support the view that short-term and long-term memory are separate stores? (18 marks)
- Give a brief account of, and evaluate, the multi-store model of memory.* (18 marks)
- Outline and evaluate **one** alternative model to the multi-store model of memory. (18 marks)

**Sample answers to this question are discussed on p. 252 of the textbook.*

Take the first of the questions above. As with all other AO1+AO2 questions, there is clear value in planning your response carefully before putting pen to paper. There are some simple guidelines for answering this question:

1. You have 18 minutes to select, plan and execute your response to this part of the question. You can expect to write about 300 words in that time (see p. 29 of the textbook).
2. This can be divided into three paragraphs, each of approximately 100 words in length. The first of these could be your AO1 content, a précised *description* of research findings that demonstrate differences in terms of encoding, capacity and duration between STM and LTM.
3. The second and third paragraphs could be your AO2 content, which might include *conclusions* that might be drawn from these studies concerning differences between STM and LTM, *criticisms* of the studies that would be relevant to the distinction between STM and LTM and any other relevant *commentary* that is more than just description.

   Answer 2 on p. 252 of the textbook is divided into three paragraphs in just this way: one of description and two of evaluation.
4. Remember that in order to make something work as AO2, it needs to be *used* as part of a sustained critical argument. This means you have to do more than just making an initial link to justify long descriptions instead of real evaluation (see p. 57 of the textbook for advice on this).
5. When deciding on appropriate content for your response – **Think**: Does it *inform* your response to the question set? Don't adopt a blunderbuss approach (firing in everything you know in a hope that some of it may be relevant) when answering these questions.

In the Expert interview on p. 18 of the textbook, Philip Beaman gives his clear assessment of value of two of the models discussed. It therefore provides some excellent material for tackling AO1+AO2-type questions.

ACTIVITY

Expert interview

Carry out the activity on p. 17 of the textbook, noting your answers in the space below. Compare your answers with the ones shown on p. 11.

Think too about how you might use this information in the AO2 ('evaluation') parts of exam questions.

1

2

3

ACTIVITY

One for you to try ...

Outline and evaluate one alternative model to the multi-store model of memory. (18 marks)

Try the question above, writing your answer on separate paper. Before you start writing, think about the following questions:

- How would you break down your response?
- What would be your AO1 and what your AO2?
- What would go in each of the three paragraphs?
- How would you ensure that your AO2 really was AO2?

CHECK YOUR UNDERSTANDING

When you have finished working through this topic, try the questions in 'Check your understanding' on p. 19 of the textbook. When you have written your answers, check them by looking at the relevant parts of the textbook or this workbook, listed below.

1. explanation of STM, textbook p. 5; definition of LTM, textbook p. 10
2. differences in capacity, duration and encoding – see workbook p. 4
3. textbook p. 5 (bottom) to p. 6 (top)
4. textbook pp. 7–8
5. textbook p. 7. See also this workbook p. 6 (remember the trigger XYZ – 9,6,3 – 3,6,9; 3 = 80%, 18 = 10%)
6. textbook pp. 8 and 12
7. textbook p. 11 – what triggers have you come up with to help you remember the key aspects of this study?
8. textbook pp. 15–16 (see Fig. 1.3); see also this workbook, p. 9 (your answer to the activity)
9. textbook pp. 16–17
10. explanation of multi-store model, textbook p. 13; evaluation of model, pp. 13–14, 18

ANSWERS TO ACTIVITIES

Understanding the specification, p. 2

1. The word 'including' tells you that you *have to* know about encoding, capacity and duration for *both* STM and LTM. In other words, there are six aspects of memory to know about here.

   The specification then lists three models of memory. One is compulsory – the multi-store model – and it is covered on pp. 13–14 of the textbook. The 'e.g.' tells you that the other two are given as examples only – in fact, the textbook covers both of them (pp. 15–17) and you can use either as an alternative to the multi-store model.
2. Yes, the specification mentions research into three aspects of STM (encoding, capacity and duration) and three aspects of LTM (encoding, capacity and duration). So, in theory you need to study six Key studies. In practice, you will only need to know about five – you will find out why when you do the activity at the top of p. 6.

Key studies, p. 6

If most psychologists agree that there is no upper limit to the LTM's capacity, it would be extremely hard to design a study that tested it. Since this research hasn't been done, there are no Key studies and so it is unlikely that you will be asked for one in the exam. In the unlikely event that you are asked for such a study, you could present a study on the *duration* of LTM because research that shows that duration is unlimited also suggests that capacity must be unlimited.

Expert interview, p. 10

1. The multi-store model suggests that information has to be rehearsed in STM before being passed to LTM. Some people cannot rehearse in STM, e.g. because of brain damage, but still have good longer-term memories. Also, we seem able to learn some information 'all in one go', without the need for rehearsal in STM.
2. Working memory acknowledges that memory is complex and suggests that memory works because it needs to be used, rather than just existing.
3. Remembering where you heard a voice or recalling touch pose a problem because they involve information that could be coded either in both the phonological loop or visuo-spatial sketchpad (e.g. the spatial location of a voice) or in neither (e.g. the memory of a touch).

Topic 2 >> Forgetting

As we know from experience, our memories can sometimes let us down. Cognitive psychologists are interested in the mechanisms involved in forgetting. In this topic, we shall look at the reasons why people sometimes fail to retrieve information. We look at explanations of forgetting in short-term and long-term memory. Because of the nature of the differences in STM and LTM, forgetting from these memory stores involves different processes. These explanations are decay and displacement (STM), and retrieval failure and interference (LTM). We will also be looking at how emotional factors influence forgetting (or not forgetting) of some types of material.

UNDERSTANDING THE SPECIFICATION

Here is what the AQA (A) specification says about this topic. It forms part of AS Module 1, Cognitive and Developmental Psychology.

Read it and then try the activity below. You'll find answers to the activity on p. 21.

Human memory

b. Forgetting

Explanations of forgetting in short-term memory (e.g. decay and displacement). Explanations of forgetting in long-term memory (e.g. retrieval failure and interference). Research into the role of emotional factors in forgetting, including flashbulb memories and repression (e.g. Freud).

ACTIVITY

Understanding the specification

1 What two factors are listed as examples of forgetting in short-term memory?
-
-

2 What two factors are listed as examples of forgetting in long-term memory?
-
-

3 Freud is mentioned as an example of what?
-

4 Which two emotional factors in forgetting do you have to study?
-
-

5 Does this topic involve Key studies (APFCCs)? If so, in what areas?
-

The specification requires you to cover two explanations of forgetting in STM and two in LTM. Examples of suitable explanations are given (and covered here), although others are also appropriate. You also need to be familiar with relevant research evidence supporting each of these explanations, and need to be able to offer criticisms (either positive or negative).

Emotion may enhance (flashbulb memory) or reduce (repression) recall of events. You should be able to define each of these and describe research appropriate to each. Although the specification does not *require* you to explain how flashbulb memory and repression work, this is a useful way of elaborating your understanding, and helps you construct a longer response to each if needed.

TOPIC MAP

The diagram on p. 13 gives you an overview of what you are about to study. If you commit this to your long-term memory, you will be less likely to forget it ...

ACTIVITY

Topic map

Look through pp. 20–9 of the textbook to see where the items shown in the topic map are covered. Note down the relevant page numbers in the spaces provided.

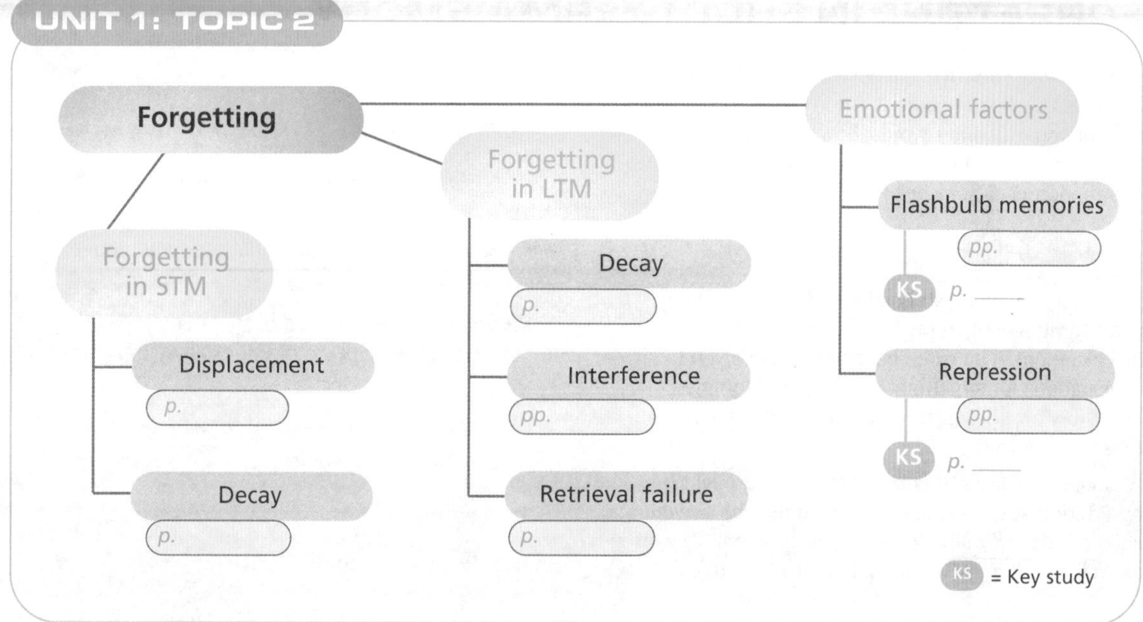

KEEPING TRACK

Use the table below to keep track of your work on this topic and plan your revision. See p. iv (Introduction) for guidance on filling it in.

What I need to learn	Where is it?	Tick if you ... could make a basic attempt	could make a good attempt	have complete mastery of this
Forgetting in short-term memory				
Definition of 'forgetting'				
Definition of 'displacement'				
Definition of 'decay'				
Explanation of the process of displacement from STM				
Explanation of the process of decay in STM				
Forgetting in long-term memory				
Definition of 'interference'				
Definition of 'retrieval failure'				
Explanation of the process of decay in LTM				
Explanation of the process of interference in LTM				
Explanation of the process of retrieval failure in LTM				
Role of emotional factors in forgetting				
Definition of 'flashbulb memory'				
Definition of 'repression'				
Description of research into the role of flashbulb memories				
Evaluation of research into the role of flashbulb memories				
Description of research into the role of repression				
Evaluation of research into the role of repression				
Description of APFCC for a Key study of flashbulb memories				
Description of APFCC for a Key study of repression				

FORGETTING IN SHORT-TERM MEMORY

To understand how the memory system works, it is important to look at some of the reasons why we lose information – in other words, how we forget. The way we forget seems to differ depending on whether the information is in STM or LTM.

Displacement and decay in STM

Pages 20–1 of the textbook look at forgetting in STM, concentrating on two processes: decay and displacement. If an exam question requires you to give explanations for forgetting in STM (see example questions on the right), you can base your answer on these two processes.

Although less likely, it *is* possible that you might be asked for just one explanation (for 6 marks), so you should have a 3-mark version of each (about 50 words) as well as a 6-mark version (about 100 words).

AO1 questions

- Outline two explanations of forgetting in STM. (3 + 3 marks)
- Explain two factors that influence forgetting in STM. (3 + 3 marks)
- Outline one explanation of forgetting in STM and give one criticism of this explanation. (3 + 3 marks)
- Describe one explanation of forgetting in STM. (6 marks)

ACTIVITY

Forgetting in STM

Read the text on displacement and decay in STM on pp. 20–1. Complete the following table summarizing these two processes, using the column heads shown below. In the 'Relevant research' column, jot down a summary of studies that investigated these processes – we have listed the relevant names to help you.

In the final column, note down your evaluation, i.e. points for and against the idea that the relevant process causes forgetting. For each +, write a sentence in favour of the process; for each –, write a sentence that describes an argument against the process. All the information you need is in the text!

Factor	Definition	Relevant research	Evaluation (criticism)
Displacement	see Key term, textbook p. 20	• **Miller (1956)**, Magic number 7: we can remember 7±2 'chunks' of information • **Waugh and Norman (1965)**, serial probe technique: 16 + probe + 1 digits Recall at start ✘, at end ✔	+ Waugh and Norman's findings support notion that items in STM get displaced – Hard to separate displacement from decay. Shallice (1967) found that decay was a factor, because faster presentation of items led to better recall, i.e. less time to decay
Decay	•	• **Hebb (1949)** • **Peterson and Peterson (1959)** • **Reitman (1974)**	+ – –

In the table on p. 14, we have again used shorthand 'triggers' to describe the research, such as '16 + probe + 1 digits' to describe the procedures in Waugh and Norman's research. This describes how participants were shown 16 digits, followed by one of the digits repeated (the probe); they then had to remember the digit that came after the probe in the original list (+1). You can devise your own triggers – the key is to find cues that will trigger your own memory.

EXAM HINT

Decay and interference

There isn't a separate heading 'Interference in STM', but much of the text on p. 21 discusses the possible effect of interference. It explains how hard it is to separate out the different factors of decay and interference. This is an important point to bring in when answering the AO2 part of exam questions, which may ask you to evaluate the factors that cause forgetting. The final paragraph on p. 21 of the textbook summarizes this quite neatly.

FORGETTING IN LONG-TERM MEMORY

Memories transferred to the long-term store are relatively stable and long lasting. However, that does not stop some of them being lost. There are various explanations for why this happens. The three most important are decay, interference and retrieval failure, covered on pp. 22–4 of the textbook.

Decay in LTM

Some psychologists have argued that, over time, material can be lost from LTM through lack of use. However, as the textbook describes, some types of knowledge and skills seem to be more prone to decay than others.

ACTIVITY

Decay in LTM

Read the text on decay in LTM on p. 22 and think about the different types of memories described and how prone to decay they are. Complete the following table to summarize the information. In the final column summarize relevant pieces of research – again, think of triggers or cues to help you memorize the key aspects of the research.

Type of activity	Knowledge/skills needed (e.g. motor/verbal skills)	Prone to decay or resistant to decay?	Relevant research (summarize)
Swimming **Riding a bicycle**	•	•	
Cardiac resuscitation	•	•	**McKenna and Glendon (1985)**
Remembering foreign vocabulary	•	•	**Bahrick and Phelps (1987)**

Using your own experience, think of more examples of each type of activity. For example, look at the following list of activities. Imagine you hadn't done any of them for several years. How easy would it be to remember how to:

- play a musical instrument
- recite lyrics of pop songs you learned years ago
- programme the timer on a piece of equipment you rarely use?

Interference in LTM

The research you summarized in the last activity suggests that decay cannot be the only factor in forgetting. The second factor that causes forgetting in LTM is interference, described on pp. 22–3 of the textbook. Here you will find descriptions of various studies showing that interference between memory traces can cause forgetting.

ACTIVITY

Interference in LTM

Use the table below to summarize the main points about interference in LTM. In particular, note the distinction between the two types of interference outlined on p. 23.

Again, use the final column note down your evaluation, i.e. points for and against the idea that interference causes forgetting. A + indicates a point in favour of the process; a – is for an argument against the process. We have included some hints to get you thinking, especially about the type of studies carried out and their relevance to everyday life.

Factor	Definition	Relevant research	Evaluation (criticism)
Interference	•	**Baddeley & Hitch (1977)**	+ Research results?
		McGeoch & MacDonald (1931)	+ Context of research?
Proactive interference	•	**'Paired associates' techniques**	+ Research results? – Context of research?
Retroactive interference	•	**Underwood (1957)**	+ Research results? – Context of research?

The terms 'retroactive' and 'proactive' can be confusing. Try to find a way of remembering what each means – for example:

- 'Retro' means 'back', so 'retroactive' means 'working backwards', i.e. new information works backwards to interfere with old information.
- 'Proactive' means 'working forwards', i.e. old information works forwards to interfere with new.

Studies into interference are often criticized for being artificial, i.e. carried out in laboratories using unrealistic tasks such as remembering nonsense syllables. Read the paragraphs under the heading 'External validity' on p. 227 of the textbook.

A second criticism comes from studies of retrieval failure, such as that of Tulving (1966).

ACTIVITY

Tulving's study of free recall

Read the panel describing Tulving's study on p. 23 of the textbook. Think about whether we forget because information isn't *available* or because it isn't *accessible*. In your own words, summarize how Tulving's study challenges interference theory.

- ______________________________

Retrieval failure in LTM

Interference theory suggests that information is not available, i.e. is lost. Retrieval failure theory suggests that information is available, but is sometimes not accessible. To make it accessible, we need cues to prompt remembering. Much of the research in this area has been into the types of cue that help us remember things best. Try the next activity now.

You should now have plenty of information to tackle exam questions on LTM, such as those shown on the right.

AO1 questions

- Describe one explanation of forgetting in LTM. (6 marks)
- Outline two explanations of forgetting in LTM.* (3 + 3 marks)
- Explain two factors that influence forgetting in LTM. (3 + 3 marks)
- Give two criticisms of an explanation for forgetting in LTM. (3 + 3 marks)
- Outline one explanation of forgetting in LTM and give one criticism of that explanation. (3 + 3 marks)

**Sample answers to this question are discussed on p. 251 of the textbook.*

ACTIVITY

Retrieval failure

Draw up a table to summarize the studies into retrieval failure and cues described on p. 24 of the textbook. Use the table headings below to organize the information. Include the studies that looked into the effect of context (where we are) and state (how we feel) on how we remember.

Research	Type of cue investigated	Findings	Conclusions

EMOTIONAL FACTORS IN FORGETTING

Cognitive theories focus on how we think, rather than how we feel, and often fail to take account of emotional factors. However, it seems likely that the way we feel has an impact on how well we remember things.

The AQA (A) specification mentions two types of emotional factor: flashbulb memories and repression.

Flashbulb memories

Flashbulb memories are memories of momentous events where heightened emotion seems to improve recollection. The events may be personal (e.g. the death of a close relative) or of worldwide interest (e.g. the September 11th terrorist attack on the World Trade Center in New York).

ACTIVITY

Flashbulb memories

1. Make a list of the key features of flashbulb memories (see textbook pp. 24–5).
2. Think of a personal event which might qualify as a flashbulb memory for you. Does it possess all the features you listed?
3. For this personal flashbulb memory, can you remember each of the six pieces of information listed near the bottom of p. 25, i.e. where you were when you heard about the event, what you were doing, etc.?

Much of the research into flashbulb memories has focused on whether they are special or not. Researchers fall into two camps:

- those that think flashbulb memories are special, i.e. the details are imprinted in the memory, and are accurate and detailed
- those that think they are no different from other types of memory, i.e. are subject to inaccuracy and forgetting.

ACTIVITY

Research into flashbulb memories

Draw up a list summarizing the main studies of flashbulb memories described in the textbook (pp. 25–7, including the Key study on p. 26). For each study, note down:

1. the name of the researcher(s)
2. the flashbulb memory investigated
3. the key findings of the research
4. whether the researcher argued for or against the idea that flashbulb memories are special
5. an evaluation of the research (points for and against it).

As with many areas of psychology, the evidence supporting the theory of repression is not conclusive. Some research supports the idea that repression causes forgetting; other researchers argue against it. The activity below will help you to evaluate the research.

ACTIVITY

Research into repression

1. Draw up two lists: one of research studies that support Freud's theory of repression, the other of research studies that challenge his theory.
2. For each study, note down:
   - the name of the researcher(s)
   - the nature of the event being 'repressed'
   - the key findings of the research
   - the conclusions drawn
   - an evaluation of the research (points for and against it).

You should now feel confident about tackling exam questions such as those below left.

AO1 questions

- Outline two factors that influence flashbulb memories. (3 + 3 marks)
- Outline findings of research into flashbulb memories. (6 marks)
- Outline conclusions of research into flashbulb memories. (6 marks)
- Outline two factors that influence repression. (3 + 3 marks)
- Outline findings of research into repression. (6 marks)
- Outline conclusions of research into repression. (6 marks)

EXAM HINT

Criticizing research into repression

In evaluating research into repression, the following criticisms are often raised:

- the difficulty of demonstrating repression in the laboratory
- the nature of evidence provided by case studies (anecdotal, often impossible to verify)
- ethical issues – if painful memories are repressed, is it right to start digging around and trying to unearth them?

These should be referred to in answers to AO1+ AO2-type questions, such as those on p. 20.

Repression

With flashbulb memories, the assumption is that heightened emotion improves memory. According to some psychologists, the opposite may also be true, that is that heightened emotion may *inhibit* memory. If memories are associated with negative emotions, anxiety or pain, we may force them from consciousness. This is termed 'repression' and was first described by Sigmund Freud.

Key studies: forgetting

Look again at the topic map on p. 13. It shows that you need to commit to memory at least two Key studies on emotional factors in forgetting, one on flashbulb memories and one on repression. This will enable you to answer questions such as those given in the panel at the top of p. 20.

Complete the following activity now.

ACTIVITY

KEY STUDIES: Emotional factors in forgetting

Write your own summaries of the Key studies on pp. 26 and 27 of the textbook, using trigger phrases, mnemonics or whatever will help you to memorize the important details. Under 'Criticisms' use the + and – columns to separate those arguments that support the study's conclusions from those that disagree with them.

KEY STUDY textbook p. 26

Subject FLASHBULB MEMORY

Researchers McCloskey et al. (1988)

Title

Aims

Procedures

Findings

Conclusions

Criticisms +

Criticisms –

KEY STUDY textbook p. 27

Subject REPRESSION

Researchers Levinger and Clark (1961)

Title

Aims

Procedures

Findings

Conclusions

Criticisms +

Criticisms –

AO1 questions (APFCC-type)

- Describe the procedures and findings of one study of flashbulb memory. (6 marks)
- Describe the aims and conclusions of one study of flashbulb memory. (6 marks)
- Describe the findings and conclusions of one study of repression. (6 marks)
- Describe the findings and give one criticism of one study of repression. (6 marks)
- Describe the aims and procedures of one study of emotional factors in forgetting. (6 marks)

AO1+AO2 QUESTIONS ON FORGETTING

Some AO1+AO2 questions have clearly indicated AO1 and AO2 content (as in the two middle questions in the panel on the right), whereas the division is less obvious in others (as in the 'to what extent' questions). Remember that all part (c) questions have the same 6+12 mark division for AO1+AO2 although this is not indicated in the question itself. What would you include as your AO1 material and your AO2 material for the first of the questions on the right?

The final question includes a quotation. These are usually intended to offer a potential route for your answer (and so are supposed to be helpful!). You do not have to address the quotation in your answer, and remember the golden rule – answer the question and not the quotation! The sample answer below shows how you could answer this question using material on pp. 27–8 of the textbook.

AO1+AO2 questions

- To what extent have flashbulb memories been shown to be accurate and reliable? (18 marks)
- Outline and evaluate research into flashbulb memories. (18 marks)
- Give a brief account of and evaluate the role of emotional factors in forgetting. (18 marks)
- "Laboratory studies have failed to provide clear-cut support for the repression hypothesis."

  To what extent can forgetting be explained through repression? (18 marks)

Sample answer

"Laboratory studies have failed to provide clear-cut support for the repression hypothesis." To what extent can forgetting be explained through repression? (18 marks)

Freud (1915) believed that repression was an unconscious process which ensured that threatening, or anxiety-provoking memories are kept from conscious awareness. Levinger and Clark (1961) compared the retrieval of associations to words that were emotionally charged with the retrieval of associations to neutral words. They found that participants took longer and had more difficulty recalling associations to the emotionally charged words, and that these words produced higher galvanic skin responses than neutral words. In a more natural setting, Williams (1992) found that 38% of abused African-American women had repressed memories of the abuse when tested some years after the event.

The results from the Levinger and Clark study appear to offer research support to Freud's claim that repression of anxiety-provoking responses causes forgetting. However, more recent evidence challenges these findings. Bradley and Baddeley (1990) ran a similar experiment but found that emotional associations were better recalled when participants were tested after 28 days. This suggests that emotionally charged words are better remembered, contrary to Freud's claim that they would be more difficult to remember. The results of the Williams study can also be criticized as it became clear that some of the apparently repressed memories were actually false memories.

Research into repressed memories is particularly controversial because memories of abuse that are 'recovered' in psychotherapy can lead to great distress and sometimes prosecution. Establishing the validity of these claims is extremely difficult as there is usually no independent objective evidence to corroborate the memories. Loftus (1997) casts further doubt on the accuracy of such recovered memories. Her research has established that even psychologically healthy individuals can alter their memories on the basis of false suggestions. Research in the laboratory on this phenomenon must also be interpreted cautiously as the experimental situation is frequently artificial and recognizably different from real-life situations.

There are two main types of material that can be used as the AO1 component of this answer. The first is the main principles of repression and the second a description of studies of forgetting through repression. Although there are other ways of structuring your response to this question, this example places all the AO1 material in the first paragraph.

If the first paragraph is all AO1, then the next two need to be all AO2 (to reflect the 6/18 mark split mentioned earlier). The second paragraph, therefore can be direct criticisms of the studies used above to demonstrate repression in action. This gives us more flexibility to introduce other forms of AO2 commentary for the third and final paragraph.

AN EYE ON THE EXAM

On p. 29 of the textbook is a very useful section on organizing your time in the exam. Read this section carefully. To understand it fully, you need to know that the AS qualification is structured into three modules, as shown in the diagram on p. 1. Each module is divided into two areas.

- For each main area of AS Psychology (Cognitive, Developmental, etc.), you have to answer just one question out of a choice of two. (The exception is Research methods, where you have to answer the one question given.)
- Each question is divided into three parts: (a), (b) and (c).
- Parts (a) and (b) test AO1 skills; part (c) tests both AO1 and AO2 skills.
- Each exam question is worth 30 marks, divided as follows:

(a) AO1 (6 marks)
(b) AO1 (6 marks)
(c) AO1+AO2 (18 marks)

- Part (c) questions always have an AO1 element (worth 6 marks) and an AO2 element (worth 12 marks).
- You'll need about 5 minutes to read the exam paper and plan your answers. This leaves you about 25 minutes' writing time. You should divide this up roughly as follows:

(a) AO1 5 minutes
(b) AO1 5 minutes
(c) AO1+AO2 15 minutes

- For part (c) questions, you should spend 5 minutes on the AO1 element and 10 minutes on the AO2 element.

CHECK YOUR UNDERSTANDING

When you have finished working through this topic, try the questions in 'Check your understanding' on p. 28 of the textbook. When you have written your answers, check them by looking at the relevant parts of the textbook or this workbook, listed below.

1 textbook p. 20
2 textbook pp. 20–1; workbook pp. 14–15
3 textbook p. 20
4 textbook p. 21
5 textbook p. 23; workbook p. 16
6 textbook p. 23; workbook pp. 16–17
7 textbook p. 24; workbook p. 17
8 textbook p. 24
9 textbook p. 27
10 textbook pp. 27–8; workbook pp. 18–20

ANSWERS TO ACTIVITIES

Understanding the specification, p. 12

1 Decay and displacement are given as examples of explanations of forgetting in STM. These are the main two explanations covered in the textbook (pp. 20–1).

2 Retrieval failure and interference are given as examples of explanations of forgetting in LTM. The textbook covers these (pp. 22–4), but also looks at decay in LTM as a third explanation.

3 Freud's research is mentioned as an example of research into repression. He is mentioned on p. 27 of the textbook, but the research of Levinger and Clark is also given as a Key study.

4 The word 'including' means that you definitely need to know about flashbulb memories and repression when investigating research into the role of emotional factors.

5 The specification mentions research into the role of emotional factors in forgetting. Two factors are listed as 'compulsory', i.e. flashbulb memories and repression. So, you need to learn at least one Key study for each of these, i.e. two Key studies.

Topic 3 >> Critical issue: eyewitness testimony

Much of the research done into memory has been quite theoretical, as you may have noticed from Topics 1 and 2. One area where it has an important practical application is eyewitness testimony.

When you try the 'Getting you thinking ...' on p. 30 of the textbook, you will realize how hard it can be to remember details accurately. There are times, though, when it is vital to remember details, such as when giving testimony about an accident or crime you have witnessed. Getting the details wrong can have very serious consequences.

UNDERSTANDING THE SPECIFICATION

Here is what the AQA (A) specification says about this topic. It forms part of AS Module 1, Cognitive and Developmental Psychology.

Read it and then try the activity below. You'll find answers to the activity on p. 30.

Human memory

Critical issue: eyewitness testimony

Memory research into eyewitness testimony, including reconstructive memory (Bartlett) and Loftus' research (e.g. role of leading questions).

ACTIVITY

Understanding the specification

1 For this part of the specification, what is compulsory and what are examples?
Clue: Look for the key words 'including' and 'e.g.'.

-
-

2 Does this topic involve Key studies (APFCCs)?
Clue: Look for the key word 'research'.

-

The main issue in this topic is reliability (or lack of reliability) of eyewitness recall. The specification emphasizes the role of reconstructive memory in this process and specifically mentions Elizabeth Loftus' research into eyewitness testimony. It also mentions 'the role of leading questions', but this is only an example and cannot be specified in an exam question. The specification requires you to be familiar with the nature of reconstructive memory and eyewitness testimony and with factors that affect each of these.

There are two APFCC studies included in this topic area – eyewitness testimony (e.g. Loftus *et al.* 1978) and reconstructive memory (Bartlett 1932). You should also be able to respond to more general questions concerning research findings (or conclusions) in both these areas. Loftus has produced a great deal of research in relation to eyewitness testimony and you are specifically required to be familiar with some of her studies, including being able to offer a critical commentary on her work.

TOPIC MAP

ACTIVITY

Topic map

The diagram below gives you a visual overview of what you are about to study in this topic. Look through pp. 30–9 of the textbook to see where the items shown are covered. Note down the relevant page numbers in the spaces left on the topic map.

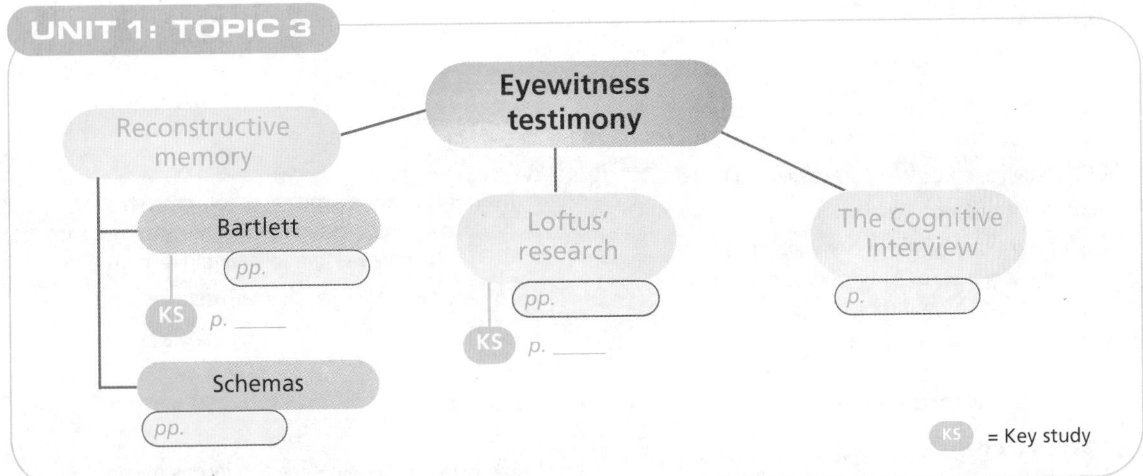

KEEPING TRACK

Use the table below to keep track of your work on this topic and plan your revision. See p. iv (Introduction) for guidance on filling it in.

What I need to learn	Where is it?	Tick if you … could make a basic attempt	could make a good attempt	have complete mastery of this
Reconstructive memory				
Definition of 'eyewitness testimony'				
Definition of 'reconstructive memory'				
Definition of 'schemas'				
Description of research into reconstructive memory				
Evaluation of research into reconstructive memory				
Description of APFCC for a Key study of reconstructive memory				
Loftus' research into eyewitness testimony				
Description of Loftus' research				
Evaluation of Loftus' research				
Description of APFCC for a Key study by Loftus				
The Cognitive Interview				
Description of the Cognitive Interview				
Evaluation of the Cognitive Interview				

RECONSTRUCTIVE MEMORY

The British psychologist, Sir Frederick Bartlett, carried out pioneering research into why people recall events inaccurately. His important work is described on pp. 31–3 of the textbook. His work is considered significant, but his ideas have also been criticized for being vague and lacking experimental rigour.

ACTIVITY

Bartlett and reconstructive memory

Write notes summarizing the main features of Bartlett's work. Your notes should include:

1 a definition of 'reconstructive memory'

2 a definition of 'schema'

3 a summary of the two Bartlett studies described on p. 31, including notes on the findings and conclusions

4 a list of criticisms made of Bartlett's work (you will find some on p. 31, some on p. 32 and some on p. 33!).

For your AS exam, you need to be able to 'explain' or 'outline' reconstructive memory (see the sample exam questions below). Be sure to know the definition and have at least one example of research you can mention.

Alternatively, you may be asked to explain factors that influence reconstructive memory. You could base your answer on culture (as in Bartlett's 'War of the Ghosts' story) and schemas.

The criticisms of Bartlett's work will be useful for any AO1 question involving 'criticisms' and for the AO2 part of questions requiring you to evaluate research into reconstructive memory.

AO1 questions

- Explain what is meant by the terms 'eyewitness testimony' and 'reconstructive memory'. (3 + 3 marks)
- Outline two factors that influence reconstructive memory. (3 + 3 marks)
- Outline findings of research into reconstructive memory. (6 marks)

Schemas

Bartlett's notion of 'schemas' has been explored in more recent years.

Do the activity below to investigate schema theory further. In answer to question 2, you may find it useful to summarize Cohen's five points in a shorthand way that you will find easy to remember, for example:

"Schemas may cause us to:

1 ignore 'difficult' details

2 remember the gist, but not the details ..."

and so on.

ACTIVITY

Schemas

Read through the explanation of schemas (textbook p. 32), including the criticisms made on p. 33. Then answer the following questions:

1 In what ways are schemas useful?

2 How can schemas lead to reconstructive memory (Cohen 1993)?

3 What are the main problems with schema theory?

EXAM HINT

Schema theory

The criticisms of schema theory will be useful for any AO1 question that asks you to give criticisms of reconstructive memory (see the example questions on p. 25).

Other research

Three more recent studies into reconstructive memory and schemas are described on pp. 32 and 33 of the textbook. These studies – with more rigorous design – have investigated various aspects of Bartlett's theories. The following activity will help you organize your reading of this research.

ACTIVITY

Further research

Read through the descriptions of the following three studies:

- Brewer and Treyens (1981)
- List (1986)
- Bransford and Johnson (1972).

Using separate paper, make notes on each of them. You could organize your notes in the form of a table under the following headings:

1 Description of study (what it investigated, method)
2 Findings
3 Conclusions
4 Support for Bartlett's idea?

Key study: reconstructive memory

As the Topic map on p. 23 shows, you need to commit to memory at least one Key study on reconstructive memory. Bartlett's important research is described in the Key study on p. 31.

ACTIVITY

KEY STUDY: Reconstructive memory

Write your own summary of the Key study on p. 31 of the textbook, using trigger phrases, mnemonics or whatever will help you to memorize the important details. Under 'Criticisms' use the + and – columns to separate those arguments that support the study's conclusions from those that disagree with them.

AO1 questions (APFCC-type)

By now you should be familiar with APFCC-type questions, which will ask for any two pieces of information about a key piece of research:

- Describe the aims and procedures of one study of reconstructive memory. (6 marks)
- Describe the findings and conclusions of one study of reconstructive memory. (6 marks)
- Describe the conclusions and give one criticism of one study of reconstructive memory. (6 marks)

KEY STUDY textbook p. 31

Subject RECONSTRUCTIVE MEMORY

Researchers Bartlett (1932)

Title

Aims

Procedures

Findings

Conclusions

Criticisms +

Criticisms –

ACTIVITY

'War of the Ghosts'

To get a good idea of how this study worked, try it out for yourself. First, track down the text of the 'War of the Ghosts' story on the Internet. Type in 'Egulac foggy' into a search engine (these words appear in the story). You will get a list of sites – mainly colleges and universities – describing Bartlett's research. Some of these will include the text of the story.

Read the story. Then set it aside for a day or so and without reading it, try to recall it as best you can. Then compare your version with the original and see what the differences are. How do they tie in with what Bartlett found?

LOFTUS' RESEARCH ON EYEWITNESS TESTIMONY

Evidence from eyewitnesses can prove crucial in convicting people of crimes. However, there is now lots of research – much of it done by Elizabeth Loftus – that shows that eyewitnesses' memories can be seriously flawed.

Factors affecting eyewitness testimony

One of the main areas of research is how our memory of information becomes distorted after the event. (This is different from schemas, where existing knowledge interferes with memories.)

ACTIVITY

Factors that affect eyewitnesses' memory

There are many factors that can affect memories after the event. Some factors serve to distort memories; others may help to improve memory. All these factors are described in the textbook starting at the bottom of p. 33, going through to the second column of p. 36.

Draw up your own summary of these factors in the form of a table. One possible format is shown below. Use the different columns to show how each factor affects memory and what studies have demonstrated this. In the column on the right, add any criticisms of the research you can think of (points in its favour and points against it).

Factor affecting testimony	How it affects witnesses' memory	Relevant research (description)	Evaluation (criticism)
Misleading information	Distorts – People may add misleading information to their memory of events.	**Loftus (1975)** – film of car accident – some Ps told of imaginary barn. Of these, 17% recalled seeing it (compared with only 2.7% of other group).	+ Results suggest memory can be influenced after the event. – Lab-based experiment. Artificial context.

EXAM HINT

Factors influencing eyewitness testimony

The information in the table from the last activity will help you to answer AO1 questions about factors that influence eyewitness testimony, such as those shown in the panel on the right. The 'Evaluation' column will provide material for the AO2 part of answers.

AO1 questions

- Outline findings of research into eyewitness testimony. (6 marks)
- Outline two factors that influence the accuracy of eyewitness testimony. (3 + 3 marks)
- Give two criticisms of eyewitness testimony research. (3 + 3 marks)
- Outline conclusions of Loftus' research into eyewitness testimony. (6 marks)

ACTIVITY

Evaluation of Loftus' research

The textbook gives a good evaluation of Loftus' research (see pp. 36–7). In the space below, draw up a short list of positive and negative aspects of her research. You should mention the disagreements about 'what happens to the original memory' (p. 36). All these points will be useful for AO2-type answers.

+ Positive aspects of Loftus' research	– Negative aspects of Loftus' research
•	•
•	•
•	•

The Cognitive Interview

The Cognitive Interview is a positive outcome of the research into eyewitness testimony. It was developed by Geiselman *et al.* (1985) in order to improve the way in which police officers question witnesses. All the research studies described in the textbook found that use of the Cognitive Interview improved witnesses' recall. Now do the activity below.

ACTIVITY

Cognitive Interview

1 What are the four main instructions of the Cognitive Interview Schedule?

-
-
-
-

2 Three pieces of research are mentioned in the text on the Cognitive Interview. Complete the following table, summarizing in note form what each study investigated and its main findings.

Research	What study investigated	Findings
Geiselman *et al.* (1985)	•	•
Fisher *et al.* (1989)	•	•
Bekerian and Dennett (1993)	•	•

Key study: eyewitness testimony

You need to commit to memory at least one Key study on Loftus' research, to answer questions such as those given in the panel on the right. A summary of her study into the effects of misleading information is given on p. 35 of the textbook.

Now complete the following activity.

AO1 questions (APFCC-type)

Below are two possible questions that could be asked about key research into eyewitness testimony.

- Describe the aims and conclusions of one study of eyewitness testimony. (6 marks)
- Describe the procedures and give one criticism of one study of eyewitness testimony. (6 marks)

ACTIVITY

KEY STUDY: Eyewitness testimony

Write your own summary of the Key study on p. 35 of the textbook, using trigger phrases, mnemonics or whatever will help you to memorize the important details. Under 'Criticisms' use the + and – columns to separate those arguments that support the study's conclusions from those that disagree with them.

KEY STUDY textbook p. 35

Subject EYEWITNESS TESTIMONY

Researchers Loftus et al. (1978)

Title

Aims

Procedures

Findings

Conclusions

Criticisms +

Criticisms –

Expert interview: Elizabeth Loftus

The topic ends with a fascinating interview with Elizabeth Loftus. In it she gives a very good summary of situations when eyewitness memory is likely to be most accurate. Do the activity on p. 38 of the textbook, writing your notes in a way that you will find easy to remember when you come to revise.

AO1+AO2 QUESTIONS ON EYEWITNESS TESTIMONY

The panel on the right shows four example AO1+AO2 questions relating to the critical issue of eyewitness testimony and reconstructive memory.

Below is a sample answer to the second of these questions. Read through the answer and our comments on it below and then try the activity at the top of the next page.

For now we will stick with the one paragraph (AO1) two paragraph (AO2) technique, although we are introducing a slight variation on that. Think of your AO2 as an opportunity for an argument with Elizabeth Loftus. She believes that eyewitness testimony is generally unreliable, so we can take issue with that position in our commentary. The example response that follows uses the material on pp. 33–9 of the textbook (including the Expert interview with Professor Loftus) to construct such a response.

AO1+AO2 questions

- Give a brief account of and evaluate research into reconstructive memory. (18 marks)
- To what extent has research into reconstructive memory helped our understanding of eyewitness testimony? (18 marks)
- To what extent has psychological research supported the idea that eyewitness testimony is unreliable? (18 marks)
- Outline and evaluate Loftus' research (theories and/or studies) into eyewitness testimony. (18 marks)

Sample answer

To what extent has research into reconstructive memory helped our understanding of eyewitness testimony? (18 marks)

Loftus (2003)* states that one reason for poor eyewitness testimony (EWT) is that information was never stored in the first place. We may look at one part of a crime and fail to notice other details, and even if we do take in an accurate picture of what we have seen, it does not stay intact in memory. Other forces erode the original experience over time or with the introduction of interfering or contradictory facts. Loftus' own research has shown that eyewitness memory can be unreliable because of conditions at the time of the event (e.g. poor lighting or high stress) or afterwards. Other reasons for unreliability are exposure to the mistaken recollections of other witnesses or being questioned in a biased way.

Loftus is able to support these claims through laboratory research showing how high levels of anxiety at the time of an incident decreased subsequent eyewitness accuracy (Loftus 1979) and how leading questions could influence later recall of material (Loftus and Palmer 1974). However, much of the research that has demonstrated the unreliability of eyewitnesses has been conducted in laboratories. It is possible that participants in experiments are less accurate because they know that inaccuracies will not lead to serious consequences. This criticism is supported by research where participants who believed that the video they were watching was of a real crime subsequently gave more accurate EWT than those who believed it was a simulation of a real crime (Foster et al. 1994).

Despite her claims that EWT is generally unreliable, Loftus does acknowledge that in some situations EWT may be more accurate. These conditions generally involve the absence of those conditions that make EWT unreliable. Hence, EWT is more likely to be reliable if the witness has longer exposure to the crime details, if there is less time between the crime and the subsequent memory report, and when the witness is questioned in a neutral rather than suggestive manner. Loftus' research methods have also been criticized for her method of testing recall. The success of the cognitive interview (Geiselman et al. 1985) is largely due to the use of memory retrieval techniques aimed at eliciting more accurate information from eyewitnesses.

**This reference is to the Expert interview with Elizabeth Loftus on p. 39 of the textbook.*

ACTIVITY

One for you to try ...

Give a brief account of and evaluate research into reconstructive memory. (18 marks)

Have a go at the question above, using the material on pp. 31–3 of the textbook. Use the same technique as in the sample answer on p. 29, and structure your response so that one third of your material is AO1 and two-thirds AO2.

CHECK YOUR UNDERSTANDING

When you have finished working through this topic, try the questions in 'Check your understanding' on p. 40 of the textbook. When you have written your answers, check them by looking at the relevant parts of the textbook or this workbook, listed below.

1 textbook p. 30 (see 'Key terms')
2 textbook p. 30
3 textbook p. 31
4 textbook p. 32
5 textbook pp. 32–3
6 textbook p. 35
7 textbook pp. 34 and 36
8 textbook p. 36
9 textbook p. 37
10 textbook pp. 33–7; workbook pp. 26–9

ANSWERS TO ACTIVITIES

Understanding the specification, p. 22

1 The word 'including' tells us that you have to know about both reconstructive memory and Loftus' research.

The 'e.g.' means that the role of leading questions is an example of Loftus' research, not compulsory. The textbook mentions leading questions (see p. 34), but covers several other aspects of her work, with a Key study into the effects of misleading information (textbook p. 35).

Note, too, that the name Bartlett is given in brackets without an 'e.g.'. This means you have to know about Bartlett's work, and you will find a Key study described on p. 31 of the textbook.

2 Yes, the specification mentions research into both aspects of eyewitness testimony (reconstructive memory and Loftus' research). So, you need to know details of two Key studies – one for each area.

2

ATTACHMENTS IN Development

PREVIEW

There are three topics in this unit. You should read them alongside the following pages in the Collins *Psychology for AS-level* textbook:

INTRODUCTION

This unit covers the AS Developmental Psychology part of Module 1 (AQA Specification A). The diagram below shows where it fits in to the overall AS qualification.

Read the Preview and Introduction on p. 42 of the textbook now. This will give you an overview of what's in the unit.

Where this unit fits in to the AS qualification

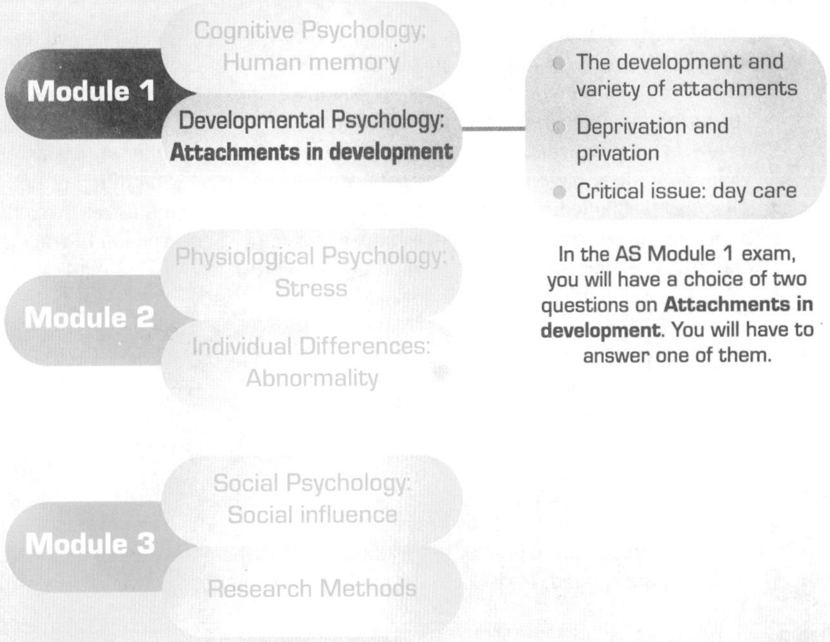

Module 1
- Cognitive Psychology: Human memory
- Developmental Psychology: **Attachments in development**
  - The development and variety of attachments
  - Deprivation and privation
  - Critical issue: day care

Module 2
- Physiological Psychology: Stress
- Individual Differences: Abnormality

Module 3
- Social Psychology: Social influence
- Research Methods

In the AS Module 1 exam, you will have a choice of two questions on **Attachments in development**. You will have to answer one of them.

Topic 1 >> The development and variety of attachments

In this topic, we will look at what it means to become 'attached' to someone. We will also look at the sequence of the development of attachments and at how development varies from one individual to another. We will then consider explanations for why an infant becomes attached, and why they become attached to one person rather than another.

UNDERSTANDING THE SPECIFICATION

Here is what the AQA (A) specification says about this topic. It forms part of AS Module 1, Cognitive and Developmental Psychology..

Read it and then try the activity below. You'll find answers to the activity on p. 41.

Attachments in development

a. The development and variety of attachments

The development of attachments (e.g. Schaffer). Research into individual differences, including secure and insecure attachments (e.g. Ainsworth) and cross-cultural variations. Explanations of attachment (e.g. learning theory, Bowlby's theory).

ACTIVITY

Understanding the specification

1 According to the specification, what two aspects of research into individual differences do you *have* to study?

- secure attachments
- insecure "

2 What two theories are given as *examples* of explanations of attachment?

- learning theory
- Bowlby's theory

3 The studies by Schaffer and Ainsworth are listed as examples of what two aspects of this topic?

-
-

4 Does this topic involve Key studies (APFCCs)? If so, how many? *Clue*: Look for the key word 'research'.

-

The attachment between infants and their caregivers follows a sequence of different stages. Schaffer's account of this sequence is given as an example in the specification, although you can use other accounts as well. The specification requires you to study the variation in the attachment process between individuals. This may be studied in general terms, but you will also be asked to comment on differences between secure and insecure attachments (as classified by Ainsworth) and cross-cultural differences in attachment. Finally, you are required to study at least two explanations of attachment (learning theory and Bowlby's theory are given as examples, but there are others) and to be able offer criticisms of your chosen explanations. To reflect the different demands of 'describe' and 'outline' questions, you should ensure you can prepare a long version of each (for 6 marks) and a short version (for 3 marks).

TOPIC MAP

ACTIVITY

Topic map

Look through pp. 43–57 of the textbook to see where the items shown in the topic map on p. 33 are covered. Note down the relevant page numbers in the spaces provided.

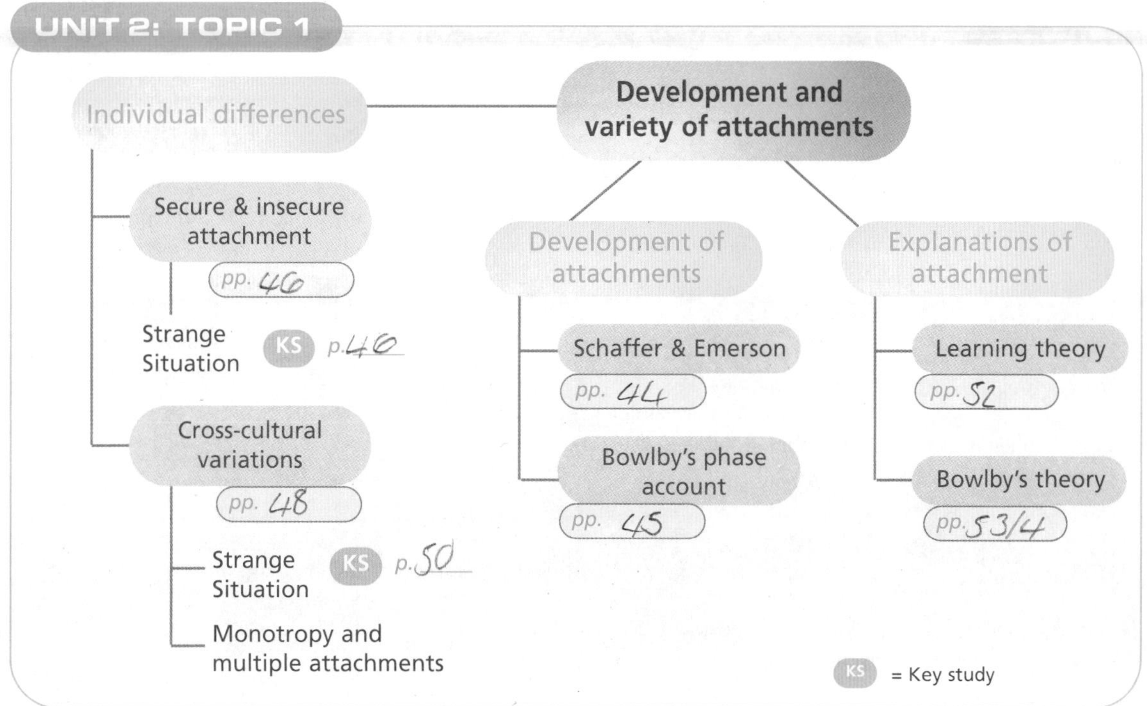

KEEPING TRACK

Use the table below to keep track of your work on this topic and plan your revision. See p. iv (Introduction) for guidance on how to fill it in.

What I need to learn	Where is it?	Tick if you ... could make a basic attempt	could make a good attempt	have complete mastery of this
The development of attachments				
Definition of 'attachment'				
Description of research into the development of attachments				
Evaluation of research into the development of attachments				
Description of phases in the development of attachment				
Variety of attachments: individual differences				
Definition of 'secure attachment'				
Definition of 'insecure attachment'				
Definition of 'cross-cultural variations'				
Description of research into individual differences in attachment				
Evaluation of research into individual differences in attachment				
Description of research into cross-cultural variations in attachment				
Evaluation of research into cross-cultural variations in attachment				
Description of APFCC for a Key study of secure and insecure attachments				
Description of APFCC for a Key study of cross-cultural variations in attachment				
Explanations of attachment				
Description of the learning theory of attachment				
Evaluation of the learning theory of attachment				
Description of Bowlby's theory of attachment				
Evaluation of Bowlby's theory of attachment				

THE DEVELOPMENT OF ATTACHMENTS

Relationships and attachments are important throughout people's lives, but have a special importance during infancy. For this reason, the focus of Topic 1 is on attachments during infancy and early childhood. (Check you know the difference between 'infancy' and 'childhood' – see Introduction, textbook p. 42.)

What is attachment?

Pages 44–6 of the textbook look at what attachments are and how they develop. When it comes to explaining what attachment is, two vital bits of information are:

- the definition on p. 43 of the textbook and further explanation at the top of p. 44
- the four key characteristics identified by Maccoby (1980), described on p. 44.

This information will be useful for the 'attachment' part of questions such as those listed on the right.

Stages of attachment

The textbook goes on to examine the important work of the following researchers into how attachments develop:

1 Schaffer and Emerson (1964)
2 Bowlby (1969).

The Schaffer and Emerson/Bowlby explanations of attachments are both described as 'phase accounts' or 'stage accounts' of development. Check that you understand what this means (see textbook p. 45). Bowlby describes early development in terms of four stages, outlined in Table 2.1 in the textbook.

Try the next two activities to summarize the key features and findings of these two stage accounts. This will provide useful material for questions asking for accounts of development, as in the last two questions in the panel below.

AO1 questions

- What is meant by the terms 'attachment', 'deprivation' and 'privation'? (2 + 2 + 2 marks)
- Explain what is meant by the terms 'attachment' and 'separation'. (3 + 3 marks)
- Describe one account of the development of attachments. (6 marks)
- Give two criticisms of the account of the development of attachment that you described above. (3 + 3 marks)

ACTIVITY

Schaffer and Emerson

Read through the text on pp. 44 and 45 of the textbook and answer the following questions about Schaffer and Emerson's research.

1 What two measures did Schaffer and Emerson use in their research to measure strength of attachment? Describe them below.

- Separation anxiety
- Stranger anxiety

2 According to Schaffer and Emerson, and Bowlby, when do the following stages appear?

	Schaffer and Emerson	Bowlby
First specific attachment	6-8mnth.	6mnth.
Multiple attachments	8+ mth	6+ mths
Stranger anxiety	7-9mth	6mth.

3 What proportion of infants had either the mother or father as first sole or joint attachment?

Mother = first sole attachment 65 %
Father = first sole attachment 3 %
Mother = first joint attachment 30 %
Father = first joint attachment 27 %

4 How important were the following factors in forming attachments?

- Time spent with infant
- Level of interaction with the infant
  higher attachment level

5 What conclusions can you draw from your answers to questions 3 and 4? (Think about what might explain the percentages in question 3.)

- the mothers interacted more with the children

ACTIVITY

Bowlby's phase account

1 **Explanation** – Make your own version of Table 2.1 (textbook p. 45), but use just a few key words or phrases instead of the longer descriptions. This will help you to memorize the important developments at each phase.

2 **Evaluation** – Summarize the criticisms of Bowlby's phase account using the following terms. For each, make a note (a) of the relevant research and (b) whether the research supports Bowlby's theory:

- infants' sociability
- ability to discriminate
- separation anxiety and role of object permanence
- role of physical development.

THE VARIETY OF ATTACHMENTS

Pages 46–51 of the textbook look at how attachments vary. It considers two aspects:

- differences between individuals
- differences between cultures.

A major tool for investigating both these types of differences is the Strange Situation, developed by Mary Ainsworth. This features in much of the research into attachments and is used in both Key studies in this section. As you read pp. 46–8 of the textbook, make sure you understand:

- what the Strange Situation is
- what it measures
- what types of attachment it is used to identify
- how it can be evaluated.

The activity below will help you to summarize the most important features of research using the Strange Situation.

Secure and insecure attachment

One of the variations in attachment is the attachment style shown by infants. These attachment styles reflect consistent patterns of thinking, feeling and behaving in interpersonal situations.

Ainsworth and Bell's study (textbook p. 47) classified infants into three groups (or attachment styles). The broad distinction they made was between securely and insecurely attached children, with the insecure group divided into two further groups: avoidant and resistant.

ACTIVITY

The Strange Situation

1 In 50 words, outline the Strange Situation (what type of research method it is, how it is used, what its purpose is, etc.).

2 What specific behaviours are measured by the Strange Situation? *Clue*: see the Key study on p. 47 of the textbook.

separation anxiety
stranger anxiety
reunion behaviour

3 The Strange Situation is often evaluated in terms of its validity and reliability. Summarize what the textbook says about these two criteria, listing any relevant studies and what they concluded:

- **Reliability**

population validity

- **Validity**

ACTIVITY

What causes attachment types

One of the major questions is what causes different attachment types. On p. 48 the textbook suggests two alternatives:

- caregiver sensitivity hypothesis*
- temperament hypothesis.

Summarize what the textbook says about these two explanations, listing any relevant studies and what they concluded.

Hypothesis	Explanation	Relevant studies
Caregiver sensitivity hypothesis	•	•
Temperament hypothesis	•	•

Hint: for an explanation of what a hypothesis is, see textbook pp. 215–17.

AO1 questions

- Explain what is mean by the terms 'secure' and 'insecure' attachment.* (3 + 3 marks)
- Outline one factor that influences the development of a secure attachment and one that influences the development of an insecure attachment. (3 + 3 marks)
- Outline one effect of secure attachment and one effect of insecure attachment. (3 + 3 marks)
- Outline findings of research into secure and insecure attachments. (6 marks)

**Sample answers to this question are discussed on p. 253 of the textbook.*

Cross-cultural differences

Researchers in many different countries have used the Strange Situation to investigate secure and insecure attachment.

ACTIVITY

Cross-cultural differences

Read the textbook pp. 48–51 on 'Cross-cultural variations in attachment' and do the following.

1 Define the following terms:
- culture
- cross-cultural study
- culture-bound theory
- subculture.

2 Answer the following questions to summarize the findings of Van IJzendoorn and Kroonenberg's analysis:
- Are infants in different cultures mainly secure or insecure in their attachments?
- Are the results consistent across cultures?
- Do any individual findings stand out?

There is another aspect of attachment formation where there may be cultural differences – the question of whether infants tend to form a single primary bond ('monotropy') or have multiple attachments. This is discussed on p. 51 and is the subject of the next activity.

ACTIVITY

Single or multiple attachments – cultural variations

1 What, according to Bowlby, is an 'internal working model' and why is it important?

-

2 Complete the following table summarizing the research into single and multiple attachments mentioned on p. 51 of the textbook.

Researcher	Culture studied	Type of childcare	Single or multiple attachments?
Thomas (1998)	Caribbean	Doesn't say	Multiple

3 Bowlby claimed that infants need one special attachment relationship in order to develop emotional maturity. Do you agree? Does the research support his claim?

-

AO1 questions

Possible questions on cross-cultural variations in attachments include the following:

- Outline two effects of cross-cultural variations in attachments. (3 + 3 marks)
- Outline findings of research into cross-cultural variations in attachments. (6 marks)
- Outline conclusions of research into cross-cultural variations in attachments. (6 marks)

Key studies: differences in attachments

There are two Key studies in this part of Topic 1, one relating to individual differences in attachments (it can also be used as a study of secure/insecure attachment) and one relating to cross-cultural variations. Both studies used the Strange Situation in their procedures.

ACTIVITY

KEY STUDIES: Differences in attachments

Using the forms on p. 38, write your own summaries of the Key studies on pp. 47 and 50 of the textbook, using trigger phrases, mnemonics or whatever will help you to memorize the important details. Under 'Criticisms', don't forget to include the points mentioned in the 'AO2 checks' at the end of each study.

KEY STUDY textbook p. 47

Subject INDIVIDUAL DIFFERENCES IN ATTACHMENT

Researchers Ainsworth and Bell (1970)

Title Measuring secure and insecure attachment in children using the Strange Situation

Aims

Procedures

Findings

Conclusions

Criticisms +

Criticisms −

KEY STUDY textbook p. 50

Subject CROSS-CULTURAL VARIATIONS

Researchers Takahashi (1990)

Title

Aims

Procedures

Findings

Conclusions

Criticisms +

Criticisms −

AO1 questions (APFCC-type)

- Describe the aims and procedures of one study of individual differences in attachment. (6 marks)
- Describe the procedures and findings of one study of secure and insecure attachment. (6 marks)
- Describe the findings and conclusions of one study of cross-cultural differences in attachment. (6 marks)
- Describe the findings of one study of individual differences in attachment and give one criticism of this study. (6 marks)

EXPLANATIONS OF ATTACHMENT

Explanations of attachment can be divided into two types: those that see attachment as a learned process and those that see it as a natural or innate aspect of human behaviour.

The textbook includes one example of each category of explanation:

- learning theory – pp. 52–3
- John Bowlby's theory – pp. 53–6.

ACTIVITY

Explanations of attachment

Using a separate sheet of A4 paper, draw up a table summarizing (in note form) the key features of each of the two explanations of attachment discussed in the textbook. Use the column headings shown in the tables below.

The questions and prompts will help you to complete the tables. The key information for each model can be found in the textbook, on the pages listed above.

Learning theory

Key features	Arguments/evidence in favour	Arguments/evidence against
• what attachment is – learned process • how it works – classical conditioning (mother as source of food – hence pleasure) • how it works – operant conditioning (mother as source of positive reinforcement)	• role of mother – see Schaffer and Emerson (1964), p. 34	• Schaffer and Emerson (1964) • Harlow and Harlow (1962) • reductionism

Bowlby's theory

Key features	Arguments/evidence in favour	Arguments/evidence against
• what attachment is – innate programming and the role of social releasers • when it takes place – the critical period • how it influences later development – the continuity hypothesis	• imprinting in non-human animals (Lorenz 1952) • Ainsworth's caregiver sensitivity hypothesis • monotropy – evidence from Schaffer and Emerson (1964) • studies supporting continuity hypothesis • influence of theory of later researchers	• children with poor attachment experiences who become well adjusted • 'post-hoc' nature of argument (check you understand what this means)

The information in these tables should provide you with plenty of material to tackle AO1 questions such as those in the panel below.

AO1 questions

- Describe one explanation of attachment. (6 marks)
- Outline two explanations of attachment. (3 + 3 marks)
- Outline one explanation of attachment and give one criticism of this explanation. (3 + 3 marks)
- Give two criticisms of one explanation of attachment. (3 + 3 marks)

AO1+AO2 QUESTIONS ON DEVELOPMENT AND VARIETY OF ATTACHMENTS

One of the skills in answering AO1+AO2 questions is knowing how to use research material in a suitably evaluative way. In the worked example of an AO1+AO2 question below, we show how material on pp. 48–51 can be used to provide a response to the question. It pays to think in advance what your opinion is about the statement in the question. In this example, it is the belief that there are some cross-cultural variations, although not as extreme as might first appear. In responding to the question, you can present arguments (and dismiss counter-arguments) that would lead to that conclusion.

In the first paragraph, the first third is AO1 and deals with one particular piece of research. The latter two-thirds offers AO2 commentary on that material. This pattern is repeated in the second and third paragraphs so that the overall AO1/AO2 proportion is maintained.

AO1+AO2 questions

- Outline and evaluate one or more explanations of the development of attachments. (18 marks)
- To what extent has research shown there to be individual differences in attachment? (18 marks)
- Consider the extent to which research has shown there to be cultural variations in attachment. (18 marks)
- Outline and evaluate two explanations of attachment. (18 marks)
- Give a brief account of, and evaluate, one explanation of attachment. (18 marks)

Sample answer

Consider the extent to which research has shown there to be cultural variations in attachment.

(18 marks)

Researchers have used the Strange Situation to investigate secure and insecure attachment in different cultures. A meta-analysis by van IJzendoorn and Kroonenberg (1988) of 32 studies carried out in eight countries found some evidence of cultural differences (e.g. 74% of Swedish infants were securely attached compared to just 50% of Chinese infants). Despite the observed differences between cultures, the researchers also found considerable consistency in patterns of secure and insecure attachment across the different cultures. Bee (1999) suggests that it is likely that the same caregiver-infant interactions have contributed to these patterns of secure and insecure attachment in different cultures. Van IJzendoorn and Kroonenberg believe this is likely to be the product of the increasing effects of the mass media, and their influence on such interactions.

Also using the Strange Situation, Takahashi (1990) found significant differences in separation anxiety between Japanese and American infants, with Japanese infants showing much greater distress when left alone. Takahashi also found an absence of avoidant-insecure attachment types in the Japanese sample. The absence of avoidant-insecure attachment behaviour can be explained in terms of cultural norms of politeness (Japanese children are taught that such behaviour is impolite and are actively discouraged from displaying it). Despite the observed differences between Japanese and American infants in the way they react to separation, it is doubtful that the Strange Situation had the same meaning for both groups, and so is not a valid form of assessment of attachment for the Japanese infants.

A key part of Bowlby's views on attachment is the claim that infants need one special attachment relationship which is qualitatively different from all others. He used the term 'monotropy' to describe this special relationship. This allows the child to build an internal working model of the world and underlies all other relationships. There is considerable debate about whether monotropy is universal. Thomas (1998) claims that in Caribbean cultures, multiple attachments are the rule rather than infants having one 'special' relationship. On the other hand, in Schaffer and Emerson's study (1964), it was found that even though infants do form multiple attachments, they appear usually to have one primary attachment. This was supported by cross-cultural research by Ainsworth (1967) and Tronick et al. (1992), both of whom found evidence of multiple carers but one primary attachment figure, who was usually the mother.

ACTIVITY

One for you to try ...

Give a brief account of, and evaluate, one explanation of attachment. (18 marks)

Using the advice in 'An eye on the exam' on p. 57 of the textbook, have a go at this question. Again, try to structure your response so that one third of your material is AO1 and two-thirds is AO2.

CHECK YOUR UNDERSTANDING

When you have finished working through this topic, try the questions in 'Check your understanding' on p. 56 of the textbook. You can check your answers by looking at the relevant parts of the textbook, listed below.

1 'interaction', see textbook p. 44 (top)
2 textbook p. 51 (1st column)
3 textbook p. 55
4 textbook p. 54
5 textbook p. 54
6 textbook p. 45
7 textbook pp. 44–5 – You might have criticized the representativeness of the sample used (working-class area of Glasgow), the accuracy of mothers' recall of separation protest, or the researchers' increasing familiarity to the infant over the course of the study.
8 textbook p. 47 – see the list of behaviours under 'Findings'
9 object permanence – see textbook, p. 46
10 textbook p. 46
11 textbook p. 47 – see 'Findings'
12 textbook p. 47 – see 'Criticisms'
13 textbook p. 49 – see Table 2.2
14 textbook p. 55, column 2
15 textbook p. 51
16 textbook p. 51, column 1
17 textbook p. 51, column 2
18 textbook pp. 52–3

ANSWERS TO ACTIVITIES

Understanding the specification, p. 32

1 The two aspects of research are secure/insecure attachments and cross-cultural variations in attachments.
2 Learning theory and Bowlby's theory.
3 Schaffer is given as an example of work into the development of attachments; Ainsworth is given as an example of work into secure/insecure attachments.
4 Yes, the specification mentions research into individual differences, and then mentions two compulsory aspects of it (see answer to 1 above). This means you will have to study two Key studies: one covering secure/insecure attachments (Ainsworth and Bell 1970, textbook p. 47) and one covering cross-cultural variations (Takahashi 1990, textbook p. 50).

Topic 2 >> Deprivation and privation

Topic 1 looked at the importance of attachments in a child's development; this topic looks at what happens when children become separated from their main caregiver(s) – the person(s) to whom they are most closely attached – or when they fail to form an attachment relationship in the first place. Although terms such as 'separation', 'deprivation' and 'privation' are frequently used interchangeably (particularly the last two), they have a more precise meaning in examination questions. It is important, therefore, to be clear in your own mind about the subtle differences between these terms before reading on. Read the definitions on p. 58 of the textbook carefully and then continue with this topic.

UNDERSTANDING THE SPECIFICATION

Here is what the AQA (A) specification says about this topic. It forms part of AS Module 1, Cognitive and Developmental Psychology.

Read it and then try the activity to the right. You'll find answers to the activity on p. 50.

Attachments in development

b. Deprivation and privation

Bowlby's maternal deprivation hypothesis. Research into the effects of deprivation/separation (e.g. Robertson & Robertson, Bowlby). Research into the effects of privation (Hodges & Tizard's study of institutionalization).

ACTIVITY

Understanding the specification

1 Whose work is given as examples of research into the effects of deprivation/separation?

- ____________________
- ____________________

2 Are you *required* to study Hodges and Tizard's research into institutionalization? Give reasons for your answer.

- ____________________

____

3 Does this topic involve Key studies (APFCCs)? If so, how many? *Clue*: Look for the key word 'research'.

- ____________________

____

____

The specification indicates three aspects of this topic. Bowlby's maternal deprivation hypothesis is explicitly mentioned as an 'including' – therefore you must be able to describe and evaluate this hypothesis (as distinct from the same psychologist's explanation of attachment). The term 'deprivation' refers to the loss of attachments (usually) as a result of separation, so the terms are used interchangeably here. The specification details appropriate research that has investigated deprivation/separation, so you should have a good working knowledge of the two examples given. Privation refers to the lack of attachments (i.e. they were never formed). Hodges and Tizard's research is given as an example of an appropriate study of the effects of privation.

TOPIC MAP

ACTIVITY

Topic map

Look through pp. 58–66 of the textbook to see where the items shown in the topic map are covered. Note down the relevant page numbers in the spaces left on the topic map.

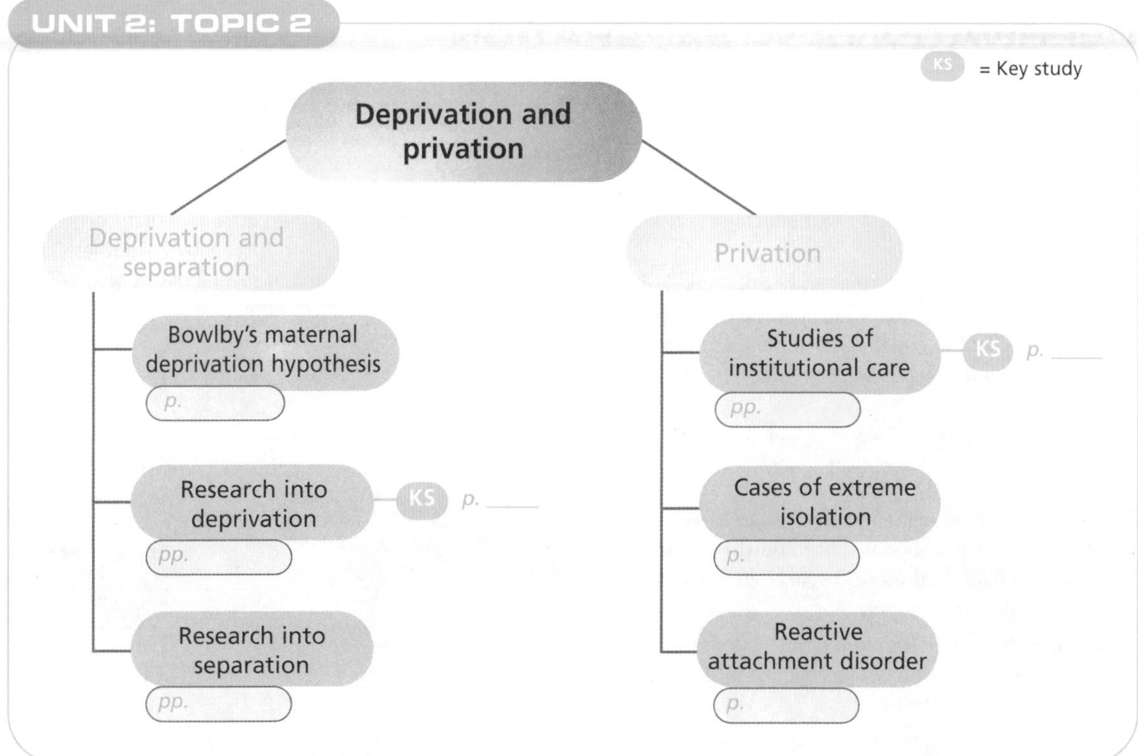

KEEPING TRACK

Use the table below to keep track of your work on this topic and plan your revision. See p. iv (Introduction) for guidance on how to fill it in.

What I need to learn	Where is it?	Tick if you ... could make a basic attempt	could make a good attempt	have complete mastery of this
Deprivation and separation				
Definition of 'deprivation'				
Definition of 'separation'				
Explanation of the difference between these two terms				
Description of Bowlby's maternal deprivation hypothesis				
Evaluation of Bowlby's maternal deprivation hypothesis				
Description of research into the effects of deprivation				
Evaluation of research into the effects of deprivation				
Description of research into the effects of separation				
Evaluation of research into the effects of separation				
Description of APFCC for a Key study of the effects of deprivation/separation				
Description of APFCC for a Key study related to Bowlby's maternal deprivation hypothesis				
Privation				
Definition of 'privation'				
Explanation of the difference between deprivation, separation, and privation				
Description of research into the effects of privation				
Evaluation of research into the effects of privation				
Description of APFCC for a Key study of the effects of privation				
Evaluation of the reversibility of early deprivation and/or privation				

DEPRIVATION AND SEPARATION

When young children are separated from their caregiver(s), it can be an upsetting, even frightening experience. The 'Getting you thinking ...' on p. 58 of the textbook describes some of the situations where children experience the unpleasant effects of separation.

When separations happen often and for long periods, this can lead to deprivation – i.e. children can end up being deprived of the emotional care and support they need in order to develop fully.

Bowlby's maternal deprivation hypothesis

The most prominent name in early research into separation and deprivation is that of Bowlby. Although his work was published over 50 years ago, it has had a lasting influence on this area.

Read the textbook's description of his hypothesis and other researchers' contributions (pp. 58–62). Then complete the activity on the right.

Research into separation

The textbook emphasizes the difference between separation and deprivation. Reread the 'key terms' on p. 58 and the description on p. 59 under 'Research into separation'. One of the crucial aspects of separation is that by itself, it does not necessarily have harmful effects, i.e. does not lead to deprivation.

Complete the activity below to summarize the key points of this research.

ACTIVITY

Bowlby's maternal deprivation hypothesis

1 What are the long-term effects of maternal deprivation, according to Bowlby's hypothesis? These are mentioned in several places on pp. 58–62. List them here.

Effects on emotional development

-
-
-
-

Effects on social development

-
-
-
-

2 Summarize the three important aspects of Bowlby's hypothesis outlined on p. 59:

- how – continuity in relationship
- when – critical period
- who – mother or mother substitute?

ACTIVITY

Research into separation

1 What two factors, according to Robertson and Robertson, help prevent separation leading to deprivation? How did their research demonstrate this?

Factor	How this was demonstrated in the Robertsons' research
•	•
•	•

2 The Robertsons' research reinforced the findings of earlier research by Skeels and Dye (1939). Note down the key findings of the Skeels and Dye research.

-

Evaluating Bowlby's hypothesis

On a positive level, Bowlby's theory has been influential, not just on other psychologists, but also on a practical level (as in the way children are treated in hospitals, outlined on p. 62 of the textbook). However, there have also been criticisms and problems identified with the hypothesis.

Now complete the activity below. The points you note down will be useful for answering AO1-type questions asking for criticisms of Bowlby's hypothesis, as well as AO2-type questions asking for an evaluation of research in the area of separation/deprivation.

After you have done the activity, you should be able to answer all the AO1-type exam questions shown on the right.

AO1 questions

- Explain what is meant by the terms 'separation' and 'deprivation'. (3 + 3 marks)
- Outline two effects of deprivation/separation. (3 + 3 marks)
- Outline two factors that influence the effects of deprivation/separation. (3 + 3 marks)
- Outline Bowlby's maternal deprivation hypothesis. (6 marks)
- Give two criticisms of the maternal deprivation hypothesis. (3 + 3 marks)
- Outline research into the effects of deprivation/separation. (6 marks)

ACTIVITY

Bowlby's maternal deprivation hypothesis

1 Is maternal deprivation the only or main form of deprivation? What other kinds of deprivation are there?

- paternal deprivation
  care-giver deprivation

2 Do all children react in the same way to deprivation?

- no.

3 Does deprivation cause maladjustment? What other factors in children's family and environment might be involved in the process?

-

PRIVATION

The term 'privation' refers to the *lack* of contact with a primary caregiver. This contrasts with 'deprivation', which refers to the *loss* of contact. In other words, those suffering deprivation have had early care, but lost it; those suffering privation never had it in the first place. Research has led psychologists to conclude that the effects of privation can be the most severe of all.

The textbook (pp. 62–4) looks at three areas of research into privation:

- longitudinal studies of children in institutional care
- case histories of children raised in extreme isolation
- studies of reactive attachment disorder.

ACTIVITY

Research into privation

Complete the table on p. 46 summarizing the details of relevant research in each of the three areas listed on the left. Organize the information in columns as shown by the first example. Doing this will help you to memorize the details you need for your answers to exam questions such as those asking you to:

- outline the effects of privation (AO1), or
- discuss whether the effects of privation are reversible (AO1+AO2).

ACTIVITY

Institutional care

Researcher	Who studied (+ ages)	Experience of deprivation	Effects of deprivation	Effects reversible?
Skeels and Dye (1939)	Two groups of orphans (ages not known)	One group raised in orphanage (control group); one raised in home for retarded women	Fall in IQ (87 → 61) in those in orphanage; rise in IQ (64 → 92) in those in home	Yes – care received by those in home reversed effects of early deprivation
Hodges and Tizard (1989)				
Rutter *et al.* (1998)	111 Romanian orphans adopted in UK before age 2			
Quinton *et al.* (1985)				

Children raised in extreme isolation

Researcher	Who studied (+ ages)	Experience of deprivation	Effects of deprivation	Effects reversible?
Koluchová (1976)	Czech twins (identical males), discovered at age 7			
Curtiss (1977)	Genie, discovered at age 13			

Reactive attachment disorder

Researcher	Who studied (+ ages)	Experience of deprivation	Effects of deprivation	Effects reversible?
Parker and Forrest (1993)	Not known	Early maternal rejection and separation		

AO1 questions

- Outline the effects of privation. (6 marks)
- Outline two effects of privation. (3 + 3 marks)
- Outline findings of research into privation. (6 marks)
- Outline conclusions of research into privation. (6 marks)

EXAM HINT

Terminology

Remember: in the exam you may be asked to outline or describe or define the terms separation, deprivation and privation. It's vital to get the differences between them very clear in your head.

ACTIVITY

Comparing separation, deprivation and privation

In the table below, summarize the main features of separation, deprivation and privation. For each one, describe what it is, what effects it has and whether those effects are reversible (and if so, how).

Institutional care

	Definition	Effects	Effects reversible?
Separation			
Deprivation			
Privation			

Key studies: deprivation and privation

There are two Key studies in this part of Topic 2, one relating to the effects of deprivation and one relating to the effects of privation. Technically there is a third (relating to Bowlby's maternal deprivation hypothesis), but if you choose the Bowlby study below, it counts both as a study of deprivation and a study relating to Bowlby's maternal deprivation hypothesis.

ACTIVITY

KEY STUDIES: Deprivation and privation

Write your own summaries of the Key studies on pp. 60 and 63 of the textbook, using trigger phrases, mnemonics or whatever will help you to memorize the important details. Under 'Criticisms', don't forget to include the points mentioned in the 'AO2 check' on p. 60.

AO1 questions (APFCC-type)

- Describe the aims and procedures of one study of deprivation/separation. (6 marks)
- Describe the procedures and findings of one study in which the effects of privation have been investigated. (6 marks)
- Describe the conclusions and give one criticism of one study of Bowlby's maternal deprivation hypothesis. (6 marks)

KEY STUDY textbook p. 60

Subject: THE EFFECTS OF DEPRIVATION

Researchers: Bowlby (1944)

Title

Aims

Procedures

Findings

Conclusions

Criticisms +

Criticisms –

KEY STUDY textbook p. 63

Subject: THE EFFECTS OF PRIVATION

Researchers: Hodges and Tizard (1989)

Title

Aims

Procedures

Findings

Conclusions

Criticisms +

Criticisms –

AO1+AO2 QUESTIONS ON SEPARATION, DEPRIVATION AND PRIVATION

So far, for these questions we've recommended a three-paragraph approach: one of AO1 and two of AO2 material. Sometimes it's easier (or simply more appropriate) to mix and match AO1 and AO2 *throughout* an answer. The following example does just that. Remember, though, that of the 18 marks available for this part of the question, 6 marks are for AO1 and 12 for AO2. There should, therefore, be far more AO2 material in answers to this part of the question. To show you what we mean by 'mix and match', we have used different colours for the AO1 and AO2 material – you should be able to work out quickly which is which!

AO1+AO2 questions

- Consider the extent to which research supports Bowlby's maternal deprivation hypothesis. (18 marks)
- Outline and evaluate Bowlby's maternal deprivation hypothesis. (18 marks)
- "Bowlby confused cause and effect with an association. The fact that early separation and later maladjustment are linked does not mean that one caused the other."

  Consider the view that early deprivation/separation has adverse effects on a child's development. (18 marks)
- Consider the view that privation has adverse effects on a child's development. (18 marks)
- To what extent are the effects of deprivation and/or privation irreversible? (18 marks)

Sample answer

To what extent are the effects of deprivation and/or privation irreversible? (18 marks)

Some research evidence suggests that the first two years of life are decisive for emotional and social development. For example, Hodges and Tizard's study (1989) showed that all the ex-institutional adolescents had difficulty coping with schoolmates. It may be, however, that they were simply less mature than their 'normal' peers and this made it more difficult to cope socially, rather than it being due to early deprivation. Quinton et al. (1985) found that ex-institutional girls went on to be less successful parents, though this may be explained in terms of a lack of adequate role models rather than poor attachment experiences. Studies of reactive attachment disorder also suggest that the effects of early privation are irreversible, though it is not certain that privation is the cause of such a disorder.

The case history of Genie suggests that early privation is not possible to recover from, even with good subsequent care, though she probably suffered a range of early privations and may have been retarded from birth. She was also quite old when discovered. Other studies of isolated children, such as the Czech twins, indicate that when children are offered good emotional care even after the age of 5, they can recover. However, they may have formed attachments with each other through their early, critical years. Harlow and Harlow (1962) also found that monkeys isolated from their mothers but reared with peers were reasonably well adjusted.

There is other evidence that at least some individuals in some circumstances can and do recover. The study of Romanian orphans, undertaken by Rutter and colleagues (1998), showed that such children could recover, although it is true that substitute care came before they were the age of 5. The answer about whether early privation is irreversible appears to be uncertain, though in general it is likely that children can recover given the right set of circumstances. However, there are many problems in interpreting the data from these studies. Perhaps most importantly, many of these children experienced more than emotional deprivation/privation, but many other forms of deprivation/privation as well (social, financial, diet, etc.). It is difficult to conduct well-controlled studies in this area of psychology, and therefore difficult to draw firm conclusions.

ACTIVITY

One for you to try ...

Consider the view that privation has adverse effects on a child's development. (18 marks)

Using the material on pp. 62–6 of the textbook, try the above question. If you haven't already done the activity on p. 66 (linked to Penelope Leach's Expert interview on p. 65 of the textbook), you might like to do that first as it will help you construct your answer to this question.

CHECK YOUR UNDERSTANDING

When you have finished working through this topic, try the questions in 'Check your understanding' on p. 66 of the textbook. You can check your answers by looking at the relevant parts of the textbook or this workbook, listed below.

1 textbook p. 58; workbook p. 47
2 textbook p. 59 (1st column)
3 textbook p. 59 (1st column)
4 textbook p. 60
5 textbook p. 60
6 textbook p. 61 (1st column)
7 textbook pp. 61–2
8 Koluchová, textbook p. 64

ANSWERS TO ACTIVITIES

Understanding the specification, p. 42

1 (a) Robertson and Robertson and (b) Bowlby.
2 Yes, you do have to know about Hodges and Tizard's research into institutionalization, because it is listed without an 'e.g.'.
3 Yes, the specification mentions research twice, so you need to know a Key study for each of two areas: the effects of separation/deprivation (Bowlby 1944 – see textbook p. 60) and the effects of privation (Hodges and Tizard 1989 – see textbook p. 63).

Topic 3 >> Critical issue: day care

Day care of children is one area where the work of psychologists has a clear practical application, rather than remaining a theoretical subject. By researching what happens when parents put their children into day care, psychologists can assess whether day care benefits or harms children's development. They can also identify which factors make day care most beneficial or harmful.

There is no clear consensus concerning the overall effects of day care and you will come across studies that appear to contradict each other. There is, however, a clear distinction between 'high-quality' day care and 'low-quality' day care. While the beneficial effects of the former are still open to debate, the negative effects of the latter are undeniable.

UNDERSTANDING THE SPECIFICATION

Here is what the AQA (A) specification says about this topic. It forms part of AS Module 1, Cognitive and Developmental Psychology.

Read it and then try the activity below. You'll find answers to the activity on p. 56.

Attachments in development

Critical issue: day care

The effects of day care on children's cognitive and social development.

ACTIVITY

Understanding the specification

1 You need to look at the effects of day care on which two aspects of children's development?

- __________
- __________

2 Does this topic involve Key studies (APFCCs)?
Clue: Look for the key word 'research'.

- __________

The specification entry for this topic is fairly short, so it is fairly easy to work out the different aspects of day care that have to be covered. The fact that this is the 'critical issue' for this section does not mean that questions set will be of a different format from other areas of the Developmental Psychology section, or (as is commonly believed) that they will necessarily be the part (c) component of developmental psychology questions.

The key issue in this area is whether day care affects both the cognitive development and the social development of children, and if so, in what ways. This is a hotly contested area of debate in developmental psychology, so you will need to be aware of the arguments on both sides, and be able to present research evidence to support (or challenge) each position.

TOPIC MAP

ACTIVITY

Topic map

Look through pp. 67–72 of the textbook to see where the items shown in the topic map are covered. Note down the relevant page numbers in the spaces left on the topic map on p. 52.

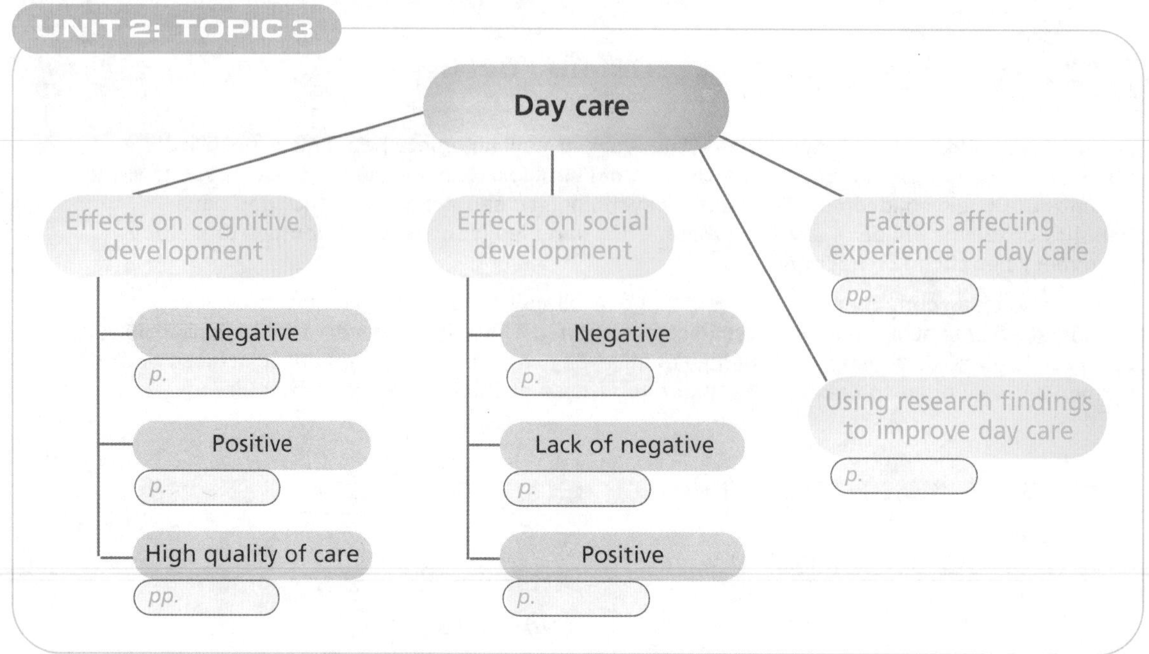

KEEPING TRACK

Use the table below to keep track of your work on this topic and plan your revision.

What I need to learn Critical issue: day care	Where is it?	Tick if you ... could make a basic attempt	could make a good attempt	have complete mastery of this
Definition of 'day care'				
Definition of 'cognitive development'				
Definition of 'social development'				
Description of research into the effects of day care on cognitive development				
Evaluation of research into the effects of day care on cognitive development				
Description of research into the effects of day care on social development				
Evaluation of research into the effects of day care on social development				
Evaluation of whether day care has harmful effects on the development of children				
Description of how research can be applied to improving day care				

EFFECTS OF DAY CARE ON COGNITIVE DEVELOPMENT

Definitions

In the AS psychology exam, you may be asked to define the terms used in the specification, including 'day care' and 'cognitive development'. On p. 67 of the textbook, detailed definitions of these terms are given. If you are answering a question such as this (right), you need to give enough detail to earn the marks available.

> **AO1 question**
>
> - Explain what is meant by the terms 'day care', 'cognitive development' and 'social development'. (2 + 2 + 2 marks)

ACTIVITY

Definitions

Read through the definition of 'day care' on p. 67 of the textbook. Complete the following table, which highlights the differences between the different types of care mentioned.

	Where are children cared for?	Who offers care?	How long for?
Day care			
Residential nursery			
Institutional care			

As you read through what the textbook says about day care, you will notice that there is a lot of disagreement between research findings on whether day care is beneficial or harmful. Some studies have found that day care has negative effects on children's development; others have found that it has positive effects. In your answers to exam questions, try and reflect this diversity of opinion. The next activity will help you to do this.

HINT

The meaning of 'cognitive'

Cognitive abilities are about how you *think*, how you *solve problems*, and how you use your *language skills*.

ACTIVITY

Effect of day care on cognitive development

Read through the text describing the effects of day care on cognitive development (textbook pp. 68–9). Summarize the findings of research by completing the tables below.

Negative effects

Researcher	Description of research (where known)	Findings – what were the effects on children's cognitive development?
Bryant *et al.* (1980)	Study of children looked after by childminders	Childminders reward quiet behaviour, encouraging passivity and understimulation
Russell (1999)		
Ruhm (2000)		

Positive effects

Researcher	Description of research (where known)	Findings – what were the effects on children's cognitive development?
Campbell *et al.* (2001)	20-year follow-up study of children who had been in day care	
Andersson (1992)		
NICHD (1997)		

EFFECTS OF DAY CARE ON SOCIAL DEVELOPMENT

ACTIVITY

Definition

Read through the definition of 'social development' on p. 67 of the textbook and then summarize the main points of the definition:

1 Social development is: ______

2 Examples of social abilities are: ______

______

3 Attachment promotes social development because: ______

______

There is also disagreement among researchers as to whether day care has a good or bad effect on social development. Again, try to reflect this range of opinion in any answers you write in the exam.

HINT

The meaning of 'social'

Social abilities are about how you *relate to other people.*

ACTIVITY

Effect of day care on social development

Read through the text describing the effects of day care on social development (textbook p. 69). Summarize the findings of research in the tables below. Note that as well as negative and positive effects, some researchers have found day care to have 'neutral' or 'non-negative' effects (see 'The lack of negative effects').

Negative effects

Researcher	Description of research (where known)	Findings – effects on social development
•		
•		

Non-negative effects

Researcher	Description of research (where known)	Findings – effects on social development
•		
•		

Positive effects

Researcher	Description of research (where known)	Findings – effects on social development
•		
•		

FACTORS WHICH AFFECT THE EXPERIENCE OF DAY CARE

Why have research studies reached such different conclusions about whether day care is harmful or beneficial? Well, you have probably already noticed that much seems to depend on the quality of care provided. Good-quality care can be stimulating and promote development; poor-quality care can increase insecurity and hinder development.

Quality of care is one important factor, but there are other factors that are thought to affect the experience of day care.

ACTIVITY

Factors affecting the experience of day care

Below is a table listing the five factors mentioned in the textbook (pp. 69–70) as affecting the experience of day care. For each factor, note down important pieces of research and some details about the research, what the research found and whether it concluded that day care had a positive or negative effect.

Factor	Researcher(s)	Who was studied, including ages	What the research found	Positive or negative
Quality of care				
Time spent in care				
Child's age				
Individual difference				
Quality of experience at home				

You should now be able to answer all the AO1-type exam questions shown below.

AO1 questions

- Explain what is meant by the terms 'day care', 'cognitive development' and 'social development'. (2 + 2 + 2 marks)
- Outline two effects of day care on cognitive development. (3 + 3 marks)
- Outline two effects of day care on social development. (3 + 3 marks)
- Describe research relating to the effects of day care on cognitive development. (6 marks)
- Outline one positive and one negative effect of day care on social development. (3 + 3 marks)
- Outline two factors that influence the effect of day care on a child's development. (3 + 3 marks)

USING RESEARCH FINDINGS TO IMPROVE DAY CARE

The final part of the topic on day care takes a positive look at how research findings can be used to improve day care. The textbook mentions several ways in which provision can be organized to improve children's experiences and promote their development.

The next activity will help you to summarize the main ideas and research findings.

ACTIVITY

Improving day care services

On a separate piece of paper, write a short letter to the head of your local social services department, outlining the ways in which day-care centres could improve the services they provide, as suggested by psychological research. Give a clear summary of possible improvements, grouping your ideas under the three headings of consistency, quality of care and staff training.

AO1+AO2 QUESTIONS ON DAY CARE

Some typical AO1+AO2-type questions are shown in the panel below. An example of a good worked answer to one of them is given on p. 254 of the textbook (along with a less good example). We have also suggested one for you to try yourself.

AO1+AO2 questions

- Consider the effects of day care on children's social development. (18 marks)
- Consider the effects of day care on children's cognitive development. (18 marks)
- To what extent has day care been shown to have beneficial effects on children's cognitive and/or social development?* (18 marks)

Detailed guidance on answering this question is given on pp. 254–5 of the textbook.

ACTIVITY

One for you to try ...

To what extent has day care been shown to have negative effects on children's development? (18 marks)

Using the material on pp. 67–72 of the textbook, construct your own answer to this question. You should pay particular attention to the comments made by Jay Belsky on p. 72, as this interview focuses on this very question.

CHECK YOUR UNDERSTANDING

When you have finished working through this topic, try the questions in 'Check your understanding' on p. 73 of the textbook. Then check your answers against the relevant parts of the textbook, listed below.

1 textbook p. 67
2 textbook p. 68
3 textbook pp. 68–9
4 textbook p. 69
5 (a) true (textbook p. 71)
(b) false (p. 68)
(c) false (p. 71)
(d) true (p. 68)
(e) false (p. 69)
6 textbook p. 69–70
7 textbook p. 70
8 in terms of social development, for example, see textbook, p. 69
9 textbook p. 71
10 textbook pp. 70–1

ANSWERS TO ACTIVITIES

Understanding the specification, p. 51

1 Cognitive development and social development.

2 The word 'research' doesn't appear in this part of the specification, so you do not need to learn any Key studies.

Stress

PREVIEW

There are three topics in this unit. You should read them alongside the following pages in the Collins *Psychology for AS-level* textbook:

INTRODUCTION

This unit covers the AS Physiological Psychology part of Module 2 (AQA Specification A). The diagram below shows where it fits in to the overall AS qualification.

Read the Preview and Introduction on p. 76 of the textbook now. This will give you an overview of what's in the unit.

Where this unit fits in to the AS qualification

- **Module 1**
  - Cognitive Psychology: Human memory
  - Developmental Psychology: Attachments in development
- **Module 2**
  - Physiological Psychology: **Stress**
    - Stress as a bodily response
    - Sources of stress
    - Critical issue: stress management
  - Individual Differences: Abnormality
- **Module 3**
  - Social Psychology: Social influence
  - Research Methods

In the AS Module 2 exam, you will have a choice of two questions on **Stress**. You will have to answer one of them.

Topic 1 >> Stress as a bodily response

As the Introduction to Unit 3 suggests (textbook p. 76), stress is thought to be linked to a wide range of illnesses, from anxiety and depression to heart attacks and strokes. This topic looks at how the body responds to stress and how this response can lead to illness and disease. Students often express their concern at the complex biology they think is needed for the first part of this topic. The required understanding of biology is actually quite basic, and questions only ever require a brief account of biological processes. We have tried to make the passage through this topic area as painless as possible!

UNDERSTANDING THE SPECIFICATION

Here is what the AQA (A) specification says about this topic. It forms part of AS Module 2, Physiological Psychology and Individual Differences.

Read it and then try the activity below. You'll find answers to the activity on p. 67.

Stress

a. Stress as a bodily response

The body's response to stressors, including the General Adaptation Syndrome (Selye). Research into the relationship between stress and physical illness, including cardiovascular disorders and the effects of stress on the immune system.

ACTIVITY

Understanding the specification

1 According to the specification, what aspect of the body's response to stressors do you *have* to study?

- ______

2 What two aspects of the relationship between stress and physical illness do you *have* to study?

- ______
- ______

3 Does this topic involve Key studies (APFCCs)? If so, how many? *Clue*: Look for the key word 'research'.

- ______

In this part of the specification you are required to know how the body responds to stressors (for example the role of the autonomic system and the pituitary gland). You are specifically required (note the use of the term 'including') to know about Selye's General Adaptation Syndrome (GAS) and should be able to summarize its three stages of stress response, as well as being able to offer criticisms of the GAS model.

The use of the term 'research' should alert you to the possibility of questions relating to studies of the relationship between stress and illness. These may specifically ask for one research study that has explored the relationship between stress and cardiovascular disorders and the effects of stress on the immune system (i.e. APFCC questions), or they may be more general in asking for research in this area.

TOPIC MAP

ACTIVITY

Topic map

Look through pp. 77–87 of the textbook to see where the items shown in the topic map are covered. Note down the relevant page numbers in the spaces left on the topic map.

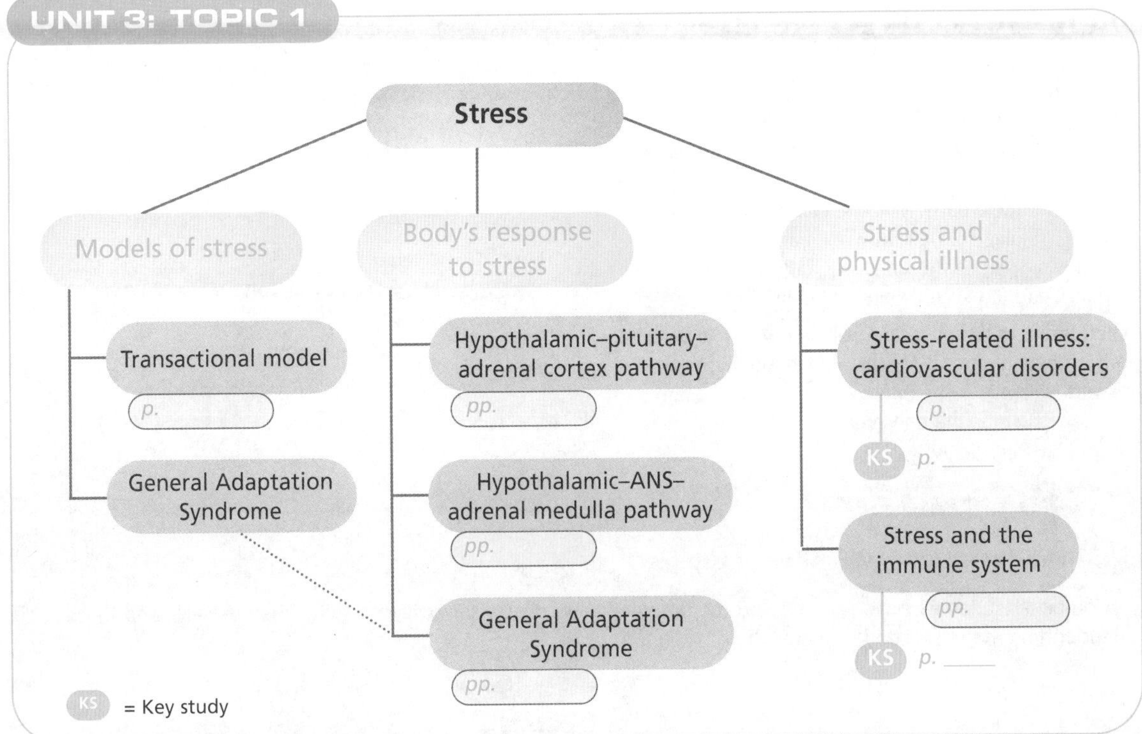

KEEPING TRACK

Use the table below to keep track of your work on this topic and plan your revision. See p. iv in the Introduction for guidance on how to fill it in.

What I need to learn	Where is it?	Tick if you ... could make a basic attempt	could make a good attempt	have complete mastery of this
The body's response to stressors				
Definition of 'stress'				
Definition of 'stressor'				
Definition of 'Selye's General Adaptation Syndrome'				
Description of at least two ways in which the body responds to stress (including the two main pathways)				
Description of the General Adaptation Syndrome				
Evaluation of the General Adaptation Syndrome				
Stress and physical illness				
Definition of 'cardiovascular disorders'				
Definition of 'immune system'				
Description of the effects of stress on the body, including physiological arousal and immunosuppression				
Description of research into stress and cardiovascular disorders				
Evaluation of research into stress and cardiovascular disorders				
Description of research into stress and the immune system				
Evaluation of research into stress and the immune system				
Description of APFCC for a Key study investigating stress and cardiovascular disorders				
Description of APFCC for a Key study investigating the effects of stress on the immune system				

MODELS OF STRESS

The study of stress is a relatively recent one, even if stress itself has been around for tens of thousands of years! The text on p. 78 of the textbook describes how psychologists' views of stress have developed over the last few decades. Early views, such as Selye's, focused on the physiological or bodily response to stressors; later views, such as the transactional model, have emphasized the psychological element.

When trying to define stress, it is important to refer to both aspects of stress. Try the activity below. Your answers will give you enough detail to tackle exam questions such as the ones shown on the right.

AO1 questions

- What is meant by the terms 'stress', 'stressor' and 'General Adaptation Syndrome'? (2 + 2 + 2 marks)
- Explain what is meant by the terms 'stress' and 'stressor'. (3 + 3 marks)

ACTIVITY

How different models define stress

Complete the table below, summarizing the different views of stress and stressors proposed by Selye and those supporting the transactional model.

	Selye's General Adaptation Syndrome	The transactional model
Stress is ...	•	•
A stressor is ...	•	•

What is the third definition of stress, given in the key terms on p. 77 of the textbook?

•

BODILY RESPONSES TO STRESS

When your brain detects a stressor, it responds by triggering an alarm reaction. This sets in motion physical changes that prepare the body for action, either to deal with the stressor or to run away from it (what Walter Cannon termed the 'fight or flight' response).

Two systems are involved in this reaction. These are described in detail on pp. 79–80 of the textbook. Don't be put off by the long names and the biological terms – the following text should help you to understand what is going on.

The full names of the two systems – or pathways – are given in the headings on p. 79. Here we refer to them using initials, HPAC and HANSAM. These acronyms are useful for triggering your memory in the exam. If you recall them, you can fill out the words they stand for and then build up a picture of the reactions. Look at the diagrams on the next page and then try the activity that follows.

EXAM HINT

Using diagrams

Diagrams are an excellent way of remembering details – especially of processes and how things relate to each other. In the exam, however, you should generally write in continuous prose as you will be given a mark for 'Quality of Written Communication'. You can use diagrams such as those shown on the next page, but you should offer some written description as well.

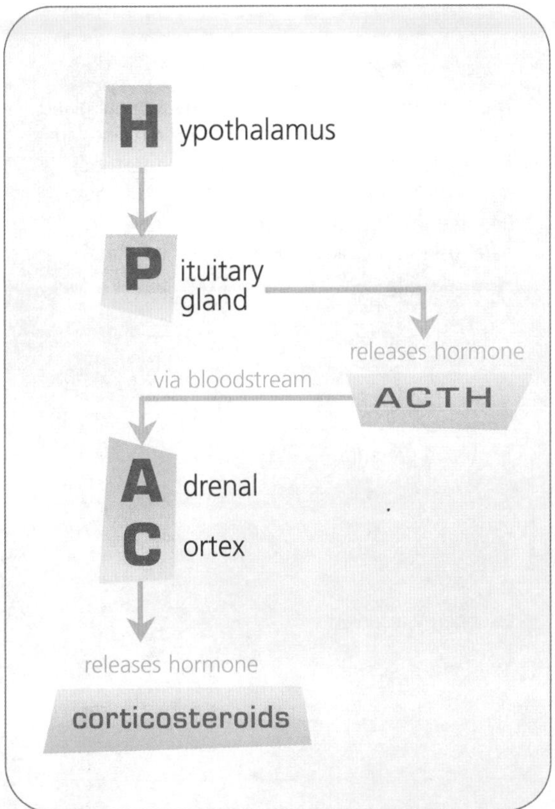

The hypothalamic–pituitary–adrenal cortex pathway (HPAC)

H ypothalamus
brainstem
A utonomic
N ervous
S ystem
via nerves
A drenal
M edulla
releases hormones
adrenaline
noradrenaline

The hypothalamic–autonomic nervous system–adrenal medulla pathway (HANSAM)

ACTIVITY

Understanding the two pathways

1 After reading the text on pp. 79–80 of the textbook, study the diagrams above and then answer the following questions.

	HPAC	HANSAM
(a) Which parts of the brain control the reaction?	•	•
(b) How does the brain stimulate the adrenal gland?	•	•
(c) Which part of the adrenal gland is involved?	•	•
(d) Which hormones are released by the adrenal gland?	•	•

2 What are the major similarities between the two systems?

-
-

3 What are the major differences? In particular, think about how the adrenal gland is stimulated by the brain into releasing hormones.

-
-

Suggested answers to the activity are given on p. 67.

Now do the activity on the right.

Once you have finished the activities and absorbed all the information here and in the textbook, you should be able to tackle questions such as the ones below.

AO1 questions

- Outline two ways in which the body responds to stress. (3 + 3 marks)
- Describe one way in which the body responds to stress. (6 marks)

The General Adaptation Syndrome

A little bit of stress may do you good – the pressure of playing in a big match or taking an exam may spur you on to perform as well as you can. However, prolonged stress can be harmful, leading to both physical and psychological damage. Selye's General Adaptation Syndrome is an attempt to explain both the short-term physical effects of stress and the long-term damage.

ACTIVITY

Activating the body's stress response

The three hormones released by the adrenal gland, corticosteroids, adrenaline and noradrenaline, are a vital part of the stress response. The textbook describes how they prepare the body to fight or flee (see pp. 79–80). Summarize the key points here, using the following phrases as prompts.

1 heart rate

2 blood pressure

3 energy reserves

ACTIVITY

Evaluating the General Adaptation Syndrome

1 The three phases of the GAS can be remembered by the acronym ARE. Complete the diagram below, by filling in the rest of the words and noting down what happens at each stage.

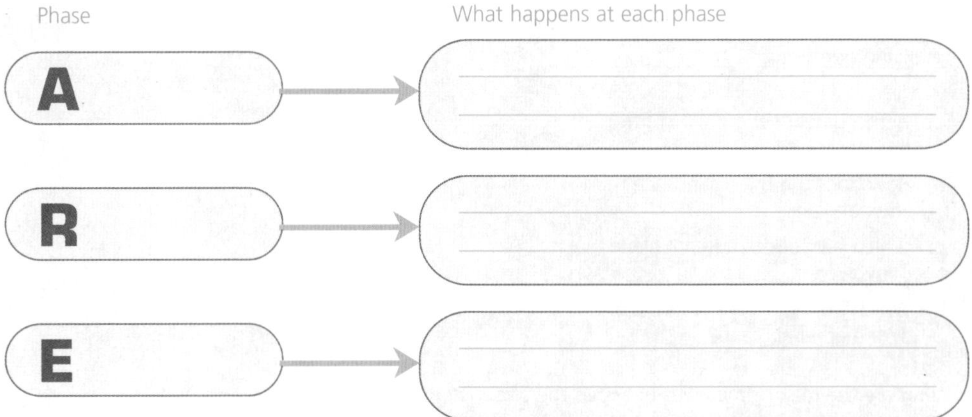

2 What are the positive aspects of Selye's GAS and what are the negative ones? Summarize these in the space below. (*Note*: read the final paragraph on p. 81 of the textbook under 'Stress and physical illness'.)

Positive	Negative
•	•
•	•
•	•
•	•

AO1 questions

- Explain what is meant by the terms 'General Adaptation Syndrome' and 'stress'. (3 + 3 marks)
- Describe Selye's General Adaptation Syndrome. (6 marks)
- Give two criticisms of Selye's General Adaptation Syndrome. (3 + 3 marks)
- Outline the main features of Selye's General Adaptation Syndrome and give one criticism of it. (3 + 3 marks)

STRESS AND PHYSICAL ILLNESS

Long-term stress is linked to several kinds of physical illness, including the five cardiovascular disorders listed on p. 82 of the textbook.

It is important to understand how the body's stress-response can lead to these disorders. The textbook discusses various ways in which the stress-response can cause illness.

HINT

Cardiovascular disorders

Check that you know which parts of the body make up the cardiovascular system. See the key term 'Cardiovascular disorder' on p. 77 of the textbook if you are unsure.

ACTIVITY

How the stress-response causes illness

Complete the following table summarizing how stress can damage the body.

Method	How it can cause damage	Illnesses it can lead to
Direct mechanical effects (textbook p. 82)	•	•
Energy mobilization (textbook p. 82)	•	•
Other effects (textbook p. 83)	•	•

During the stress-response, the body activates some systems to help meet the threat of the stressor. At the same time it shuts down or inhibits other systems, not immediately needed to deal with the stress. Over a prolonged period, this can lead to physical damage or illness.

ACTIVITY

The effect of the stress-response on the body's systems

Draw up a list of systems that are shut down or inhibited during the body's stress-response. These are mentioned on pp. 82 and 83. An example is given below.

Systems inhibited or shut down	How this can lead to physical damage
• Digestive system	•
•	•
•	•

Stress and the immune system

The immune system is the body's defence mechanism that helps protect us from infection. The textbook explains how this works (see pp. 82–3).

ACTIVITY

Stress and the immune system

1 The diagram below summarizes the information given in the textbook about the immune system. Fill in the gaps describing what the various components are and how they work.

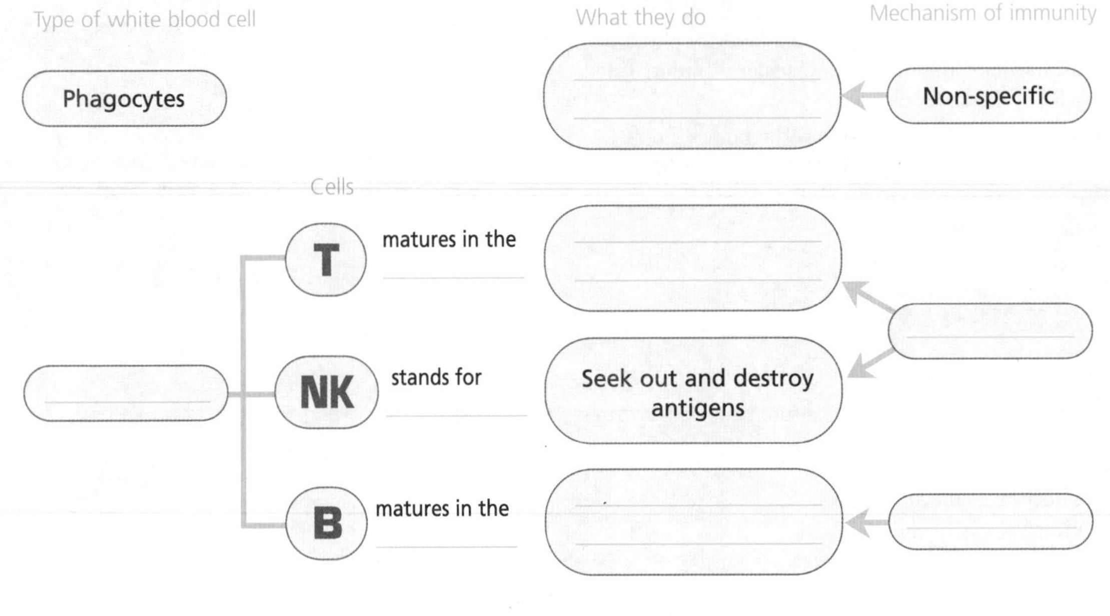

2 How does stress affect the immune system? Read the text on p. 83, the Key study on p. 85, the Expert interview on p. 86 and the text at the top of p. 87.

On a separate piece of paper, write notes to describe:

- how stress can suppress the immune system
- what factors can improve immune function
- how personal relationships can affect immune function
- any evidence of gender differences.

AO1 questions

- Outline the effects of stress on the immune system. (6 marks)
- Outline two effects of stress on the cardiovascular system. (3 + 3 marks)
- Outline findings of research into the relationship between stress and physical illness. (6 marks)
- Outline findings of research into the relationship between stress and cardiovascular disorders. (6 marks)
- Outline conclusions of research into the relationship between stress and the immune system. (6 marks)

Key studies: stress and physical illness

There are two Key studies in this topic. The first relates to stress and physical illness (textbook p. 84) and the second to stress and the immune system (textbook p. 85).

A third Key study is relevant to this topic: the study of stress and cardiovascular disorders by Friedman and Rosenman (see textbook p. 95).

You can use either of the latter two studies as a response to a question asking about 'stress and physical illness'. Both cardiovascular disorders and immunosuppression count as physical illness.

ACTIVITY

KEY STUDIES: Stress and physical illness

Write your own summaries of the Key studies on pp. 84 and 85 of the textbook, using trigger phrases, mnemonics or whatever will help you to memorize the important details. Under 'Criticisms', don't forget to include the points mentioned in the 'AO2 checks' at the end of each study.

KEY STUDY textbook p. 84

Subject STRESS AND PHYSICAL ILLNESS

Researchers Brady et al. (1958)

Title

Aims

Procedures

Findings

Conclusions

Criticisms +

Criticisms −

KEY STUDY textbook p. 85

Subject STRESS AND THE IMMUNE SYSTEM

Researchers Kiecolt-Glaser et al. (1984)

Title

Aims

Procedures

Findings

Conclusions

Criticisms +

Criticisms −

AO1 questions (APFCC-type)

- Describe the procedures and findings of one study of stress and physical illness. (6 marks)
- Describe the aims and conclusions of one study of stress and cardiovascular disorders. (6 marks)
- Describe the findings of one study of stress and the immune system and give one criticism of this study. (6 marks)

AO1+AO2 QUESTIONS ON STRESS AS A BODILY RESPONSE

This is an area where the number of possible AO1+AO2 questions is reasonably limited. You can, therefore, afford the luxury of being quite creative when preparing your responses. The relationship between stress and cardiovascular disorders spans many different areas. In the worked example (opposite) we have used material from several different parts of the stress chapter of the textbook in order to construct an informed and critical response to the question set. We have used information from:

- the Key study (Friedman and Rosenman, textbook p. 95)
- the 'Hardy personality' (textbook p. 96)
- 'Gender differences in coping' (textbook p. 97)
- 'An eye on the exam' (textbook p. 99).

AO1+AO2 questions

- To what extent does research support a link between stress and the immune system? (18 marks)
- To what extent does research support a link between stress and cardiovascular disorders? (18 marks)
- To what extent does research support a link between stress and physical illness?* (18 marks)
- Outline and evaluate research into the relationship between stress and physical illness.* (18 marks)

**It pays to look very closely at the requirements of each question. If a question that you are prepared for appears in a slightly different format, it could still be asking for the exactly the same material (as illustrated here). This is not always the case, so don't try to shoehorn a prepared answer into a question where it clearly doesn't fit!*

ACTIVITY

One for you to try ...

To what extent does research support a link between stress and the immune system? (18 marks)

Using information on pp. 84–7, write your own answer to this question. The Expert interview with Janice Kiecolt-Glaser will give you some invaluable help in constructing your response. You might want to refer back to the worked example on pp. 48–9 of this workbook, as well as the example opposite for advice on how to tackle a question such as this.

CHECK YOUR UNDERSTANDING

When you have finished working through this topic, try the questions in 'Check your understanding' on p. 87 of the textbook. Check your answers by looking at the relevant parts of the textbook or this workbook, listed below.

1 textbook pp. 77–8; workbook p. 60
2 textbook p. 78
3 textbook pp. 78–9; workbook p. 61
4 textbook p. 80
5 textbook pp. 82–3
6 textbook p. 84
7 textbook p. 85
8 textbook p. 85
9 textbook p. 87
10 textbook p. 87

Sample answer

To what extent does research support a link between stress and cardiovascular disorders? (18 marks)

Psychological research has demonstrated that stress can adversely affect the cardiovascular system. Friedman and Rosenman (1974) described Type A behaviour as a major behavioural risk factor for cardiovascular disorders. Different characteristics mark out the Type A individual whose risk of coronary heart disease is greatest. The issue of control, for example, is an important one and may distinguish between the vulnerability of Type As and the resistance of 'hardy' types (Kobasa 1979). Kobasa's hardy types report feeling in control of their work and their lives. Type A behaviour predicts cardiovascular disorders, while hardiness predicts general good health. The relationship between Type A behaviour and cardiovascular disorders is not always consistent across studies. Other studies (e.g. Shekelle et al. 1985) have failed to show a relationship between Type A behaviour and heart disease. The experience of stress, therefore, does not inevitably contribute to the development of cardiovascular disorders. For some, stress may adversely affect health. At the same time, however, a state of ill health can act as a significant source of stress, reducing an individual's ability to cope with other sources of stress.

Although research has generally established a relationship between stress and cardiovascular disorders, it is also clear that there are gender differences in this vulnerability. Vogele et al. (1997) found that men show more stress-related arousal than women across a range of psychological and physical stressors. Taylor et al. (2000) offer an evolutionary explanation for this, claiming that high sympathetic nervous system activation (targeted primarily at the cardiovascular system) and high cortisol responses are characteristic biological components of the male stress response. In contrast, neurophysiological mechanisms within the female brain inhibit the fight-or-flight response, and instead promote attachment behaviour (tend-and-befriend). Taylor and colleagues believe that these gender differences have evolved to allow the individual to maximize their chances of survival when confronted with a stressor, and could play a role in the fact that men are more likely than women to die of cardiovascular disorders.

ANSWERS TO ACTIVITIES

Understanding the specification, p. 58

1 The word 'including' means that you have to know about Selye's General Adaptation Syndrome when studying the body's response to stressors.

2 The second 'including' means that when studying the relationship between stress and physical illness, you have to know about both cardiovascular disorders and the effects of stress on the immune system.

3 Yes, the specification mentions research into the relationship between stress and physical illness. Two aspects of this relationship are mentioned (cardiovascular disorders and the effects of stress on the immune system) and so you need to learn about two Key studies, one for each aspect.

Understanding the two pathways, p. 61

1 The answers are all in the diagram!

2 Similarities include:

- Both pathways start in the brain and work through to the adrenal gland.
- Both pathways are controlled by the hypothalamus.
- The end result is the same: the adrenal gland releases hormones that help the body deal with or escape from the stress.

3 A major difference is that in the HPAC pathway, the adrenal cortex is stimulated by hormones in the bloodstream. The HANSAM pathway depends on messages being carried via the autonomic nervous system.

The hormones released by the different parts of the adrenal gland are different (see diagrams on p. 61).

Topic 2 >> Sources of stress

In Topic 1 we defined a stressor as something that produces the stress-response – in other words, a source of stress. In this topic we look at some of the many aspects of life and the world that cause us stress and how psychologists have attempted to measure them. The first source of stress that we look at here is 'life changes' (also known as life events), which are events that necessitate a significant transition or adjustment in important aspects of a person's life. The second is 'workplace stressors', i.e. aspects of the working environment that may cause us stress. The number of workplace stressors is potentially endless, but the textbook considers four in detail.

Stress does not affect everyone the same way – it is modified by factors such as gender and personality (i.e. individual differences).

UNDERSTANDING THE SPECIFICATION

Here is what the AQA (A) specification says about this topic. It forms part of AS Module 2, Physiological Psychology and Individual Differences.

Read it and then try the activity below. You'll find answers to the activity on p. 77.

Attachments in development

b. Sources of stress

Research into sources of stress, including life changes (e.g. Holmes and Rahe), and workplace stressors (e.g. work overload, role ambiguity). Individual differences in modifying the effects of stressors, including the roles played by personality (e.g. Friedman and Rosenman), culture and gender.

ACTIVITY

Understanding the specification

1 What **two** areas of research into sources of stress do you have to know about?

- ______________________
- ______________________

2 Whose work is given as an example of research into life changes as a source of stress?

- ______________________

3 What two examples of workplace stressors are given in the specification?

- ______________________

____

4 The specification mentions three types of individual differences which can modify the effects of stress. What are they?

- ______________________
- ______________________
- ______________________

Are these 'compulsory' or merely examples?

- ______________________

5 Does this topic involve Key studies (APFCCs)? If so, how many? *Clue*: Look for the key word 'research'.

- ______________________

____

In this part of the specification you are expected to know about the sources of stress, and specifically research into the role of life changes and workplace stressors as sources of stress. Unlike specification entries which are preceded by the term 'including', you cannot be asked specifically about the work of Holmes and Rahe, or about work overload or role ambiguity. These are merely examples used in the specification to guide your response. The second aspect of this topic deals with individual differences – stress does not affect everybody in the same way. You are required to show your understanding of how the effects of stress might be modified by personality differences (e.g. the Type A and non-Type A difference demonstrated by Friedman and Rosenman), cultural differences and gender differences.

TOPIC MAP

ACTIVITY

Topic map

Look through pp. 88–100 of the textbook and fill in the relevant page numbers in the spaces left on the topic map below.

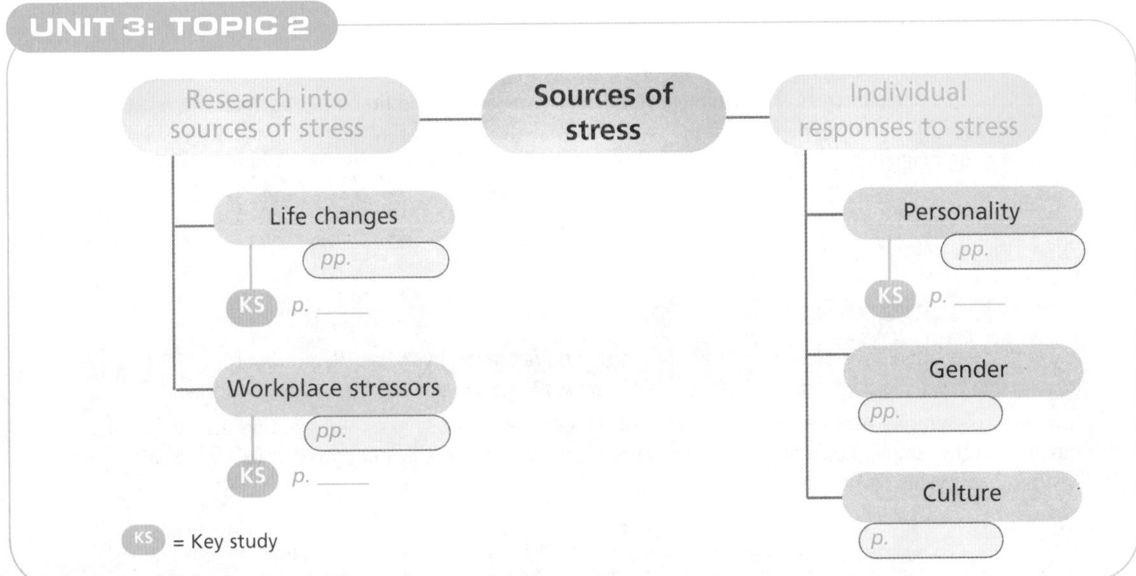

KEEPING TRACK

Use the table below to keep track of your work on this topic and plan your revision.

What I need to learn	Where is it?	Tick if you ... could make a basic attempt	could make a good attempt	have complete mastery of this
Research into sources of stress				
Definition of 'life changes'				
Definition of 'control (psychological)'				
Definition of 'workplace stressor'				
Description of research into life changes as a source of stress				
Evaluation of research into life changes as a source of stress				
Description of APFCC for a Key study investigating life changes as a source of stress				
Description of research into workplace stressors				
Evaluation of research into workplace stressors				
Description of APFCC for a Key study investigating workplace stressors				
Individual differences in modifying the effects of stress				
Description of research into the role played by personality in modifying the effects of stressors				
Evaluation of research into the role played by personality				
Description of research into the role played by gender				
Evaluation of research into the role played by gender				
Description of research into the role played by culture				
Evaluation of research into the role played by culture				

RESEARCH INTO SOURCES OF STRESS

Sources of stress are many and varied. In fact, there are so many possible causes of stress that psychologists have found it hard to devise effective ways of investigating and measuring them. Here we look at two areas that have interested researchers: life changes and workplace stressors.

Life changes

On pp. 89–92, the textbook describes several different scales that have been developed in order to measure aspects of life that can cause stress. The Holmes–Rahe scale was one of the first and has been the most widely used for over 30 years. Holmes and Rahe were doctors who noticed that their patients often seemed to experience several significant life events prior to becoming ill – for example, divorce or bereavement.

ACTIVITY

How different models define stress

Life-event scales often have quite complicated names and are known by initials. Read through pp. 89–92 and complete the table below to summarize what each scale is, who devised it and how it works.

In the final column give examples from the scale where possible. Choose examples you find easy to remember – for example, beginning or ending school has a value of 26 life change units (LCU), while Christmas has a value of 12.

Scale	What initials stand for	Who devised it	How it works	Examples of things it measures
SRRS	•	•	•	• Life changes, e.g. death of spouse = 100 LCU
LES	•	•	• Users rate 57 items on a scale from -3 to +3	•
HUS	• Hassles & Uplifts Scales	•	•	•
LSSRI	•	• Moos and Swindle (1990)	•	•

As the textbook explains on p. 91, several problems have been identified with the Holmes–Rahe scale. In an attempt to improve the way life changes were measured, other researchers developed their own scales. Nevertheless, the life-event approach has been successful in identifying and measuring stress. It is important to remember that scales like the 'Hassles and Uplift' scale do not measure life events but daily stressors and 'uplifts'. This material can, however, be used as part of your evaluation of life events scales such as the SRRS.

AO1 questions

- Explain what is meant by the terms 'life changes' and 'stress'. (3 + 3 marks)
- Outline two ways in which life changes may cause stress. (3 + 3 marks)
- Describe one source of stress. (6 marks)
- Outline research into life events as a source of stress. (6 marks)
- Give two criticisms of research measuring life changes as a source of stress. (3 + 3 marks)

Now try the activity below. The information you note down will provide plenty of material for answering AO1 questions that ask you to give criticisms of research measuring life changes. You can also use it in the AO2 part of questions that require you to evaluate these sorts of scales (see textbook, pp. 256–7).

You should now be able to attempt all the AO1-type questions shown at the bottom of p. 70.

ACTIVITY

Evaluating life changes scales

In the table below, summarize all the positive and negative aspects of life-event scales as a way of measuring the amount of stress in people's lives.

Positive aspects	Negative aspects
•	•
•	•
•	•
•	•

Workplace stressors

The study of workplace stress is one area of psychology that has a clear practical application. By identifying sources of stress, researchers can offer employers and employees pointers about how to reduce stress. In the exam, you may need to identify at least two workplace stressors and describe how they create stress. This will enable you to answer questions such as those shown on the right.

AO1 questions

- Outline two ways in which the workplace can cause stress. (3 + 3 marks)
- Explain what is meant by the terms 'stress' and 'workplace stressor'. (3 + 3 marks)
- Outline findings of research into the effects of workplace stress. (6 marks)

ACTIVITY

Workplace stressors

1 Why is the study of workplace stress an important area:

- for employees?
- for employers/organizations?

2 The textbook lists four main areas of workplace stress. If you carry out the activity on p. 93 of the textbook, you may identify other ones. For each category, summarize the key factors in the table below and on p. 72. We have included some details about the physical environment to start you off.

Category	Factors	Relevant research	How these factors increase stress
Physical environment	• space		Make it harder to work
	• temperature	Halpern (1995)	Increased arousal, leading to frustration
	• lighting		
	• arrangement		
	• noise	Evans et al. (1998)	

continued on next page

ACTIVITY

Workplace stressors – *continued from p. 71*

Category	Factors	Relevant research	How these factors increase stress
Work overload	●	●	●
Lack of control	●	●	●
Role ambiguity	●	●	●
Other	●	●	●

Key studies: stress and physical illness

There are two Key studies in this topic. The first relates to life changes as a source of stress (textbook p. 90) and the second to stress in the workplace (textbook p. 94).

ACTIVITY

KEY STUDIES: Sources of stress

Write your own summaries of the Key studies on pp. 90 and 94 of the textbook, using trigger phrases, mnemonics or whatever will help you to memorize the important details. Under 'Criticisms', don't forget to include the points mentioned in the 'AO2 check' on p. 90.

KEY STUDY textbook p. 90

Subject LIFE CHANGES AND STRESS

Researchers Rahe et al. (1970)

Title

Aims

Procedures

Findings

Conclusions

Criticisms +

Criticisms –

KEY STUDY textbook p. 94

Subject STRESS IN THE WORKPLACE

Researchers Johansson et al. (1978)

Title

Aims

Procedures

Findings

Conclusions

Criticisms +

Criticisms −

AO1 questions (APFCC-type)

- Describe the procedures and conclusions of one study of life events as a source of stress. (6 marks)
- Describe the aims and findings of one study of the workplace as a source of stress. (6 marks)
- Describe the findings of one study relating to the sources of stress, and give one criticism of this study. (6 marks)

INDIVIDUAL RESPONSES TO STRESS

We have already seen that individuals can respond very differently to the same sort of stress (remember the cartoons on p. 78 of the textbook). The study of individual differences is an important area of stress research. The textbook looks at three aspects of this:

- personality (Type A personality and hardy personality)
- gender
- culture.

Personality

The textbook looks at two aspects of personality, one which is claimed to make people more vulnerable to stress (Type A personality, textbook pp. 95–6) and one which is claimed to protect people from the effects of stress (the hardy personality, textbook p. 96).

Key study: individual responses to stress

The Key study on p. 95 of the textbook looks at the research into stress and cardiovascular disorders done by Friedman and Rosenman. This Key study will be useful for answering APFCC questions on stress as a bodily response (see workbook pp. 64 and 66), but you will not be asked an APFCC question about individual responses to stress.

ACTIVITY

KEY STUDY: Individual responses to stress

Using the form on p. 74, write your own summary of the Key study on p. 95 of the textbook, in a way that will help you to memorize the important details. Don't forget to include the points mentioned in the 'AO2 check'.

KEY STUDY textbook p. 95

textbook p. 95

Subject STRESS & CARDIOVASCULAR DISORDERS

Researchers Friedman and Rosenman (1974)

Title

Aims

Procedures

Findings

Conclusions

Criticisms +

Criticisms –

ACTIVITY

Behaviour patterns

Complete the diagram below, summarizing the personality types identified by Friedman and Rosenman.

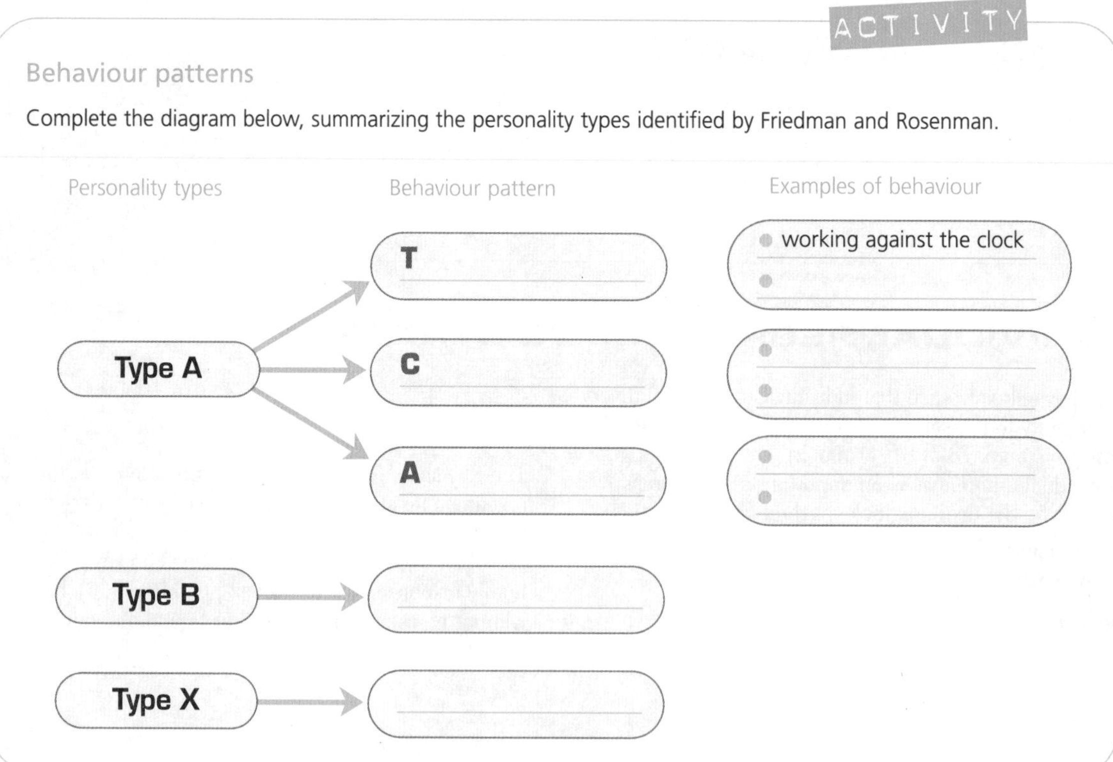

AO1 questions

- Outline two ways in which personality can modify the effects of stressors. (3 + 3 marks)
- Outline the role of personality in modifying the effects of stressors. (6 marks)
- Outline research relating to the role of personality in modifying the effects of stressors. (6 marks)

Hardiness

The concept of hardiness as a defence against stress was developed by Kobasa and is easily remembered as the three Cs. Complete the activity on the right.

ACTIVITY

Hardy personality

Makes notes on Kobasa's research into the hardy personality. In particular, note down:

1 what the three Cs stand for
2 how they provide defences against sources of stress
3 what two other factors help protect against stress
4 what criticisms have been levelled against Kobasa's ideas.

Gender

Two facts have interested researchers into stress:

1 on average women live longer than men
2 men are more likely to die of cardiovascular disorders.

Of course, these facts may well be connected! Psychologists have sought to investigate whether there are differences between men and women in their bodily responses to stress.

ACTIVITY

Gender and bodily responses to stress

1 Research has found different physiological responses to stressors between men and women. In the space below, summarize what each of the following found.

- Frankenhaeuser *et al.* (1976)
- Stoney *et al.* (1990)
- Taylor *et al.* (2000)

2 What do Taylor and colleagues mean by females' 'tend-and-befriend' response?

How does evolution explain this difference between men's and women's responses?

Researchers have also investigated whether there are differences in how men and women cope with stress (textbook p. 97). Carry out the activity on p. 97 of the textbook to find out for yourself whether such differences exist.

The panel on the right contains examples of questions you might be asked about the role of gender in modifying the effects of stress.

AO1 questions

- Outline the role of gender in modifying the effects of stressors. (6 marks)
- Outline two ways in which gender can modify the effects of stressors. (3 + 3 marks)
- Outline findings of research relating to the role of gender in modifying the effects of stressors. (6 marks)

Culture

Psychologists agree that culture is an important factor in modifying an individual's experience of stress. However, they also agree that it is very hard to pinpoint what aspects of culture account for these differences.

ACTIVITY

Culture and responses to stress

The textbook describes several research studies into how people of different cultures respond to stress. Read the text on pp. 98 and 99, and summarize the key points below.

Factor	Researcher	Findings
Differences in social support	• Kim and McKenry (1998)	• White Americans used children for social support less than other ethnic groups in USA.
	• Connell and Gibson (1997)	
Other dimensions of culture	•	•
Cultural diversity as a stressor	•	•

AO1 questions

- Outline the role of culture in modifying the effects of stressors. (3 + 3 marks)
- Outline two ways in which culture can modify the effects of stressors. (3+ 3 marks)
- Outline conclusions of research relating to the role of culture in modifying the effects of stressors. (6 marks)

AO1 +AO2 QUESTIONS ON SOURCES OF STRESS

Possible AO1+AO2 questions on sources of stress are shown on the right. Two sample answers to the first question can be found on p. 256 of the textbook. Look at the two answers and think about the following questions:

- What are the main differences between the answers that warrant the difference in marks?
- Unpack the question into specific requirements (outline of first attempt to explain the relationship, outline of second attempt to explain, etc.).
- If you were to outline and evaluate two attempts to explain the relationship between life changes and stress (as here) and had a 'budget' of approximately 360 words, how many words would you allocate to each 'portion' of your answer?
- Do a rough comparison between your plan and Answer 2. Are they close?
- What does that tell you about the value of planning?

AO1+AO2 questions

- Outline and evaluate attempts to explain the relationship between life changes and stress.* (18 marks)
- To what extent have the effects of stressors been shown to be modified by gender and/or culture? (18 marks)
- To what extent have the effects of stressors been shown to be modified by individual differences? (18 marks)
- Outline and evaluate research into the workplace as a source of stress. (18 marks)

*See p. 256 for sample answers to this question.

ACTIVITY

One for you to try ...

Outline and evaluate research into the workplace as a source of stress. (18 marks)

Using the material on pp. 92–4 of the textbook, construct a plan for the above question, and then write out your answer. You should think carefully about how you will ensure that two-thirds of your answer is AO2. Try to incorporate insights from the second heading under 'An eye on the exam' (p. 99 of the textbook) into your answer. The following two points can also be used as an evaluation of the workplace as a source of stress.

- In a recent study of night-shift nurses, Kobayashi *et al.* (1999) found that the cortisol and NK cell activity levels were low during the night shift, suggesting that night shift work is highly stressful and may lower resistance to illness.
- Vaernes *et al.* (1991) reported a study of Norwegian air force personnel in which they showed a strong relationship between perceived work stress and illnesses related to immune system activity. While this shows that a linkage between work-stress and immunosuppression exists, the direction of this relationship is not yet clear as the data are correlational.

CHECK YOUR UNDERSTANDING

When you have finished working through this topic, try the questions in 'Check your understanding' on p. 100 of the textbook. Check your answers against the relevant parts of the textbook or this workbook, listed below.

1 textbook p. 89
2 textbook p. 91; workbook p. 71
3 textbook p. 91; workbook p. 70
4 hassles, textbook pp. 91–2
5 textbook pp. 91–2
6 textbook p. 94
7 textbook p. 94
8 textbook p. 93; workbook pp. 71–2
9 textbook p. 95
10 hostility, textbook p. 96
11 textbook p. 96
12 textbook pp. 97–8; workbook p. 75
13 textbook pp. 97–8; workbook p. 75
14 textbook pp. 98–9; workbook p. 76
15 textbook pp. 98–9; ; workbook p. 76

ANSWERS TO ACTIVITIES

Understanding the specification, p. 68

1 Life changes and workplace stressors.

2 Holmes and Rahe – the textbook also examines other research, including the Life Experiences Survey, and the Hassles and Uplifts Scales.

3 Work overload and role ambiguity – the textbook also looks at physical environment and lack of control.

4 Personality, culture and gender.

The word 'including' means that they are compulsory.

5 Yes, the specification mentions research into sources of stress and specifies two aspects: life changes and workplace stress. You will need to learn two Key studies, one for each of these two aspects (see textbook pp. 90 and 94). There is a third Key study in this topic, on p. 95 of the textbook, but it relates to Topic 1, Stress as a bodily response (see workbook pp. 64 and 67).

Topic 3 >> Critical issue: stress management

Having looked at what causes us stress and how we react to it physically and mentally, we now move on to look at ways of managing stress. This includes both physiological methods (such as using drugs) and psychological methods (such as meditation). Physiological methods are designed to change the activity of the body's stress-response system, whereas psychological methods are designed to help people cope better with stressful situations or to alter their perception of the demands of a stressful situation.

One factor that has a major impact on whether a situation is likely to cause us stress is how far we believe we can control the situation. The most stressful situations are those in which we feel entirely helpless, believing that nothing we can do will significantly alter the outcome.

UNDERSTANDING THE SPECIFICATION

Here is what the AQA (A) specification says about this topic. It forms part of AS Module 2, Physiological Psychology and Individual Differences.

Read it and then try the activity below. You'll find answers to the activity on p. 86.

Stress

Critical issue: stress management

Methods of managing the negative effects of stress, including physiological (e.g. drugs, biofeedback) and psychological approaches (e.g. stress-inoculation, increasing hardiness). The role of control in relation to stress. The strengths and weaknesses of methods of stress management.

ACTIVITY

Understanding the specification

1 What are the two main methods of managing stress that you need to know about?
- ______
- ______

2 The specification lists two examples of physiological methods of managing stress. What are they?
- ______
- ______

3 The specification lists two examples of psychological methods of managing stress. What are they?
- ______
- ______

4 Does this topic involve Key studies (APFCCs)?
- ______

The use of the plural 'methods' in the specification means that you might be asked for *more than one* physiological method or *more than one* psychological method of stress management. The examples given are not compulsory, there are other examples of each approach that would be relevant. Make sure you are clear about the difference between a *physiological* and a *psychological* approach to stress management.

You are also required to know about the strengths and weaknesses of each of your chosen methods of stress management, as well as being able to summarize these in an overview of the strengths and weaknesses of physiological and psychological methods in general. The textbook takes an 'all-in-one' approach – it gives a description of each method of stress management and, immediately after, discusses the strengths and weaknesses of that method.

The 'role of control in relation to stress' requires you to know how control (e.g. through the nature of the stressor itself or through personality differences) alters the experience and effects of stress.

TOPIC MAP

ACTIVITY

Topic map

Look through pp. 101–10 of the textbook. Then fill in all the blank boxes and add the missing page numbers in the topic map below.

UNIT 3: TOPIC 3

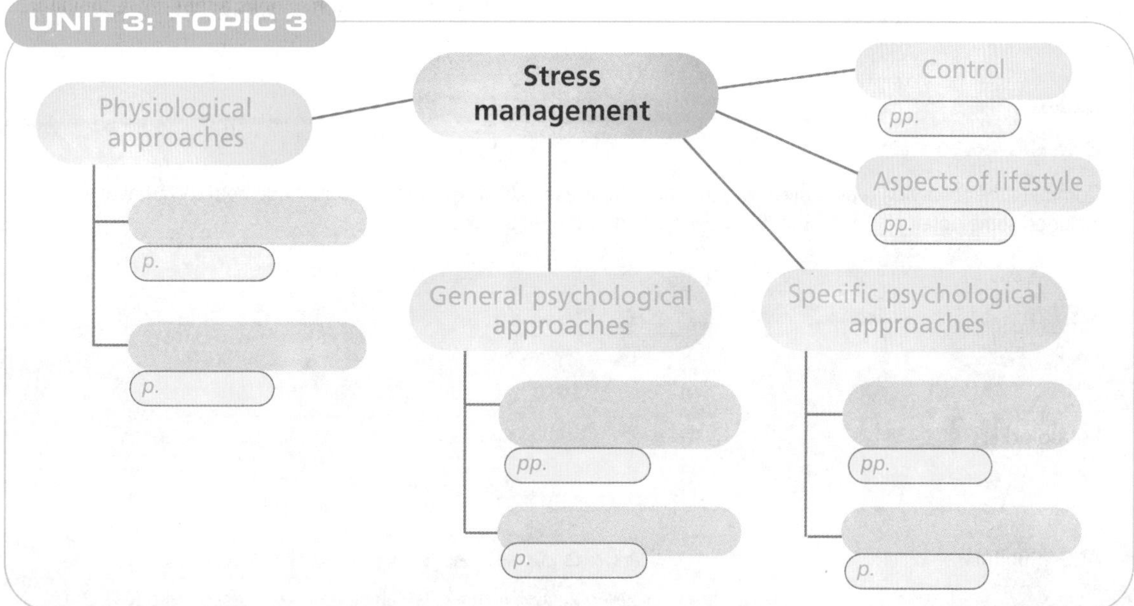

KEEPING TRACK

Use the table below to keep track of your work on this topic and plan your revision.

What I need to learn	Where is it?	Tick if you ... could make a basic attempt	could make a good attempt	have complete mastery of this
Methods of managing the negative effects of stress				
Definition of 'stress management'				
Definition of 'physiological approaches to stress management'				
Definition of 'psychological approaches to stress management'				
Description of physiological approaches to stress management (drugs and biofeedback)				
Evaluation of the strengths and weaknesses of these physiological approaches				
Description of general psychological approaches to stress management (progressive muscle relaxation and meditation)				
Evaluation of the strengths and weaknesses of these general psychological approaches				
Description of specific psychological approaches to stress management (stress-inoculation and hardiness training)				
Evaluation of the strengths and weaknesses of these specific psychological approaches				
Description of aspects of lifestyle in relation to stress management (physical exercise and social support)				
Evaluation of the strengths and weaknesses of these aspects of lifestyle				
The role of control in relation to stress				
Description of the role of control				
Evaluation of the role of control				

MODELS OF STRESS

As you saw in Topic 1, the body responds to stressors in quite specific ways. Logically, one way of dealing with stress is to manipulate the way that the body responds. This can be done either through drugs or biofeedback.

Drugs

The textbook describes two main families of drugs, BZs and beta-blockers, and mentions a third, ACE-inhibitors.

ACTIVITY

Drugs used to combat stress

Complete the following table which lists the three families of drugs used in stress management. (We have included some detail about ACE-inhibitors not given in the textbook.)

Family of drugs	Examples	How it works
BZs	● *Librium*	●
Beta-blockers	●	●
ACE-inhibitors	●	● *Prevents release of ACE, an enzyme that activates the hormone angiotensin, which causes blood vessels to constrict*

Biofeedback

This process is explained clearly on p. 102 of the textbook. In particular, try to memorize the information in Fig. 3.3 as it gives a good summary of how this technique works.

You can use the information about drugs and biofeedback to answer the questions shown on the right.

AO1 questions

- Describe one physiological method of stress management. (6 marks)
- Outline two physiological methods of stress management. (3 + 3 marks)

ACTIVITY

Strengths and weaknesses of physiological approaches

In the space below, summarize the strengths and weaknesses of using drugs and biofeedback in stress management.

Approach	Strengths	Weaknesses
Drugs	●	●
Biofeedback	●	●

Strengths and weaknesses questions

According to the AQA specification, you need to know the strengths and weaknesses of all types of stress management. You may be tested on these, in questions such as the ones shown here.

These are typical part (a) or (b) questions, testing AO1 skills and each worth 6 marks in total. As outlined on p. 29 of the textbook (Unit 1, Topic 2, 'An eye on the exam'), you will have about 5 minutes to answer a 6-mark question. This is just enough time to write about 100 words. With the third question, for example, that's 50 words for the description of one physiological method and 50 words for one weakness.

AO1 questions

- Describe one physiological method of stress management. (6 marks)
- Outline two physiological methods of stress management. (3 + 3 marks)
- (i) Outline one physiological method of stress management (e.g. drugs, biofeedback). (3 marks)

  (ii) Outline one weakness of the method you have outlined in (i). (3 marks)

ACTIVITY

Strengths and weaknesses

Answer the third question in the panel, giving yourself 5 minutes in total, to write about 100 words. Choose either drugs or biofeedback.

GENERAL PSYCHOLOGICAL APPROACHES

The textbook focuses on two general psychological approaches: progressive muscle relaxation and meditation. After reading the text about progressive muscle relaxation, try the activity on p. 103 of the textbook. That will give you a good idea of what it involves and how it can help.

ACTIVITY

General psychological approaches

In the space below, summarize the main points of the text regarding general psychological approaches. Note down strengths and weaknesses of using drugs and biofeedback in stress management.

Approach	Brief description	Strengths	Weaknesses
Progressive muscle relaxation	•	•	•
Meditation	•	•	•

SPECIFIC PSYCHOLOGICAL APPROACHES

Relaxation and meditation can relieve stress by bringing about a more general state of calm. Other psychological approaches take a more targeted approach. They help people to work out what it is that causes them stress and try to reduce it in a two-pronged attack:

- by taking a more positive view of potentially stressful situations
- by learning or improving ways of dealing with stress, such as relaxation techniques.

The textbook describes two specific psychological approaches:

- Meichenbaum's stress-inoculation training
- Kobasa's method of increasing hardiness.

ACTIVITY

Specific psychological approaches

In the space below, summarize the main points of the two psychological approaches described on pp. 104–6 of the textbook. Note down the three stages of each approach, and list the strengths and weaknesses of each approach.

Approach	Brief description	Strengths	Weaknesses
Meichenbaum's stress-inoculation training	1	•	•
	2		
	3		
Kobasa's method of increasing hardiness	1	•	•
	2		
	3		

AO1 questions

- Outline two psychological methods of stress management. (3 + 3 marks)
- Give one strength and one weakness of a psychological method of stress management. (3 + 3 marks)
- (i) Outline one psychological method of stress management. (3 marks)
  (ii) Outline one strength of the method you have outlined in (i). (3 marks)

ASPECTS OF LIFESTYLE AND STRESS MANAGEMENT

Two aspects of lifestyle are thought to play an important role in reducing levels of stress: physical exercise and social support.

Physical exercise

In the space below, summarize the main points, strengths and weaknesses of the use of physical exercise to reduce stress, described on p. 106 of the textbook. Check that you understand the biology – it may help to re-read the paragraphs on 'Energy mobilization' on p. 82 of the textbook.

How physical exercise reduces stress	Strengths	Weaknesses
•	•	•

ACTIVITY

Social support

Complete the following table to summarize the main points of the use of social support networks to reduce stress, described on pp. 107–8 of the textbook. As you fill in the 'Evaluation' column, think about the types of research study that have been carried out.

Categories of social support	How social support reduces stress	Evaluation
Emotional	•	•
Practical	•	•
Advice	•	•

CONTROL

A sense of not being in control is a feature of many people's experience of stress.

ACTIVITY

Types of control

The textbook describes five types of control (p. 108). Think of a situation relevant to you (e.g. studying for AS psychology) and note down how you might try to exercise control in each of these five different ways.

Situation •

Type of control	How you might try to exercise it
1 informational	
2 decisional	
3 behavioural	
4 cognitive	
5 retrospective	

ACTIVITY

Locus of control

Read the description of Rotter's concept of locus of control on pp. 108–9 of the textbook and then answer the following questions:

1 Who generally copes better with stress: people with an *internal* locus of control or those with an *external* locus of control? Why?

2 Do you have an internal or external locus of control? Give examples to support your answer.

ACTIVITY

Research into control

The textbook describes several research studies into stress and the role of control. Some examine how stress increases when there is a perceived lack of control, while others investigated the benefits of giving people more control. Summarize the findings of these research studies in the table below.

Research into the effects of lack of control	Research into the effects of increasing control
•	•
	•
•	
	•

AO1 questions

- Outline research relating to the role of control in stress. (6 marks)
- Explain the role of control in stress. (6 marks)
- Outline two ways in which control might influence stress and/or stress management. (3 + 3 marks)

AO1 + AO2 QUESTIONS ON STRESS MANAGEMENT

Possible AO1+AO2 questions on stress management are shown below. A sample answer to the last question in the list is given opposite.

This question needs some careful thought. It requires AO1 description as well as AO2 analysis and evaluation. Remember that analysis and evaluation come in several forms, and we will use several different types in this answer (taken from material in the textbook pp. 108–9, the 'Hardy personality' textbook pp. 96–7, and 'Increasing hardiness' textbook p. 106).

AO1+AO2 questions

- Outline and evaluate the physiological approach to stress management. (18 marks)
- Give a brief account of, and evaluate, two psychological methods of stress management. (18 marks)
- Consider two physiological methods of stress management (e.g. drugs, biofeedback) in terms of their strengths and weaknesses. (18 marks)
- To what extent is control important in stress and/or stress management? (18 marks)

Sample answer

To what extent is control important in stress and/or stress management? (18 marks)

Green (2003)* states that several different forms of control are important in how we manage stress. These include behavioural control – taking direct action to deal with the stressor, and retrospective control – thinking about how the stressful event happened and how it could be avoided in the future. Kobasa suggests that having the belief that we can control what happens in our life is an important aspect of the hardy personality (Kobasa and Maddi 1977). Some people develop learned helplessness (Seligman 1975) because of stressful experiences that they have tried to control and failed. As a result they develop a sense of being unable to exercise control over their life. This impairs their performance in situations that can be controlled, a characteristic of many people who fail to initiate coping strategies when faced with stress.

Kobasa's concept of hardiness overlaps substantially with issues of personal control, and she has demonstrated how our sensation of control can be increased through stress-management techniques. This gives the concept of control considerable value as a method of stress management. However, there are few systematic studies of the effectiveness of this technique, and it has the additional problem of aspects of personality and learned habits that are difficult to modify. In particular Rotter's concept of locus of control indicates that whereas people with a strong internal locus cope better with stress and are more likely to take behavioural control, those with an external locus of control are more passive in their stress management and so suffer more stress-related illness (Kamen and Seligman 1989). Locus of control is a fundamental part of personality and is hard to modify.

Research has, however, generally supported the importance of control in stress management. A study by Langer and Rodin (1976) in a nursing home for elderly people found clear evidence that those patients who were given the opportunity to exercise more control over everyday decisions were rated as more active and generally more improved, compared to a control group. Experimental research has also shown that even the illusion of control can have a significant effect on our experience of stress, with participants who thought they were exercising some control experiencing smaller activation of the stress-response (Glass and Singer 1972). Green suggests that this could explain why, for many people, air travel is more stressful than car travel – we have more control when driving than when flying.

**This reference is to Unit 3 in the textbook, which was written by Simon Green.*

ACTIVITY

One for you to try ...

Consider two physiological methods of stress management (e.g. drugs, biofeedback) in terms of their strengths and weaknesses. (18 marks)

Have a go at the above question, but spend time before you start allocating space (i.e. the appropriate number of words) and time (i.e. the number of minutes) for each part. Assuming you choose the two examples given in the question, this is what you should aim to cover:

- Outline of drug(s) as a method of stress management.
- Outline of biofeedback as a method of stress management.
- Strengths of drug(s) as a method of stress management.
- Weaknesses of drug(s) as a method of stress management.
- Strengths of biofeedback as a method of stress management.
- Weaknesses of biofeedback as a method of stress management.

CHECK YOUR UNDERSTANDING

When you have finished working through this topic, try the questions in 'Check your understanding' on p. 111 of the textbook. Check your answers against the relevant parts of the textbook or this workbook, listed below.

1. drugs or biofeedback, textbook p. 102
2. workbook p. 80
3. textbook p. 102
4. progressive muscle relaxation, meditation, stress-inoculation or hardiness training, textbook pp. 103–6
5. textbook pp. 103–6; workbook pp. 81–2
6. textbook pp. 104–5
7. the three Cs, textbook p. 96
8. textbook p. 106
9. textbook p. 106
10. textbook p. 106
11. textbook p. 107
12. textbook p. 108
13. textbook pp. 108–9
14. textbook p. 109
15. textbook p. 109; workbook p. 84

ANSWERS TO ACTIVITIES

Understanding the specification, p. 78

1. Physiological and psychological.
2. Drugs and biofeedback are given as examples of physiological approaches; the textbook considers these on p. 102.
3. Stress-inoculation and increasing hardiness are given as examples of psychological approaches; these are covered on pp. 104–6. The textbook also covers other psychological approaches, including progressive muscle relaxation and meditation (pp. 103–4), as well as aspects of lifestyle, such as exercise and social support (pp. 106–8).
4. No, the specification doesn't specifically mention research here, so there are no Key studies for this topic.

4 Abnormality

PREVIEW

There are three topics in this unit. You should read them alongside the following pages in the Collins *Psychology for AS-level* textbook:

Topic	Textbook pages
1 Defining psychological abnormality	pp. 115–26
2 Biological and psychological models of abnormality	pp. 127–38
3 Critical issue: eating disorders	pp. 139–51

INTRODUCTION

This unit covers the AS Individual Differences part of Module 2 (AQA Specification A). The diagram below shows where it fits in to the overall AS qualification.

Read the Preview and Introduction on p. 114 of the textbook now. This will give you an overview of what's in the unit.

Where this unit fits in to the AS qualification

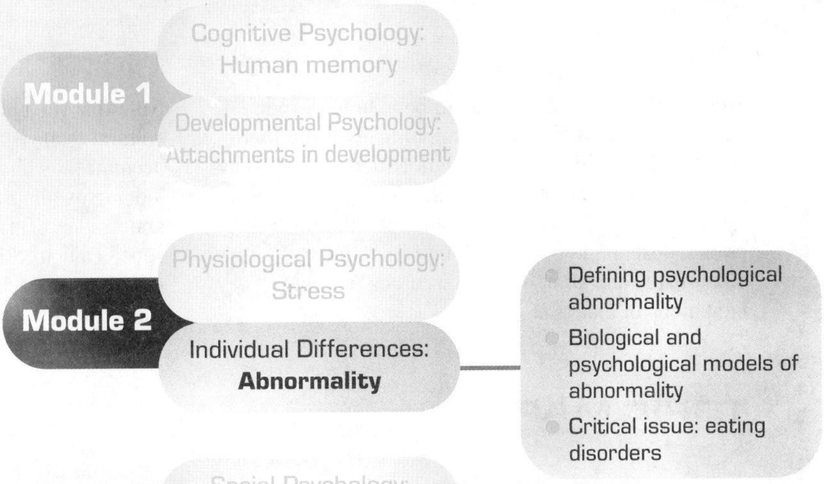

Module 1
- Cognitive Psychology: Human memory
- Developmental Psychology: Attachments in development

Module 2
- Physiological Psychology: Stress
- Individual Differences: **Abnormality**
  - Defining psychological abnormality
  - Biological and psychological models of abnormality
  - Critical issue: eating disorders

Module 3
- Social Psychology: Social influence
- Research Methods

In the AS Module 2 exam, you will have a choice of two questions on **Abnormality**. You will have to answer one of them.

Topic 1 >> Defining psychological abnormality

Defining psychological abnormality is no easy task – as the introduction on p. 114 of the textbook explains. Have a go at the 'Getting you thinking...' on p. 115 – you will probably find it hard to make judgements about whether the people described are 'normal' or 'abnormal'. Psychologists have made several attempts to come up with definitions of psychological abnormality based on different approaches. In this topic you will read about four such attempts. You will also examine what the limitations are of their efforts.

An important, yet often overlooked, issue is that of cultural differences. What may be seen as socially normal or ideal functioning in one society may not be accepted as such in another. Psychologists call this 'cultural relativism', and it is a clear problem in this area.

UNDERSTANDING THE SPECIFICATION

Here is what the AQA (A) specification says about this topic. It forms part of AS Module 2, Physiological Psychology and Individual Differences.

Read it and then try the activity below. You'll find answers to the activity on p. 96.

Abnormality

a. Defining psychological abnormality

Attempts to define abnormality in terms of statistical infrequency, deviation from social norms, a failure to function adequately, and deviation from ideal mental health. Limitations associated with these attempts to define psychological abnormality (including cultural relativism).

ACTIVITY

Understanding the specification

1 How many attempts to define abnormality do you need to know about, and what are they?
- ______
- ______
- ______
- ______

2 Which one limitation of attempts to define abnormality do you need to know about?
- ______

3 Does this topic involve Key studies (APFCCs)? *Clue*: Look for the key word 'research'.
- ______

The specification requires you to be able to describe each of the four definitions of abnormality listed there. You are also required to be able to criticize (i.e. give the limitations of) each of these definitions of abnormality. Again, the textbook takes an 'all-in-one' approach – it gives a description of each attempt to define abnormality and straight after discusses possible limitations of that attempt.

Note that the specification includes the problem of cultural relativism (the view that one must take into account the cultural context of a behaviour before judging its abnormality) in all these attempts to define abnormality. This means that you may be asked specifically to comment on the problem of cultural relativism in each of the four definitions, or may be asked to write more generally about cultural relativism in the definition of abnormality.

TOPIC MAP

ACTIVITY

Topic map

Look through pp. 115–25 of the textbook to see where the items shown in the topic map are covered. Note down the relevant page numbers in the spaces left on the topic map.

UNIT 4: TOPIC 1

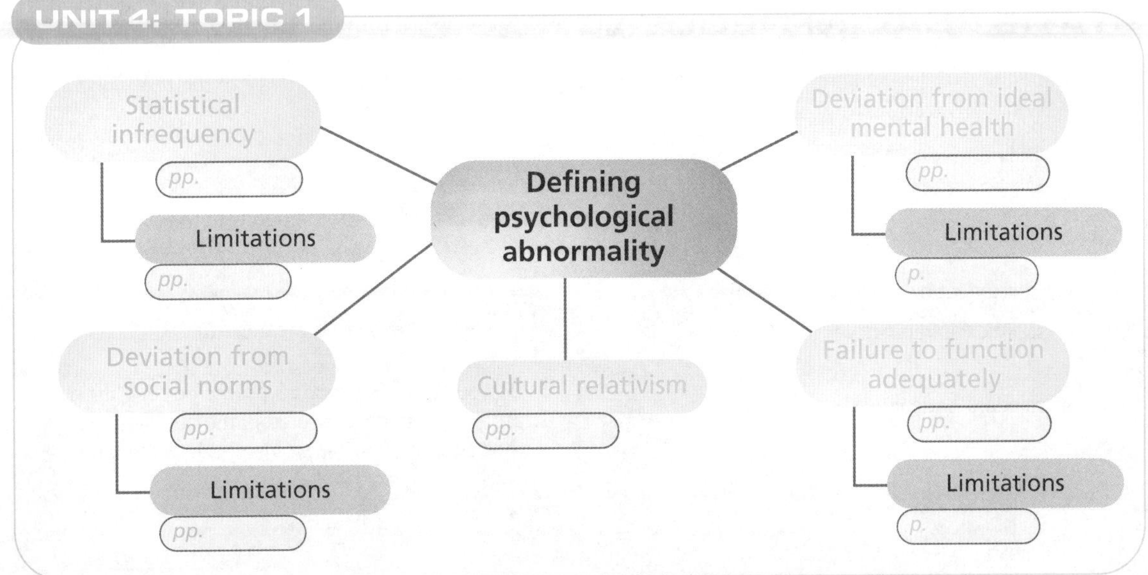

KEEPING TRACK

Use the table below to keep track of your work on this topic and plan your revision. See p. iv (Introduction) for guidance on filling it in.

What I need to learn	Where is it?	Tick if you ... could make a basic attempt	could make a good attempt	have complete mastery of this
Statistical infrequency definition				
Definition of 'statistical infrequency'				
Description of how the statistical infrequency definition has been used to define abnormality				
Explanation of the limitations associated with the statistical infrequency definition				
Deviation from social norms definition				
Definition of 'deviation from social norms'				
Description of how the deviation from social norms definition has been used to define abnormality				
Explanation of the limitations associated with the deviation from social norms definition				
Deviation from ideal mental health definition				
Definition of 'deviation from ideal mental health'				
Description of how the deviation from ideal mental health definition has been used to define abnormality				
Explanation of the limitations associated with the deviation from ideal mental health definition				
Failure to function adequately definition				
Definition of 'failure to function adequately'				
Description of how the failure to function adequately definition has been used to define abnormality				
Explanation of the limitations associated with the failure to function adequately definition				
Cultural relativism				
Definition of 'cultural relativism'				
Explanation of how cultural relativism affects the definition of abnormality				

STATISTICAL INFREQUENCY

The first attempt to define abnormality is in terms of statistical infrequency. Read pp. 116–17 of the textbook and then try the following activity.

ACTIVITY

Statistical infrequency

1 What is meant by the following terms?

- statistical infrequency
- standard deviation (SD)
- mean
- spread

2 What percentage of the population falls within:

- 1 SD either side of the mean?
- 2 SDs either side of the mean?
- 3 SDs either side of the mean?

3 Do you think that people's psychological attributes can be measured in the same way as their shoe size? What problems might there be with this approach?

-

ACTIVITY

Limitations of the statistical infrequency definition

Complete the following table, summarizing limitations with this definition of abnormality (textbook pp. 116–17).

Limitation	Key points	Researcher	Findings of research
Which characteristics to choose	• Not clear which characteristics are abnormal • Very low IQ is seen as abnormal; very high IQ is not		•
Where to draw the line	•		•
Common disorders	•	Angst (1992) Kessler et al. (1994)	• 1 in 20 Americans severely depressed •
Misleading statistics	•		•
Cultural issues	•		•

DEVIATION FROM SOCIAL NORMS

To understand (and answer questions on) this definition, you need to be sure of what is meant by 'social norms', as well as the different types of social norms that exist. Read pp. 118–19 of the textbook and then try the following activity.

ACTIVITY

Deviation from social norms definition

1 What is meant by the following terms?

- social norms
- explicit norms
- implicit norms

2 Give two examples each of explicit norms and implicit norms, and how other people would react to someone breaking those norms.

Type of norm	Reaction to someone breaking the norm
(a) explicit norms	
•	
•	
(b) implicit norms	
•	
•	

ACTIVITY

Limitations of the deviation from social norms definition

The textbook describes five possible limitations with this definition of abnormality (pp. 118–19). Complete the following table, summarizing these limitations.

Limitation	Key points
Eccentric or abnormal?	• There are some 'deviant' behaviours which we would regard just as eccentric, not abnormal, e.g. ...
The role of context	•
Changes with the times	•
Abnormal or criminal?	•
Cultural issues	•

DEVIATION FROM IDEAL MENTAL HEALTH

This definition differs from the others in that it concentrates on the positive aspects of mental health. To answer exam questions on this definition, you will need to cite as many of Jahoda's six criteria for mental health as you can. Read pp. 119–20 of the textbook and then try the following activity.

ACTIVITY

Deviation from ideal mental health

1 For each of Jahoda's six criteria, think of someone you know who displays that quality. Note down what it is about them that makes them 'healthy' in that respect. Don't forget yourself in answering this activity.

Quality	Person illustrating this
Positive attitudes towards self	
Self-actualization of one's potential	
Resistance to stress	
Personal autonomy	
Accurate perception of reality	
Adapting to the environment	

2 Write a 50-word précis of the deviation from mental health definition. This is something you might have to do when answering either part of an AO1 question or the first part of an AO1+A02 question.

When you have completed your précis, compare it with the 'model answer' on p. 259 of the textbook. The second part of the first paragraph (starting in line 9) contains a 54-word précis that is both accurate and detailed enough.

ACTIVITY

Limitations of the deviation from ideal mental health definition

The textbook describes three limitations with this definition of abnormality (p. 120). Complete the following table, summarizing these limitations.

Limitation	Key points
Difficulty of self-actualizing	
Possible benefits of stress	
Cultural issues	

FAILURE TO FUNCTION ADEQUATELY

The basic assumption of this definition is that if someone becomes so unwell that they cannot carry out everyday activities, then they may be considered abnormal. Read pp. 121–2 of the textbook, including Fig. 4.2, which is a scale used to assess how well people are functioning.

ACTIVITY

Failure to function adequately

1 In your opinion, at what point on the GAF scale would someone be so unwell as to need medical help?

-

2 Would everybody agree with your view? If possible, ask one or two other people studying AS psychology to answer question 1.

-

3 What about people who have mental health problems, but are functioning adequately on a day-to-day basis? Should they be given medical help?

-

When describing the failure to function adequately definition in an exam, you could refer to the Global Assessment of Functioning Scale as an example of a diagnostic scale used to assess how well people are functioning.

ACTIVITY

Limitations of the failure to function adequately definition

The textbook describes three limitations with this definition of abnormality (p. 122). Complete the following table, summarizing these limitations. Include the names of any researchers mentioned and brief notes of the findings of their research.

Limitation	Key points	Researcher	Findings of research
Not the whole picture	•		•
Exceptions to the rule	•		•
Cultural issues	•		•

ANSWERING AO1 QUESTIONS ON DEFINITIONS OF ABNORMALITY

These are typical part (a) or (b) questions, testing AO1 skills and worth 6 marks. As outlined on p. 57 of the textbook, you will have about 5 minutes to answer questions such as these. This is just enough time to think about, plan and write about 100 words. If the question is divided into (3 + 3 marks), you will have 2.5 minutes on each part, i.e. about 50 words.

AO1 questions

- Explain what is mean by the terms 'abnormality' and [XXX] definition of abnormality. (3 + 3 marks)
- Outline the [XXX] and [XXX] definitions of abnormality. (3 + 3 marks)
- Outline the [XXX] definition of abnormality and give one limitation of this definition. (3 + 3 marks)
- Describe two limitations of the [XXX] definition of abnormality. (3 + 3 marks)

[XXX] stands for a named definition

CULTURAL RELATIVISM

You may have noticed that 'cultural issues' appear in every one of the four 'Limitations' tables you have completed in this topic. This points to a clear problem in defining abnormality: cultural relativism. Read the definition of the term on p. 115 of the textbook and then read pp. 122–5.

ACTIVITY

Different cultural groups

1 Why is it in impossible to find a definition of abnormality that applies to the whole of humankind?

-

2 The textbook describes how subgroups within society often receive inappropriate diagnosis and treatment for mental health disorders. This applies particularly to members of minority ethnic communities. This is discussed by Ray Cochrane in the Expert interview on p. 125. Answer the questions in the Activity on p. 124 of the textbook, noting down your answers here.

1

2

3

3 Give an example of a mental illness that is recognized in almost all cultures as something abnormal and undesirable.

-

Other 'subcultures'

The textbook also describes the experiences of other subgroups within Western culture, i.e. the socially disadvantaged, women and gay people (pp. 123–4). In what ways do these subgroups experience particular problems (e.g. in assessment, diagnosis or treatment of their mental health) because of their vulnerable position within Western society?

Complete the following table to summarize the most important points.

Group	Problems faced	Reason for problem	Relevant research
Socially disadvantaged	•	•	•
Women	•	•	•
Gay people	•	•	•

AO1 + AO2 QUESTIONS ON DEFINING PSYCHOLOGICAL ABNORMALITY

Sample answers to the first question on the right are discussed on pp. 258–9 of the textbook. If you read through these answers, you should see that the main difference between them is the effectiveness of the AO2 in Answer 2. It is important that your AO2 (the second two paragraphs in Answer 2) is used as effectively as it can be so that you pick up marks in the higher mark bands.

What is it about the AO2 in Answer 2 that makes it so effective? There is an easy-to-remember rule concerning the effectiveness of AO2 commentary.

- Identify the critical point – what is the problem or advantage?
- Justify it – what evidence allows me to make this point?
- Judge the consequences – so what? Why is this a good or bad thing for the study, theory, etc., being evaluated?

AO1+AO2 questions

- "The main problem with abnormality as a concept is that we cannot agree exactly what constitutes abnormal behaviour."

  Outline and evaluate two or more attempts to define abnormality.* (18 marks)
- To what extent are definitions of abnormality limited by cultural relativism? (18 marks)

**Two sample answers to this question are shown on pp. 258–9 of the textbook, together with a commentary.*

ACTIVITY

One for you to try ...

To what extent are definitions of abnormality limited by cultural relativism? (18 marks)

Bearing in mind the advice about making your AO2 effective, construct an answer to the above question. You will find the interview with Ray Cochrane on p. 125 of the textbook and the activities on pp. 94–5 of this workbook particularly helpful. Remember to restrict yourself to a maximum of 18 minutes' writing time (15 would be more realistic), as this is the time available in the exam for this task.

CHECK YOUR UNDERSTANDING

When you have finished working through this topic, try the questions in 'Check your understanding' on p. 126 of the textbook. You can check your answers by looking at the relevant parts of the textbook or this workbook, listed below.

1 textbook p. 116
2 textbook pp. 116–7; workbook p. 90
3 textbook p. 118; workbook p. 91
4 attitudes towards unmarried women and homosexuality, textbook p. 124
5 textbook p. 119
6 textbook p. 120; workbook p. 92
7 textbook pp. 119–20; workbook p. 92
8 textbook p. 122
9 textbook p. 122
10 textbook pp. 122–5; workbook p. 94

ANSWERS TO ACTIVITIES

Understanding the specification, p. 88

1 Four: statistical infrequency, deviation from social norms, a failure to function adequately, and deviation from ideal mental health. The textbook covers each of these.
2 The 'including' in the last sentence means that you have to know about cultural relativism as a limitation of attempts to define psychological abnormality. The textbook explores this issue on pp. 122–5.
3 No, the specification doesn't specifically mention research here, so there are no Key studies for this topic.

Topic 2 >> Biological and psychological models of abnormality

Numerous theories or 'models' have been developed to explain psychological disorders (abnormality). Different models make different assumptions and hence result in different kinds of treatment. This topic looks in detail at four models: one based in biology and three based more in psychology. Each of these models makes very different assumptions regarding what *causes* abnormality, and therefore what would be the most appropriate way to *treat* abnormal behaviour.

UNDERSTANDING THE SPECIFICATION

Here is what the AQA (A) specification says about this topic. It forms part of AS Module 2, Physiological Psychology and Individual Differences.

Read it and then try the activity below. You'll find answers to the activity on p. 106.

Abnormality

b. Biological and psychological models of abnormality

Assumptions made by biological (medical) and psychological (including psychodynamic, behavioural and cognitive) models of abnormality in terms of their views on the causes and treatment of abnormality.

ACTIVITY

Understanding the specification

1 What biological model of abnormality do you need to know about?

- __________

2 What three psychological models of abnormality do you need to know about?

- __________
- __________
- __________

3 What two aspects of abnormality does each model make assumptions about?

- __________
- __________

4 Does this topic involve Key studies (APFCCs)? If so, how many? *Clue*: Look for the word 'research'.

- __________

There are *four* models specified here (biological, psychodynamic, behavioural and cognitive). The specification requires you to explore the assumptions made by each model both about causes and treatment of abnormality. The textbook will help you do this, as it takes a structured approach, looking at each model in turn and discussing:

- the basic *assumptions* the model makes about causes of mental disorders
- the approach to *treatment* using this model
- an *evaluation* of the model – positive and negative aspects.

Questions that ask about assumptions relating to the treatment of abnormality are not an invitation to describe specific treatments, but to consider, in broad terms, how that model's views of the causes of abnormality might influence its treatment. For example, the biological/medical model may claim that one cause of abnormality is a *chemical imbalance* in the body (e.g. a neurotransmitter deficiency), and so would advocate treating that imbalance through the use of drugs. Likewise, the behavioural model may claim that abnormal behaviours are *learned* and supporters of this model would therefore advocate treatments that 'unlearn' these learned associations (classical conditioning) or change the consequences for abnormal behaviours (operant conditioning).

TOPIC MAP

ACTIVITY

Topic map

Look through pages pp. 127–38 of the textbook and fill in the blanks below.

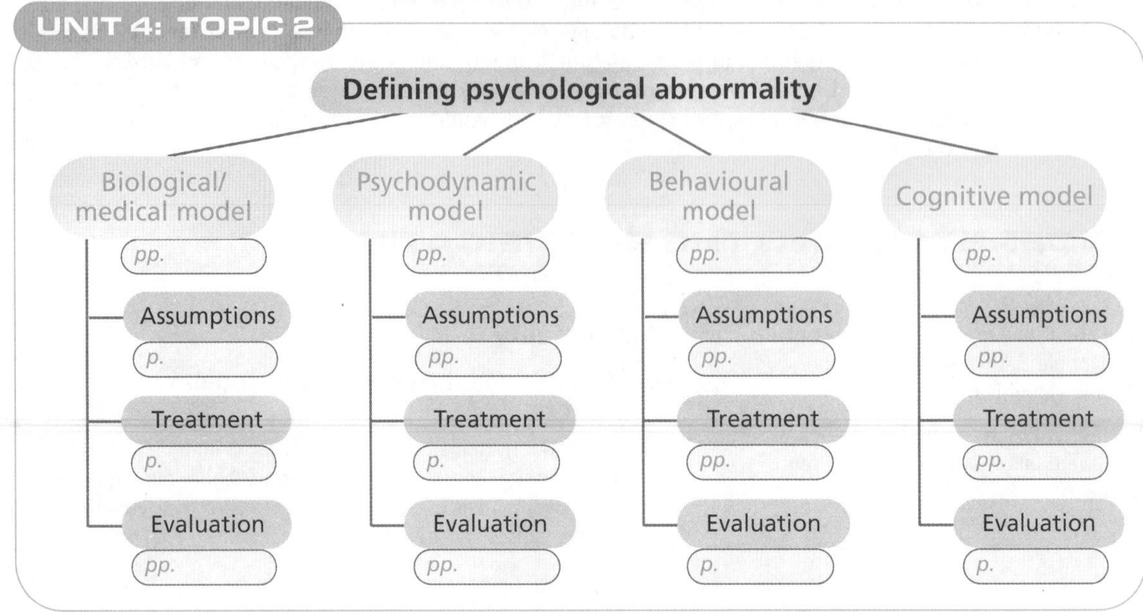

KEEPING TRACK

Use the table below to keep track of your work on this topic and plan your revision.

What I need to learn	Where is it?	*Tick if you ...* could make a basic attempt	could make a good attempt	have complete mastery of this
Biological/medical model				
Definition of 'biological/medical model'				
Explanation of the model's assumptions about causes of abnormality				
Explanation of the model's assumptions about treatment				
Evaluation of the model's strengths and weaknesses				
Psychodynamic model				
Definition of 'psychodynamic model'				
Explanation of the model's assumptions about causes of abnormality				
Explanation of the model's assumptions about treatment				
Evaluation of the model's strengths and weaknesses				
Behavioural model				
Definition of 'behavioural model'				
Explanation of the model's assumptions about causes of abnormality				
Explanation of the model's assumptions about treatment				
Evaluation of the model's strengths and weaknesses				
Cognitive model				
Definition of 'cognitive model'				
Explanation of the model's assumptions about causes of abnormality				
Explanation of the model's assumptions about treatment				
Evaluation of the model's strengths and weaknesses				

BIOLOGICAL/MEDICAL MODEL

Before looking at the first model, check that you understand what is meant by the term 'model'. Read the first paragraph at the top of p. 128 of the textbook. Then read the text about the biological model (pp. 128–30) and try the following activities.

ACTIVITY

Assumptions of the biological model

1 What is the underlying assumption of the biological model?

2 Who are the model's main supporters and how do they approach psychological abnormality?

ACTIVITY

Causes of abnormality (biological model)

According to the biological model, there are several factors that can contribute to psychological disorders. The textbook describes four of them on p. 128. Complete the following table summarizing them. In the right-hand column, note down examples of psychological disorders caused by each factor.

Causal factor	Main assumption	Example
Brain damage	Damage to structure of brain leads to abnormal behaviour	Alzheimer's disease – dementia caused by malformation and loss of cells in brain
Infection		
Biochemistry		
Genes		Schizophrenia
		Muscular dystrophy

ACTIVITY

Treatment and the biological model

Under the biological model, physical treatments are the most appropriate for mental disorders. Complete the table on the next page which summarizes the three categories of treatment described in the textbook.

Treatment and the biological model

Treatment	How it works	Other key points
Drug therapy	• Relieves symptoms by tackling chemical imbalance. Examples include ...	• They can have severe side effects. •
ECT	•	•
Psychosurgery	•	•

ACTIVITY

Evaluation of the biological model

The textbook lists several issues to consider when evaluating this model (pp. 129–30). Pick out which are positive and which are negative, and list them under the relevant heading below. Note that some of the issues have both positive and negative aspects (e.g. 'Research').

Positive aspects	Negative aspects
•	•
•	•
•	•
•	•
•	•

PSYCHODYNAMIC MODEL

The psychodynamic model is the first of three psychological models discussed in the textbook. The assumptions underlying the model are described on pp. 130–2 of the textbook. Freud worked out quite a complex analysis of what goes on in our mind – especially at the unconscious level. Your challenge in the exam will be to summarize the important points in far fewer words than the textbook uses. For example, you may have to answer a question such as the one below. To answer this 6-mark question, you have time to write only about 100 words (at most 120).

AO1 question

- Outline the psychodynamic model with respect to the causes of abnormality. (6 marks)

ACTIVITY

Assumptions

Write a 120-word précis of the assumptions made by the psychodynamic model about the causes of abnormality. Use the following questions to guide you. Remember how few words you have for your answers.

1 How and where do mental problems originate?

2 What three aspects of the personality are involved?

3 How does the ego try to keep psychological balance?

4 When does psychical conflict have greatest impact?

Write your précis on your PC. That way you can not only edit your answer to fit 120 words, but also use the 'word count' option to keep a tally of your words. Remember you are outlining the psychodynamic explanation of *abnormality* – don't spend too long talking about the *normal* personality.

ACTIVITY

Treatment and the psychodynamic model

Read the text on p. 132 of the textbook about treatment and the psychodynamic model. Describe what is meant by the following terms and how each type of therapy is intended to help the client.

Type of therapy	What it is	How it helps
Psychoanalysis	•	•
Analysis of dreams	•	•
Free association	•	•

ACTIVITY

Evaluation of the psychodynamic model

The textbook lists several issues to consider when evaluating this model (pp. 132–3). Work out which are positive and which are negative, and list them under the relevant heading below.

Positive aspects	Negative aspects
•	•
•	•
•	•
•	•
•	•

BEHAVIOURAL MODEL

The second psychological models covered in the textbook is the behavioural model. This model takes a very different approach from the psychodynamic model, as it focuses primarily on how people behave, not on what is going on inside their heads. Behaviourists believe that the abnormal behaviour itself is the problem whereas psychodynamic theorists believe abnormal behaviour is merely a symptom of the real problem.

ACTIVITY

Assumptions of the behavioural model

Read the text on pp. 133–4 of the textbook. What is meant by the following terms?

- 'maladaptive behaviour'
- 'dysfunctional behaviour'

ACTIVITY

Behavioural processes

Complete the following table to summarize the three processes that underpin the behavioural model.

Process	Brief description	Relevant research
Classical conditioning	Behaviour is learned through stimulus-response associations. A stimulus (e.g. white rat) produced a learned response (e.g. fear).	Pavlov (1927)
Operant conditioning		
Social learning		

ACTIVITY

Treatment and the behavioural model

Read the text on pp. 134–5 of the textbook about treatment and the behavioural model.

1 What is the basic assumption of behavioural therapies?

2 What is the therapist's role?

3 Complete the following table.

Type of therapy	What it is	How it helps
Systematic desensitization		
Aversion therapy		
Token economy		

ACTIVITY

Evaluation of the behavioural model

The textbook lists several issues to consider when evaluating this model (p. 135). Work out which are positive and which are negative, and list them under the relevant heading below.

Positive aspects	Negative aspects
•	•
•	•
•	•
•	•
•	•

COGNITIVE MODEL

The third and final psychological model we will look at is the cognitive model. This model is similar to the behavioural model in that it concentrates on what causes people to behave in the way they do; it is different in that it sees the cognitive element as being important, i.e. how we think.

ACTIVITY

Assumptions of the cognitive model

Read the text on pp. 135–6 of the textbook about the assumptions of the cognitive model.

1 What is the underlying belief of the cognitive model?

•

2 How does 'faulty' or irrational thinking lead to maladaptive behaviour?

•

3 Study Fig. 4.3 on p. 136 of the textbook. Using this as an example, what would be adaptive and maladaptive responses to the following stimulus?

Stimulus >> seeing your girl/boyfriend sitting close to someone else and laughing

Maladaptive response

thinking > feelings > behaviour > outcome

Adaptive response

thinking > feelings > behaviour > outcome

ACTIVITY

Treatment and the cognitive model

Read the text on pp. 136–7 of the textbook about treatment and the cognitive model.

1 What is the basic assumption of cognitive therapies?

- ______________________

2 What is the therapist's role?

- ______________________

3 What is the client's role?

- ______________________

4 Who might benefit from cognitive therapies?

- ______________________

ACTIVITY

Evaluation of the cognitive model

The textbook lists several issues to consider when evaluating this model (p. 137). Work out which are positive and which are negative, and list them under the relevant heading below.

Positive aspects	Negative aspects
•	•
•	•
•	•
•	•
•	•

AO1 QUESTIONS ON MODELS OF ABNORMALITY

In order to understand fully the different requirements of questions such as these, and how to answer them, you might refer to 'An eye on the exam' on p. 138 of the textbook.

AO1 questions

- Outline two assumptions of the [XXX] model with respect to the causes of abnormality. (3 + 3 marks)
- Outline two assumptions of the [XXX] model with respect to the treatment of abnormality. (3 + 3 marks)
- Outline the [XXX] model with respect to the causes of abnormality. (6 marks)
- Outline the [XXX] model with respect to the treatment of abnormality. (6 marks)
- Outline one assumption of the [XXX] model with respect to the causes of abnormality and give one criticism of this model. (3 + 3 marks)
- Give two criticisms of the [XXX] model of abnormality. (3 + 3 marks)

[XXX] stands for a named model

AO1+AO2 QUESTIONS ON MODELS OF ABNORMALITY

AO1+AO2 questions

- "The biological (medical) model of abnormality has dominated the field of mental health for the last 200 years. This is an indication of its unrivalled position as the most valuable explanation of abnormal behaviour." To what extent can it be claimed that the biological (medical) model offers the best explanation of both the causes and treatment of abnormal behaviour? (18 marks)
- Outline and evaluate the behavioural model of abnormality and consider its strengths and limitations. (18 marks)
- Give a brief account of and evaluate the cognitive model of abnormality. (18 marks)
- Outline key features of the psychodynamic model of abnormality and consider its strengths and/or weaknesses. (18 marks)

One of the trickiest things to have do in an examination is summarize down a lot of information into just 100 or so words. That's why we have emphasized the skill of précis throughout this book. To answer the first question above, the descriptive material on pp. 128–9 of the textbook must be précised down considerably. Remember there is no one definitive way to do this – you cannot include everything, so just a flavour of the material would do. Note that both causes and treatments need to be considered, so that makes our task even harder.

A sample answer to the first question is given on p. 106 of this workbook. The first paragraph is the AO1 paragraph and is 129 words long. It covers both causes and treatments in précis. Although this would be one of the most demanding tasks that you might be asked to perform in an examination, it does pay to be ready for it. We have already mentioned the importance of having a 120-word précis of each model with respect to the causes of abnormality, and another with respect to the treatment, but it would clearly pay you to be able to précis each of these down to 60 words as well. This would then cover the eventuality of a question such as "Outline the main features of two models ... (3 + 3 marks)" as well as giving you material that you could simply combine together to answer questions such as the question we are dealing with here.

On with the AO2 material. In this second paragraph we could restrict ourselves to critical commentary on the biological model's value in terms of explaining the *causes* of abnormality. The final paragraph can then give the same treatment to this model's views on the *treatment* of abnormality. In order to make this evaluation effective, it is best not to be too ambitious about the number of points made in each paragraph. Remember the advice given about effective evaluation on p. 57 of the textbook.

ACTIVITY

One for you to try ...

Outline key features of the psychodynamic model of abnormality and consider its strengths and/or weaknesses. (18 marks)

If you completed the activity on p. 100 of this workbook, you will now have a 100- to 120-word précis of the key features of the psychodynamic model of abnormality. This question does not specify 'causes' or 'treatment', so either would do here (causes would be preferable as it gives more opportunities to express the key features). That is the AO1 part of your response to this question.

You then have to produce two more paragraphs of approximately the same length each for the AO2 content. The question allows you to cover strengths and/or weaknesses. It is up to you whether you go for strengths, weaknesses or both. The relevant pages of the textbook are pp. 132–3. Alternatively, you could do a bit of research yourself to add flavour to your evaluation. Try this article by ex-England cricket captain turned psychoanalyst, Mike Brearley, 'The Practice of Psychoanalysis', available at www.psychoanalysis.org.uk/brearley2.htm

Sample answer

"The biological (medical) model of abnormality has dominated the field of mental health for the last 200 years. This is an indication of its unrivalled position as the most valuable explanation of abnormal behaviour."

To what extent can it be claimed that the biological (medical) model offers the best explanation of both the causes and treatment of abnormal behaviour? (18 marks)

The basic assumption of the biological model is that mental disorders are caused by abnormal physiological processes. Research has shown that many mental disorders (e.g. schizophrenia) have a strong genetic influence, i.e. they appear to run in families. Biochemical explanations propose that many disorders can be explained in terms of dysfunctions in neurotransmitter action. Depression may be caused by a lowered level of activity in the neurotransmitters serotonin or noradrenaline, which can be corrected by the use of drugs. As mental disorders are seen essentially as physical illnesses, the major implication of this approach is that alterations in bodily functioning will be effective in their treatment, e.g. the use of psychosurgery reflects the belief that some disorders are due to abnormal functioning of a specific area of the brain.

Research relating to the biological model has greatly increased our understanding of the possible biological factors underpinning psychological disorders. However, much of the evidence is inconclusive and findings can be difficult to interpret. In family studies, for example, it is difficult to disentangle the effects of genetics from the effects of the environment, or to establish cause and effect. In schizophrenia, for example, raised levels of dopamine activity may be a consequence rather than a cause of schizophrenia. The biological explanation of abnormality is also criticized for being reductionist in trying to explain complex phenomena such as schizophrenia and depression in terms of brain cell activity or dysfunction. This underestimates the possible contribution of other factors, such as learning or disordered thinking.

Many psychologists criticize psychiatry for focusing attention primarily on symptoms and for assuming that relieving symptoms with drugs cures the problem. In most cases, however, when the drug treatment is ceased, symptoms recur, suggesting that drugs are not addressing the true cause of the problem. Another criticism of the medical model is that people are encouraged to become 'patients', handing over responsibility for their 'wellness' to professionals, so not feeling responsible for their own recovery. Some successful treatments have arisen from the medical model that have helped people with psychological disorders. However, many treatments have been criticized as being unethical or ineffective. There is an expectation that patients will comply with medication despite the fact that most medication carries side effects and often long-term dependency upon the drugs.

CHECK YOUR UNDERSTANDING

When you have finished working through this topic, try the questions in 'Check your understanding' on p. 137 of the textbook. Check your answers by looking at the relevant parts of the textbook or this workbook, listed below.

1 biological model, textbook p. 128
2 textbook p. 128; workbook p. 99
3 textbook p. 129; workbook p. 100
4 workbook p. 100
5 textbook p. 131
6 textbook p. 131
7 textbook p. 132
8 textbook pp. 133–4
9 workbook p. 103
10 textbook pp. 135–6

ANSWERS TO ACTIVITIES

Understanding the specification, p. 97

1 The medical model.
2 Psychodynamic, behavioural and cognitive.
3 The causes of abnormality and the treatment of abnormality.
4 The specification doesn't mention research here, so there are no Key studies for this topic.

Topic 3 >> Critical issue: eating disorders

Eating disorders are 'serious disruptions to healthy eating habits or appetite' (Cardwell 2000). Anorexia nervosa and bulimia nervosa are two of the most common types of eating disorder. In this topic you will examine the characteristics of these two disorders, as well as examining the explanations of them offered by biological and psychological models of abnormality and research into their origins.

UNDERSTANDING THE SPECIFICATION

Here is what the AQA (A) specification says about this topic. It forms part of AS Module 2, Physiological Psychology and Individual Differences.

Read it and then try the activity below. You'll find answers to the activity on p. 116.

Abnormality

Critical issue: eating disorders

The clinical characteristics of anorexia nervosa and bulimia nervosa. Explanations of these disorders in terms of biological and psychological models of abnormality, including research studies on which these explanations are based.

ACTIVITY

Understanding the specification

1 How many eating disorders do you have to study and what are they?

- __________
- __________

2 What kinds of explanation do you need to know about and what are they?

- __________
- __________

3 Does this topic involve Key studies (APFCCs)? If so, how many?

- __________

For this topic, you need to cover the *clinical characteristics* (i.e. the diagnostic criteria) of anorexia nervosa and bulimia nervosa, *explanations* (biological and psychological) of both, and *research studies* relating to these explanations.

The specification requires you to consider both *biological* and *psychological* explanations for both eating disorders. It is wise to cover more than one biological explanation (e.g. the influence of genes and biochemical explanations) and more than one psychological explanation (e.g. psychodynamic and behavioural) for each, so that means eight explanations in total.

As you know from Topic 2, psychological explanations fall into at least three categories (psychodynamic, behavioural and cognitive), and the textbook covers all of these (see pp. 145–9). In addition, biological explanations can be divided into two categories: genetic inheritance and biochemical dysfunction. The textbook covers these on pp. 142–5.

TOPIC MAP

ACTIVITY

Topic map

Look through pp. 139–51 of the textbook to see where the items shown in the topic map on the next page are covered. Add the missing page numbers.

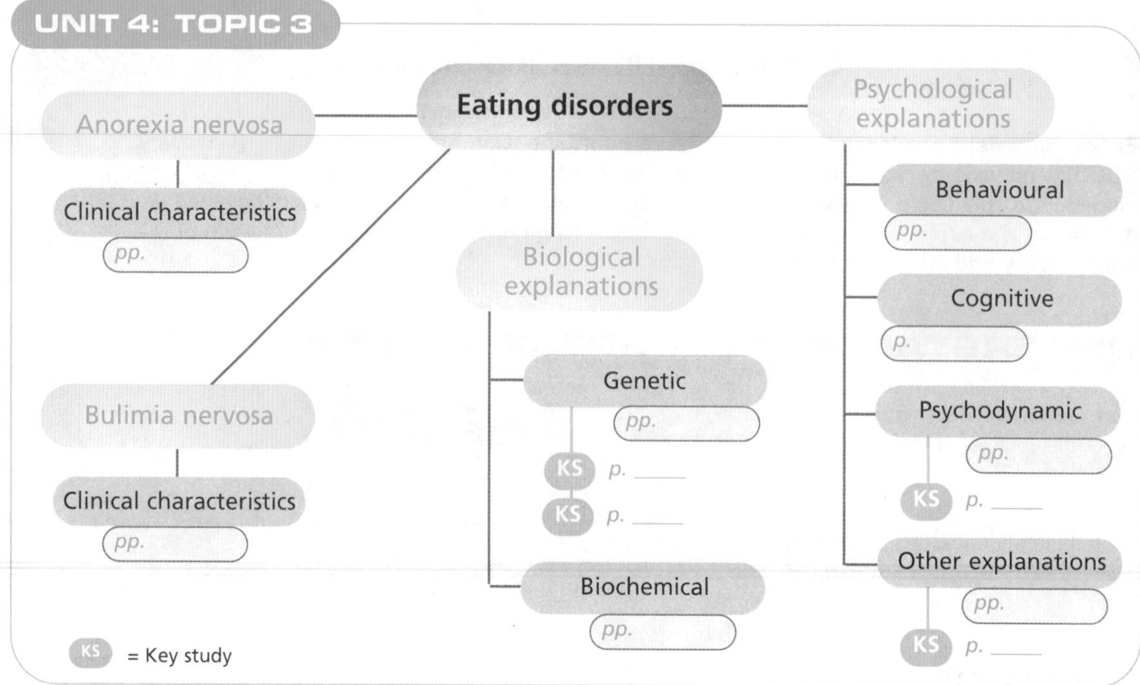

KEEPING TRACK

Use the table below to keep track of your work on this topic and plan your revision.

What I need to learn	Where is it?	Tick if you ... could make a basic attempt	could make a good attempt	have complete mastery of this
Clinical characteristics of eating disorders				
Definition of 'anorexia nervosa'				
Outline of the clinical characteristics of anorexia nervosa				
Definition of 'bulimia nervosa'				
Outline of the clinical characteristics of bulimia nervosa				
Biological explanations for eating disorders				
Explanation of eating disorders in terms of the biological model of abnormality				
Description of research into biological explanations				
Evaluation of research into biological explanations				
Description of APFCC for a Key study investigating biological explanations of anorexia nervosa				
Description of APFCC for a Key study investigating biological explanations of bulimia nervosa				
Psychological explanations for eating disorders				
Explanation of eating disorders in terms of psychological models of abnormality				
Description of research into psychological explanations				
Evaluation of research into psychological explanations				
Description of APFCC for a Key study investigating psychological explanations of anorexia nervosa				
Description of APFCC for a Key study investigating psychological explanations of bulimia nervosa				

CHARACTERISTICS OF ANOREXIA AND BULIMIA

The characteristics of these two disorders are described on pp. 140–2 of the textbook. The clinical characteristics are described in the two panels on pp. 140 and 141. (Clinical characteristics are those characteristic physical or behavioural symptoms that a clinician would look for in order to diagnose a particular disorder.) More general characteristics are also described, such as who tends to develop the disorder, and what the course and outcome of each disorder tend to be. There is plenty of ammunition here for answering questions asking you to describe characteristics of either disorder (as in the first four questions on the right).

Alternatively, you may be asked to compare the characteristics (either clinical or general) of anorexia and bulimia, as in the final three questions on the right. To prepare yourself for such questions, complete the tables outlined in the next two activities.

AO1 questions

- Outline the clinical characteristics of anorexia nervosa. (6 marks)
- Outline three clinical characteristics of anorexia nervosa. (2 + 2 + 2 marks)
- Outline the clinical characteristics of bulimia nervosa.* (6 marks)
- Outline three clinical characteristics of bulimia nervosa. (2 + 2 + 2 marks)
- Outline two clinical characteristics that are common to anorexia nervosa and bulimia nervosa. (3 + 3 marks)
- Outline three characteristics that are common to anorexia nervosa and bulimia nervosa. (2 + 2 + 2 marks)
- Give two differences in the clinical characteristics of anorexia nervosa and bulimia nervosa. (3 + 3 marks)

**Sample answers to this question are discussed on p. 257 of the textbook.*

ACTIVITY

Clinical characteristics of anorexia and bulimia

Complete the table below which compares the clinical characteristics of the two eating disorders. In the final column state whether the characteristics of the two disorders are similar or different.

Characteristic	Anorexia	Bulimia	Similar or different?
Body weight	• Below 85% of normal for height and age	•	✘ Different
Menstruation	•	•	✔ Similar
Eating behaviour	•	•	
Other food-related behaviour	•	•	
Body perception	•	•	
Mood disturbance	•	•	
Physical effects of disorder	•	•	
Awareness of disorder	•	•	

ACTIVITY

General characteristics of anorexia and bulimia

Complete the table below which compares the general characteristics of the two eating disorders.

Characteristic	Anorexia	Bulimia
% population diagnosed	• 0.5 to 1 per cent of women in late teens and early twenties	• 1 to 2 per cent of women 16–40
Gender	•	•
Age	•	•
Course and outcome	•	•

BIOLOGICAL EXPLANATIONS OF EATING DISORDERS

Two biological explanations are discussed in the textbook: genetic inheritance and biochemical disorders (pp. 142–5).

ACTIVITY

Biological explanations of anorexia and bulimia

Read through pp. 142–5 of the textbook and complete the table below, summarizing the main points. In the column on the right, add criticisms of the research (points in its favour and points against it).

Explanation	Key points	Relevant research (description)	Evaluation (criticism)
Genetic inheritance	• No genes identified yet for specific behaviours	• Anorexia – Holland et al. (1984) Concordance MZ = 55%, DZ = 7% (female twins) • Bulimia – Kendler et al. (1991)	+ –
Biochemical dysfunction	•	•	+ –

AS Individual Differences

Exam questions may ask you to describe *either* biological or psychological explanations of *either* anorexia or bulimia. Be prepared for any eventuality! There are a number of combinations here, but all are completely predictable. The following selection of questions gives you a flavour of the different combinations possible. Do remember that the word 'explanations' indicates a plurality requirement, and you will lose marks if you only write about one.

AO1 questions

- Describe one biological explanation of anorexia nervosa. (6 marks)
- Outline two biological explanations of bulimia nervosa. (3 + 3 marks)
- Outline one biological explanation of anorexia nervosa and give one criticism of this explanation. (3 + 3 marks)
- (i) Outline one explanation of bulimia nervosa. (3 marks)
  (ii) Give one criticism of the explanation of bulimia nervosa that you gave in (i). (3 marks)
- Outline research into the biological origins of anorexia nervosa. (6 marks)
- Outline findings of research into the biological origins of bulimia nervosa. (6 marks)

Key studies: biological explanations of eating disorders

There are two Key studies relating to biological explanations of eating disorders. The first relates to anorexia (textbook p. 143) and the second to bulimia (textbook p. 144). These will help you to tackle APFCC-type questions such as those shown on p. 112 of this workbook.

ACTIVITY

KEY STUDIES: Biological explanations of eating disorders

Write your own summaries of the Key studies on pp. 143 and 144 of the textbook, using trigger phrases, mnemonics or whatever will help you to memorize the important details. Under 'Criticisms', don't forget to include the points mentioned in the 'AO2 check' on p. 143.

KEY STUDY textbook p. 143

Subject GENETICS AND ANOREXIA NERVOSA

Researchers Holland et al. (1984)

Title

Aims

Procedures

Findings

Conclusions

Criticisms +

Criticisms –

KEY STUDY textbook p. 144

Subject GENETICS AND BULIMIA NERVOSA

Researchers Kendler et al. (1991)

Title

Aims

Procedures

Findings

Conclusions

Criticisms +

Criticisms −

AO1 questions (APFCC-type)

- Describe the procedures and findings of one study of the biological origins of eating disorders. (6 marks)
- Describe the aims and findings of one study of the biological origins of anorexia nervosa. (6 marks)
- Describe the conclusions of one study of the biological origins of bulimia nervosa and give one criticism of this study. (6 marks)
- Describe two criticisms of one study of the biological origins of anorexia nervosa. (6 marks)

PSYCHOLOGICAL EXPLANATIONS OF EATING DISORDERS

Psychological explanations of eating disorders (EDs) are covered on pp. 145–9 of the textbook. It looks in turn at:

- behavioural explanations (pp. 145–6)
- the cognitive explanation (p. 146)
- psychodynamic explanations (pp. 146–8)
- other explanations (pp. 148–9).

Behaviourists explain the development of eating disorders through conditioning processes linked to slimming (textbook p. 146). Cross-cultural studies have provided many useful findings to support the view that the pressure in Western cultures to conform to a slim body ideal contributes to the development of eating disorders.

ACTIVITY

Cross-cultural research studies

Draw up a table summarizing the cross-cultural research studies described on p. 146 of the textbook. Use the format shown below. In the final column, note down what you conclude from the findings described.

Researcher	People studied	Rate of eating disorder	Conclusion
APA (1994) diagnosed	• Immigrants to US from cultures where EDs are rare	• Same for immigrants as for those born in USA	• Immigrants adopt Western body ideal and become vulnerable to EDs.

ACTIVITY

Psychological explanations of eating disorders

Read through pp. 145–8 and complete the table below to summarize the main points of the behavioural, cognitive and psychodynamic explanations. Make a note of the findings of any research. In the final column add any criticisms of each explanation (its strengths and its weaknesses).

When giving criticisms in response to APFCC questions, remember to include enough information to gain the full 3 marks (see p. 57 of the textbook for advice on this).

Explanation	Key points	Relevant research (description)	Evaluation (criticism)
Behavioural explanation	• *According to classical conditioning, slimming is a learned response* •	• *See table of cross-cultural studies from last activity*	+ *A convincing 'common-sense' explanation* + – *Doesn't explain how EDs originate* –
Cognitive explanation	•	•	+ –
Psychodynamic explanation	•	•	+ –

The final part of this topic considers other explanations of eating disorders, focusing on individual identity and self-esteem, and family pressures.

ACTIVITY

Other psychological explanations of eating disorders

Read through pp. 148–9 and draw up a table similar to the one in the last activity to summarize the main points of the 'Other psychological explanations'. Use the same column headings as in the table above. Include separate rows for each of the four bulleted points described ('Individual identity', 'Pressures to succeed', etc.).

Key studies: psychological explanations of eating disorders

There are two Key studies relating to psychological explanations of eating disorders. Use the first of these studies (textbook p. 147) for questions on bulimia, and the second (p. 149) for questions on anorexia. For questions that ask for '... one study of the psychological origins of eating disorders', either can be used.

ACTIVITY

KEY STUDIES: Psychological explanations of eating disorders

Write your own summaries of the Key studies on pp. 147 and 149 of the textbook. Use the space provided on p. 114 of this workbook for your notes.

KEY STUDY textbook p. 147

Subject CHILDHOOD ABUSE AND BULIMIA

Researchers Wonderlich et al. (1996)

Title

Aims

Procedures

Findings

Conclusions

Criticisms +

Criticisms −

KEY STUDY textbook p. 149

Subject SELF-ESTEEM AND EATING DISORDERS

Researchers Button et al. (1996)

Title

Aims

Procedures

Findings

Conclusions

Criticisms +

Criticisms −

AO1 questions (APFCC-type)

- Describe the aims and conclusions of one study of the psychological origins of eating disorders. (6 marks)
- Describe the findings and conclusions of one study of the psychological origins of anorexia nervosa. (6 marks)
- Describe the conclusions of one study of the psychological origins of bulimia nervosa and give one criticism of this study. (6 marks)

Psychological explanations of eating disorders stress the influence of psychological factors in their development. You have looked at a number of psychological explanations, covered in the textbook on pp. 145–50. Most of these apply to both anorexia *and* bulimia so can be used either for *general* questions (i.e. psychological explanations of eating disorders) or *specific* questions (i.e. psychological explanations of anorexia *or* bulimia).

AO1 questions

- Describe one psychological explanation of anorexia nervosa. (6 marks)
- Outline two psychological explanations of bulimia nervosa. (3 + 3 marks)
- Outline one psychological explanation of anorexia nervosa and give one criticism of this explanation. (3 + 3 marks)
- Outline research into the psychological origins of bulimia nervosa. (6 marks)
- Outline conclusions of research into the psychological origins of eating disorders. (6 marks)

AO1 + AO2 QUESTIONS ON EATING DISORDERS

AO1+AO2 questions

- Outline and evaluate two or more biological explanations of anorexia and/or bulimia nervosa. (18 marks)
- Consider whether research (theories and/or studies) supports the view that eating disorders are caused by psychological factors. (18 marks)
- To what extent is it possible to explain anorexia nervosa from a biological perspective? (18 marks)

The skill of transferring material from textbook to examination script can be achieved through anticipation and preparation. There is clearly far too much material in the textbook for you to have any hope of representing it all, so the advice is not to try. The anticipation part of this solution is *knowing* the type of question you are likely to be asked (see above), and the preparation part is *practising* how you would answer each possible question in advance.

Take the second question above, for example. There is no single correct answer to this question, so you are free to use whatever material you feel comfortable with provided you feel that it is addressing the question set. You may even incorporate alternative (biological) explanations, but you must use this material as part of a sustained critical argument rather than just presenting a different 'non' psychological explanation.

You also need to keep a very close eye on your AO1/AO2 ratio. Imagine yourself as a newspaper editor who has a maximum of 120 words for AO1 and 240 words for AO2. In the sample answer on p. 116, there are a total of 120 words of AO1 and 242 words of AO2 (we have used different colours to distinguish AO1 and AO2). You don't have to be as precise as this and examiners certainly won't be counting them. However, you should try to balance your answer in such a way as to reflect the number of marks available for AO1 (6) and AO2 (12) in this type of question.

Have a go at the question below, following the advice given.

ACTIVITY

One for you to try ...

To what extent is it possible to explain anorexia nervosa from a biological perspective? (18 marks)

Although many of the AO1+AO2 questions on this topic will invite you to write about eating disorders in general, this one is specifically on anorexia nervosa. It is important, therefore, to ensure that whatever explanations, research studies or evaluative points you use are relevant to anorexia.

Material on biological explanations of anorexia nervosa is covered on pp. 142–5 of the textbook. You could simply construct your answer by using *descriptions* of biological explanations and then evaluate these using material on p. 145 (which effectively makes this the same question as the first of the AO1+AO2 questions listed above). However, in order to expand your AO2 material, and take advantage of the expertise of an active researcher in this field, you should read and incorporate the Expert interview with Gill Harris (textbook p. 150).

Sample answer

Consider whether research (theories and/or studies) supports the view that eating disorders are caused by psychological factors. (18 marks)

*Classical conditioning theory suggests that slimming becomes a habit as people learn to associate being slim with feeling good about themselves. Operant conditioning then comes into play as admiration from others further reinforces this dieting behaviour. Refusing to eat may provide an additional reward in the form of attention from parents. Cross-cultural studies support these explanations. It has been noted that eating disorders are more common in industrialized societies where there is an abundance of food, yet being attractive is associated with being slim. The fact that studies have discovered that people who move from a non-industrialized to an industrialized country are more at risk of developing an eating disorder is further support of the influence of Western ideals of attractiveness rather than genetics or biochemical influences. The idea that pressures to be slim in Western cultures play a part in eating disorders is also supported in studies conducted on groups of people for whom slimness is essential, such as gymnasts and ballet dancers. In a group of ballet students, Garner et al. (1987) found that 25% developed anorexia nervosa over the two years of their study.

Family systems theory suggests that the development of anorexia serves to prevent disagreements within the family by diverting attention onto the person with the eating disorder. Research has supported this view with the finding that parents sometimes become more anxious and depressed when their adolescent child starts to regain weight, reinforcing the idea that anorexia may be a way of defusing family conflict. It has been argued that the drive to succeed comes from the family of those girls who develop anorexia nervosa, and it is the stresses of the family environment and not a genetic predisposition that triggers dietary restraint as a response to stress. However, much of this work has been carried out with families after the eating disorder has developed, and the effect of caring for an adolescent who is trying to starve herself has not been taken into account. It is possible, therefore, that the family stress frequently found in the families of people with anorexia may be a consequence of the disorder, rather than the cause of it.

*orange text = AO1, purple text = AO2

CHECK YOUR UNDERSTANDING

When you have finished working through this topic, try the questions in 'Check your understanding' on p. 151 of the textbook. Check your answers by looking at the relevant parts of the textbook or this workbook, listed below.

1 textbook p. 140; workbook p. 109
2 textbook p. 141
3 textbook p. 141; workbook p. 109
4 textbook p. 143
5 textbook pp. 142–5 – *Note:* biochemical explanations are not specifically mentioned in the specification, therefore cannot be asked for in an exam.
6 textbook p. 146
7 textbook p. 146
8 textbook pp. 146–7
9 textbook pp. 148–9
10 textbook p. 150

ANSWERS TO ACTIVITIES

Understanding the specification, p. 107

1 You have to study two eating disorders: anorexia nervosa and bulimia nervosa.

2 You need to know about biological and psychological explanations for both eating disorders.

3 Yes, the word 'research' indicates that Key studies are involved. According to the specification, you need to learn at least one Key study for *both* kinds of explanation (biological and psychological) of *both* eating disorders. In other words you need to learn four Key studies.

SOCIAL Influence

PREVIEW

There are three topics in this unit. You should read them alongside the following pages in the Collins *Psychology for AS-level* textbook:

Topic		Textbook pages
1	Conformity and minority influence	pp. 155–68
2	Obedience to authority	pp. 169–80
3	Critical issue: ethical issues in psychological research	pp. 181–91

INTRODUCTION

This unit covers the AS Social Psychology part of Module 3 (AQA Specification A). The diagram below shows where it fits in to the overall AS qualification.

Read the Preview and Introduction on p. 154 of the textbook now. This will give you an overview of what's in the unit.

Where this unit fits in to the AS qualification

Topic 1 >> Conformity and minority influence

Social influence is the process by which an individual's attitudes, beliefs or behaviours are modified by the presence or actions of others. Traditionally (and particularly in North America), researchers have concentrated on the power of the majority over the minority in exerting social influence. However, if people conformed to the majority at all times, there would never be change or innovation. Researchers (particularly in Europe) have also focused on the power of the minority to produce such change and innovation.

In this topic we look at explanations of the different psychological processes involved in majority and minority influence, as well as important research studies related to these forms of social influence.

UNDERSTANDING THE SPECIFICATION

Here is what the AQA (A) specification says about this topic. It forms part of AS Module 3, Social Psychology and Research Methods.

Read it and then try the activity on the right. You'll find answers to the activity on p. 127.

Social influence

a. Conformity and minority influence

Research studies into conformity (e.g. Sherif, Asch, Zimbardo) and minority influence (e.g. Moscovici, Clark). Explanations of why people yield to majority (conformity) and minority influence.

ACTIVITY

Understanding the specification

1 Whose work might you study when looking at research into conformity?

- ______________
- ______________
- ______________

2 And whose work might you study when looking at research into minority influence?

- ______________
- ______________

3 Does this topic involve Key studies (APFCCs)? If so, how many? *Clue*: Look for the key word 'research'.

- ______________

The specification mentions *conformity* and *minority influence* as the two forms of social influence that you must study in this section. You are specifically required to be able to define these terms, and know at least two explanations of why people yield to these two forms of social influence. Note that *conformity* and *majority influence* are the same thing, whereas *minority influence* is something completely different.

There are three APFCC studies in this topic – two studies of conformity and one of minority influence. It is also important to be able to relate research on social influence to the real world – we will refer to this later.

TOPIC MAP

Topic map

Look through pp. 155–68 of the textbook to see where the items shown in the topic map are covered. Note down the relevant page numbers in the spaces left on the topic map.

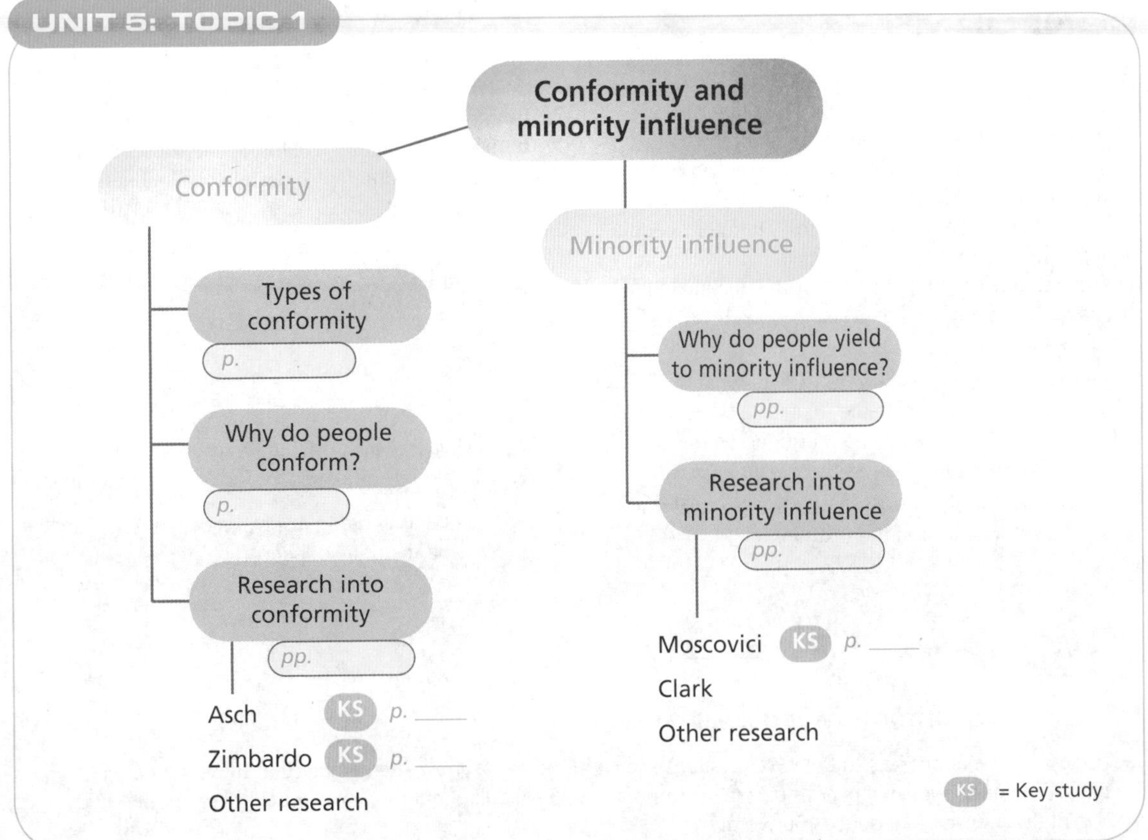

KEEPING TRACK

Use the table below to keep track of your work on this topic and plan your revision. See p. iv (Introduction) for guidance on filling it in.

What I need to learn	Where is it?	Tick if you ... could make a basic attempt	could make a good attempt	have complete mastery of this
Conformity				
Definition of 'social influence'				
Definition of 'majority influence' or 'conformity'				
Explanations of why people yield to majority influence				
Description of research into majority influence				
Evaluation of research into majority influence				
Description of APFCC for a Key study investigating majority influence				
Minority influence				
Definition of 'minority influence'				
Explanations of why people yield to minority influence				
Description of research into minority influence				
Evaluation of research into minority influence				
Description of APFCC for a Key study investigating minority influence				
Outline of the differences between majority and minority influence				

CONFORMITY

The first part of the topic examines conformity or majority influence. Technically there is a difference in the meaning of these terms. *Majority influence* is the pressure that people experience when exposed to the prevailing group norm; *conformity* is the action of the individual in yielding to this pressure. Therefore people conform (or not) to majority influence. However, you don't need to worry too much about this distinction, as these two terms are used interchangeably in texts and exam papers.

In the exam you may be asked to explain what is meant by the terms 'majority influence'/'conformity' or 'social influence'. Look at the example questions on the right. In answering questions such as these, you can:

- first provide a definition of the term – you will find definitions on p. 154 of the textbook
- describe different types of influence (with a brief example) and who identified them – different types of majority influence/conformity are described on p. 156, while different types of social influence are described on p. 157.

AO1 questions

- Explain what is meant by the terms 'social influence' and 'majority influence'. (3 + 3 marks)
- (i) What is meant by the terms majority and minority influence? (2 + 2 marks)

  (ii) Give one difference between majority and minority influence. (2 marks)

ACTIVITY

Explaining conformity and social influence

Using a PC, write answers to the two questions shown in the panel above. Remember that these are AO1 questions and so would appear as part (a) or (b) of a full AS Module 3 question. You would have about 5 minutes in which to produce 100 words.

For this activity, don't limit yourself to 5 minutes, but aim to produce answers which you feel would score high marks in the exam. You can check what the examiners are looking for by reading pp. 249–50 of the textbook.

Remember, too, that a question part worth 3 marks is asking for more detail than one worth just 2 marks – obvious, really, as you have more time to write more words. But make the extra words count – for instance add a really telling example, don't just put in more 'padding'.

ACTIVITY

Making your answers 'psychological'

As well as being accurate, your answers to exam questions need to sound 'psychological', as the textbook puts it on p. 268. Below are a couple of descriptions of terms made by one candidate in response to the two questions above. What is wrong with them? Why aren't they 'psychological'?

1 "Social influence is something you feel because you are part of a society. It may get to you and so you try to ignore it."

-

2 "Majority influence is when you are a member of the majority rather than just being a member of the minority. You have more power over other people."

-

Compare your answers with those given on p. 127.

Research into conformity

Asch's study into conformity is a classic piece of research that provoked much debate and further studies by other psychologists. It is described in detail on pp. 158–60 of the textbook. The Key study on p. 159 describes his original procedure. He went on to repeat the study several times, changing aspects of the test to see whether different factors produced varying results.

ACTIVITY

Summarize the results of Asch's studies in the table below. This will provide you with an at-a-glance summary of how levels of conformity rose and fell according to the situations set up by Asch in his tests. Note that the percentage level of conformity is a measure of the percentage number of *trials* where participants conformed (not the percentage of *participants* who conformed).

Situational factor	Features of the test	Level of conformity	Other key points
Original	• 6 vs 1 – incorrect answers on 12/18 trials	32%	• 74% conformed at least once • 26% never conformed
Non-unanimous majority			
Size of majority			
Losing a partner			
Gaining a partner			
Nature of task (easy/difficult)			
Mode of response			

Further research into conformity

Asch's procedures have been used and adapted by lots of researchers investigating conformity. Several of these studies are described on pp. 160–2 of the textbook. Their aim was generally to investigate factors that influence conformity levels.

The activity on p. 122 of this workbook will help you to summarize the main points of their research in a table. This information will give you plenty of material for answering questions such as the ones shown in the panel on the right. Note that the first two questions would use the same material, and are essentially the same question.

The final important piece of research you will look at under the heading of conformity is Zimbardo's controversial study set in a mock prison. This aimed to investigate how people conformed to social roles, in this case the stereotyped roles of prisoner and prison guard. The results are fascinating, but also disturbing. Read the textbook pp. 162–3 and complete the 'Key studies' activity that follows.

AO1 questions

- Describe two factors that influence majority influence. (3 + 3 marks)
- Outline two explanations of why people conform. (3 + 3 marks)
- Briefly describe findings of research into majority influence. (6 marks)

ACTIVITY

Further research into conformity

Asch's procedures have been used and adapted by lots of researchers investigating conformity. Several of these studies are described on pp. 160–2 of the textbook. Their aim was generally to investigate factors that influence conformity levels.

Factor	Researcher(s)	Description of study	Key findings
Mode of response (other Ps visible or not)	Crutchfield (1955)	•	•
Individual differences	Crutchfield (1955)	•	•
	Furman and Duke (1988)	•	•
Historical and cultural contexts		•	•

Key studies: conformity

There are two Key studies relating to conformity. The first is Asch's classic study of 1951 (textbook p. 159) and the second is Zimbardo's prison simulation study (p. 163). One very important point is that when using Zimbardo's study in the context of conformity, you *must* emphasize those aspects of the study that showed conformity (i.e. to social roles) rather than just offering a general account of this piece of research.

ACTIVITY

KEY STUDIES: Research into conformity

Write your own summaries of the Key studies on pp. 159 and 163 of the textbook, using trigger phrases, mnemonics or whatever will help you to memorize the important details. Don't forget to include the points mentioned in the 'AO2 checks' at the end of each study.

AO1 questions (APFCC-type)

- Describe the procedures and findings of one study of conformity/majority influence. (6 marks)
- Describe the aims and conclusions of one study of conformity/majority influence. (6 marks)
- Describe the conclusions of one study of conformity/majority influence and give one criticism of this study. (6 marks)

KEY STUDY textbook p. 159

Subject MAJORITY INFLUENCE

Researchers Asch (1951)

Title

Aims

Procedures

Findings

Conclusions

Criticisms +

Criticisms –

KEY STUDY textbook p. 163

Subject CONFORMITY TO SOCIAL ROLES

Researchers Zimbardo et al. (1973)

Title

Aims

Procedures

Findings

Conclusions

Criticisms +

Criticisms –

MINORITY SOCIAL INFLUENCE

Minority social influence – where a minority exerts influence over the majority – is outlined on pp. 162–7 of the textbook.

Research into minority influence

Two main pieces of research into minority influence are described in the textbook: Moscovici's 'blue-green' slide study (see Key study on p. 124) and Clark's *Twelve Angry Men* study.

ACTIVITY

KEY STUDY: Research into minority influence

In the table below, write your own summary of the Key study into minority influence (the 'blue–green' slide experiment by Moscovici and colleagues). Use trigger phrases, mnemonics or whatever will help you to memorize the important details.

AO1 questions (APFCC-type)

- Describe the aims and findings of one study of minority influence. (6 marks)
- Describe the procedures and conclusions of one study of minority influence. (6 marks)
- Describe the findings of one study of minority influence and give one criticism of this study. (6 marks)

KEY STUDY textbook p. 164

Subject	MINORITY INFLUENCE	Findings
Researchers	Moscovici et al. (1969)	
Title		
Aims		
Procedures		Conclusions
Criticisms +		Criticisms –

ACTIVITY

Juries and minority influence

1 According to Clark (textbook p. 165), when were participants in his 'juries' most persuaded by the minority viewpoint? What two factors were most important?

-
-

2 The Tanford and Penrod experiment and Chicago Jury Project (textbook p. 165) highlight potential criticisms of Clark's research. What are they? *Hint*: think about the size of the minorities and the types of setting investigated.

-

3 According to Charlan Nemeth (textbook p. 167), how does the 'unanimity requirement' of juries help serve justice? Your answer should refer specifically to minority views.

-

HINT

Twelve Angry Men

Clark's *Twelve Angry Men* study used the plot of a famous 1957 film as the basis for his research into minority influence. If you're interested in seeing the original film, you can easily get hold of a video or DVD through a local or Internet video retailer. Beware, though: when describing this *study*, don't fall into the trap (as many do) of describing the *film*.

Explanations of minority influence

The textbook discusses four main factors in explaining why people yield to minority influence (p. 166).

ACTIVITY

Explanations of minority influence

Read through p. 166 and look at the 'Hint' below. Then note down what is meant by the following terms:

- intra-individual consistency
- inter-individual consistency
- snowball effect
- in-group
- out-group
- dissociation model
- social cryptoamnesia

Differences between majority and minority social influence

In the exam you may be asked to compare majority influence and minority influence, as in the example question and answers given on p. 259 of the textbook. The next activity will help you to clarify the differences between them.

HINT

Terminology

- 'Intra' means 'inside' (for example, an intravenous drip goes inside the vein).
- 'Inter' means 'between' (for example, an international match is one between countries).
- 'Crypto' means hidden (as in a crypt!).

ACTIVITY

Differences between majority and minority social influence

Complete the following table to summarize the differences between majority and minority social influence. Read the panel on p. 166 of the textbook and refer also to the pages mentioned below.

Factor	Majority influence	Minority influence
Type of conformity (textbook p. 156)	•	•
Type of influence (textbook p. 157)	•	•
Timescales	•	•
Other difference	•	•

AO1+AO2 QUESTIONS ON CONFORMITY AND MINORITY INFLUENCE

AO1+AO2 questions

- "Research into majority influence tells us very little about conformity in real life." To what extent is majority influence research a valid representation of real-life situations? (18 marks)
- Outline criticisms of majority influence research, and consider whether these are justified. (18 marks)
- Outline and evaluate minority influence research. (18 marks)
- To what extent has research into minority influence been shown to apply to real life? (18 marks)

Part (c) questions in psychology often ask you to go beyond simply detailing research and describing criticisms, and ask you to reflect on such criticisms. The questions above are some of the most demanding, but can be answered with some careful planning.

Take the last question. First of all we need to break it down into its constituent parts so that we really are answering the question. This might include the following:

- description of important research findings/ conclusions in minority influence (AO1)
- arguments to show situations where these do not apply to real life (AO2)
- arguments to show situations where these do apply to real life (AO2).

Note that the latter two paragraphs are completely AO2 in this plan, and so we cannot get away with lengthy descriptions of studies where minority influence has been studied in more realistic situations. These must be used to construct a convincing argument. The following answer is constructed from material on pp. 162–7 of the textbook, including the Expert interview with Charlan Nemeth on p. 167, cited in the answer as 'Nemeth (2003)'.

Sample answer

To what extent has research into minority influence been shown to apply to real life? (18 marks)

Research has established that for minorities to exert an influence on the majority, they must be consistent in their opposition to the majority, maintaining a consistent viewpoint over time and showing agreement among different members of the minority (Mosovici et al. 1969). Moscovici also established that the minority must not appear dogmatic by rigidly reiterating the same arguments, but must demonstrate a degree of flexibility. Minority influence has been shown to be more influential if the minority appear to acting out of principle, and are seen to have made sacrifices in order to maintain their position. Minorities may be more influential over time, particularly if they are advocating views that are consistent with current social trends.

The artificiality of the laboratory setting in research by Moscovici et al. has been criticized as being unlike real-life situations where minorities attempt to exert their influence on the prevailing majority position. The ecological validity of these conclusions has been challenged by research studying minority influence in more realistic settings, and with more important issues than the colour of slides. Tanford and Penrod, for example, found little evidence of minority influence in simulated jury discussions. It appeared from this study that when people are discussing serious issues, it is majorities, not minorities, that are influential. Likewise, in the Chicago Jury Project, in only 5 per cent of the cases did the initial minority prevail, and then only if the minority began with at least three members of the jury.

The fact that the minority viewpoint may not prevail does not, however, detract from the importance of minority influence. Nemeth (2003) has shown in her own research that exposure to dissenting minority views stimulates us to be better decision makers and more creative in our thought. This suggests that the value of the minority position in jury deliberations is that it stimulates better decision making and increases the perception of justice. The principle of unanimity rather than majority rule in juries provides some protection from legal injustice. Nemeth also argues that the true value of minority dissent is that it acts as a safeguard against tyranny. Democracies allow for the airing of different views and gives us the opportunity for the detection of truth.

ACTIVITY

One for you to try ...

Outline criticisms of majority influence research, and consider whether these are justified. (18 marks)

This is an occasion when it pays you to work backwards. Think of potential criticisms of majority influence research, and then consider for which of these you could provide a convincing case for or against. For example, a criticism of Asch's research is that the deception and stress experienced by his research participants was ethically unacceptable. Aronson (textbook p. 190) suggests that this criticism may not be justified. Likewise, in the Key study on p. 159 of the textbook, you are told that the time and place when the research was carried out might have affected the findings. Perrin and Spencer (1980) found evidence to support this criticism, but also found that when the perceived costs of not conforming were high, conformity effects would still be demonstrated (Perrin and Spencer 1981, textbook p. 161).

Remember that when answering this question, a description of criticisms would be AO1 and your consideration of whether they are justified would be AO2.

CHECK YOUR UNDERSTANDING

When you have finished working through this topic, try the questions in 'Check your understanding' on p. 168 of the textbook. You can check your answers by looking at the relevant parts of the textbook, listed below.

1 textbook pp. 154, 155 and 162
2 textbook p. 157
3 textbook p. 156
4 textbook p. 159
5 textbook p. 161
6 textbook p. 163
7 textbook p. 166
8 textbook p. 164
9 textbook p. 166; workbook p. 125
10 textbook p. 167

ANSWERS TO ACTIVITIES

Understanding the specification, p. 118

1 The work by Sherif, Asch and Zimbardo can be used as examples of research into conformity (note the 'e.g.' in the specification). The textbook looks in detail at Asch's and Zimbardo's work (see Key studies on pp. 159 and 163).

2 The research of Moscovici and of Clark can be used as examples of research into minority influence; the textbook contains a Key study of an experiment by Moscovici (p. 164) while Clark's *Twelve Angry Men* study is described on p. 165.

3 The specification specifically mentions research into both conformity and minority influence, so you need to know at least two Key studies. In fact, the textbook contains three studies in total: two on conformity and one on minority influence (see answer to question 1).

Making your answers 'psychological', p. 120

1 This is too imprecise. The term is not really understood although there is a glimmer of truth in what is being said. Also, the answer is not 'psychological' because it doesn't use terms that psychologists use to describe things accurately. For example, it could have included the phrase 'the process by which a person's attitudes ... are modified by the presence or actions of others' – this describes accurately what social influence means (and isn't the same as 'it may get to you'!).

2 This answer makes the mistake of defining a term ('majority influence') in an almost circular way ('it's when you are a member of the majority'). It needs to find a different way of explaining the term, such as 'adopting the views or behaviour of a reference group as a result of perceived group pressure'.

While 'having more power over other people' is part of majority influence, the key (psychological) point is that people experience this as pressure to adopt the behaviours, attitudes and values of other members of a reference group. Having 'more power' is not precise enough and doesn't describe the important effects of conformity.

Topic 2 >> Obedience to authority

To start thinking seriously about obedience, try the 'Getting you thinking…' activity on p. 169 of the textbook. This gives a startling example of the appalling actions people can carry out in the name of obedience. It is worth bearing the My Lai massacre in mind as you come to think about what makes people obey and how people might resist obedience. Before launching into this topic, you should be clear what is meant by the term 'obedience to authority'. The My Lai and Holocaust examples provide stark illustrations of these processes in action. Obedience, therefore, is carrying out an act that we probably would not have done without a direct order from someone in a position of authority over us.

UNDERSTANDING THE SPECIFICATION

Here is what the AQA (A) specification says about this topic. It forms part of AS Module 3, Social Psychology and Research Methods.

Read it and then try the activity on the right. You'll find answers to the activity on p. 136.

Social influence

b. Obedience to authority

Research studies into obedience to authority (e.g. Milgram, Hofling, Meeus and Raaijmakers). Issues of experimental and ecological validity associated with such research. Explanations of psychological processes involved in obedience, the reasons why people obey and how people might resist obedience.

ACTIVITY

Understanding the specification

1 Whose work might you study when looking at research into obedience to authority?

- ______
- ______
- ______

2 What two types of validity do you have to know about when considering research into obedience?

- ______
- ______

3 Does this topic involve Key studies (APFCCs)? If so, how many?

- ______

______

This part of the specification is concerned with *obedience to authority* as a form of social influence. You need to know the aims, procedures, findings, conclusions and criticisms (i.e. APFCC) of *one study* of obedience. This will probably be Milgram's 1963 study, as this is the one we have covered in the most detail in the textbook. You should know about *experimental* and *ecological validity* in the context of obedience research. It is worth finding out what critics of Milgram's research (e.g. Orne and Holland) said about validity issues, and how Milgram responded to such claims. Finally, you are required to be able to define the term 'obedience', and know at least two explanations of why people obey, and at least two explanations of how they might *resist* obedience.

TOPIC MAP

ACTIVITY

Topic map

Look through pp. 169–80 of the textbook to see where the items shown in the topic map are covered. Fill in the blank boxes with the names of the people whose research into obedience is covered in the textbook. Add page numbers in all the relevant boxes.

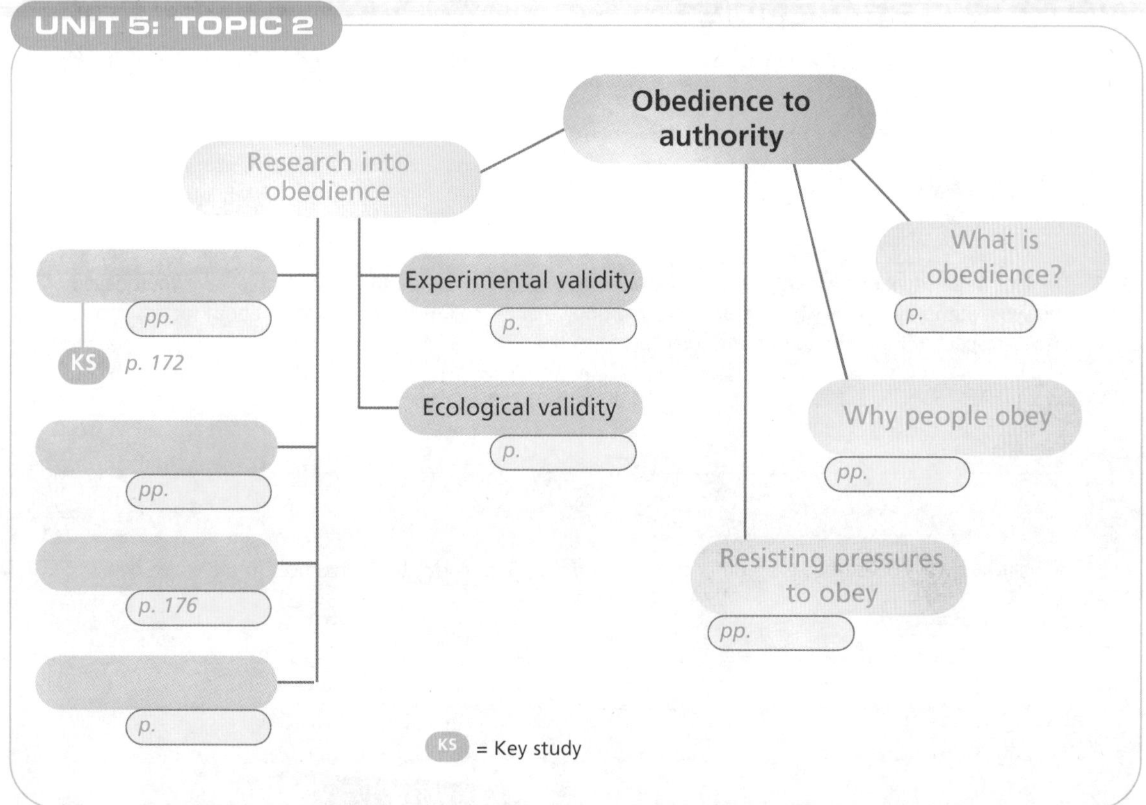

KEEPING TRACK

Use the table below to keep track of your work on this topic and plan your revision. See p. iv (Introduction) for guidance on filling it in.

What I need to learn	Where is it?	Tick if you ... could make a basic attempt	could make a good attempt	have complete mastery of this
Obedience				
Definition of 'obedience to authority'				
Definition of 'ecological validity'				
Definition of 'experimental validity'				
Outline of the differences between conformity and obedience				
Description of research into obedience to authority				
Evaluation of research into obedience to authority				
Evaluation of the experimental and ecological validity of research into obedience				
Description of APFCC for a Key study investigating obedience				
Explanations of obedience				
Explanations of why people obey				
Explanations of how people might resist obedience				

WHAT IS OBEDIENCE?

Page 170 of the textbook gives a good introduction to obedience, including both a full definition (see 'Key terms') and an outline of the differences between obedience and conformity.

ACTIVITY

Conformity or obedience?

1 Think of three situations where you have obeyed other people in the past. Which people have you obeyed and what authority did they have that made you obey them? (You might like to think about factors such as power, respect and the threat of punishment.)

People	What authority they had
•	•
•	•
•	•

2 In what two ways does obedience differ from conformity? Summarize the differences in the space below.

-
-

Milgram's studies of obedience

Stanley Milgram's studies in the 1960s have been without doubt the most influential pieces of research into obedience. For that reason, the textbook uses it for the basis of a Key study (see p. 172). Milgram actually carried out 18 variations of his initial baseline study. It is acceptable to include material from any of these variations in your description of the original study.

Now complete the activity on the right. The information you note down will help you answer APFCC-type questions such as those in the panel below.

AO1 questions (APFCC-type)

- Describe the findings and conclusions from one study of obedience.* (6 marks)
- Describe aims and findings of one study of obedience. (6 marks)
- Describe the procedures of one study of obedience and give one criticism of this study. (6 marks)

**Possible answers to this question are discussed on p. 260 of the textbook.*

ACTIVITY

KEY STUDY: Milgram's research into obedience

In the table on p. 131, write your own summary of the Key study into obedience (Milgram 1963).

The procedures are quite complicated, but it is important to understand them and, in particular, the role the 'teacher' (the one giving the shocks) thought he was playing in the mock experiment. Answer the following questions (you may need to read p. 171 as well as the Key study on p. 172):

1 What did the participants in Milgram's experiment think they were doing?

-

2 All the participants went to 300 volts. What was the 'learner' saying at that point?

-

3 What exactly does the figure of 65% describe?

-

4 What is meant by 'a subordinate role in a dominance hierarchy'?

-

KEY STUDY textbook p. 172

Subject OBEDIENCE

Researchers Milgram (1963)

Title

Aims

Procedures

Findings

Conclusions

Criticisms +

Criticisms –

Milgram repeated the experiment described in the Key study many times (in all he tested over 1000 participants). By varying features of the experiment, he was able to work out which features of the experiment set-up ('situational variables') would affect levels of obedience, and in which direction (i.e. whether increasing or decreasing the percentage).

Complete the activity below to summarize some of effects Milgram found.

ACTIVITY

Variations on Milgram's basic procedure

Read the text about how Milgram varied his procedure on p. 173 of the textbook, including Table 5.2.

1 In which situation was the obedience rate at its highest?

-

2 What factor brought obedience levels down to their lowest?

-

3 How does this tie in with Asch's findings about conformity (see p. 158)?

-

4 What other factors reduced obedience levels and why do you think they had that effect?

Factor	Why factor reduced obedience levels
•	•
•	•
•	•
•	•
•	•

Evaluating Milgram's work

In the Key study on p. 172, two main criticisms of Milgram's work are mentioned:

- *ethical issues* – in particular, whether or not participants were harmed
- *validity of the experiment* – including both experimental (internal) validity and ecological validity (mundane realism).

Milgram's work raises other ethical issues apart from potential harm to participants. These include the need for informed consent, avoiding deception and debriefing. You will consider those later in this topic. David Mandel (textbook p. 174) also discusses some of the wider ethical criticisms of Milgram's research.

Issues of experimental and ecological validity

As you read through this unit, you will realize that most of the studies of social influence are carried out in artificial settings. This is because of the many practical difficulties involved in observing social influence in natural settings. However, because of their artificiality, these studies raise important questions such as:

- Does the experimental manipulation work?
- How realistic or true to life is the study?
- Can the results of the study be applied to settings outside the laboratory?

Now try the activity below.

ACTIVITY

Milgram's research and validity

Complete the table below, summarizing the arguments criticizing and supporting the validity of Milgram's research. Note down the name of any researchers who provided evidence in favour of or against the validity of Milgram's work.

Issue	Arguments against	Arguments in support
Experimental (internal) validity	•	•
Ecological validity (mundane realism)	•	•

Experimental and ecological validity are mentioned specifically in the specification for this topic, so you may be asked direct questions about these issues – some possible questions are listed below. There is plenty of relevant material in the textbook – the key thing is to limit your answers to what the question asks for.

For example, with the first question, you could base your answer on Milgram's study or you could take the research by Hofling and colleagues as your main study of obedience (see next activity).

HINT

What is mundane realism?

'Mundane' means 'worldly', so 'mundane realism' refers to whether results can apply to the 'real world'.

AO1 questions

- Explain what is meant by the term 'ecological validity' and illustrate your answer with reference to one study of obedience. (3 + 3 marks)
- Explain what is meant by the terms 'obedience' and 'experimental validity'. (3 + 3 marks)

ACTIVITY

Other researchers into obedience

On pp. 175–6, the textbook describes three other studies into obedience. They are interesting in their own right, but also because they are often used to argue for or against Milgram's conclusions (as in the last activity). Complete the table below to summarize the main points of these research studies.

Researcher	Brief description of research	Findings	Validity of research
Hofling *et al.* (1966)	•	•	•
Rank and Jacobson (1977)	•	•	•
Bickman (1974)	•	•	•

WHY PEOPLE OBEY – EXPLANATIONS OF OBEDIENCE

The textbook lists five factors that might explain why people obey (pp. 177–8). All of these explanations are illustrated by one or other of Milgram's studies.

ACTIVITY

Why people obey

Complete the following table which summarizes the various explanations for obedience. In the right-hand column, note down how each factor is illustrated by Milgram's studies.

Factor	Key features	How illustrated in Milgram's research
Legitimate authority	• We respect people seen to hold positions of power and hence are more likely to obey them. • Bickman's study (1974) showed the power of uniforms to prove authority & encourage obedience.	• Change of venue from Yale to less prestigious offices reduced authority in participants' eyes. Levels of obedience fell.
Gradual commitment	•	•
Agency theory	•	•

continued on next page

Why people obey – *continued from previous page*

Factor	Key features	How illustrated in Milgram's research
Buffers	•	•
Personality factors	•	•

ACTIVITY

True or false?

Carry out the activity on p. 178 of the textbook and then compare your answers with those given on p. 136.

AO1 questions

- Outline two reasons why people obey. (3 + 3 marks)
- Explain what is meant by 'obedience' and give one reason why people obey. (3 + 3 marks)

RESISTING PRESSURES TO OBEY

The textbook lists several factors that might explain why people resist pressures to obey (pp. 179–80), with illustrations from Milgram's studies as well as other research.

ACTIVITY

Why people don't obey

Read the text about why people resist pressures to obey and then answer the following questions.

Factor	Question
Feeling responsible	What percentage of people in Milgram's original study did not go to the full 450-volt shock? •
	Look at Table 5.2 on p. 173. In which of these variations would participants have felt more responsible for the 'pain' being inflicted on the 'learner' and how did the levels of obedience change? •
Disobedient models	In Milgram's studies, what happened when the participant had the support of another 'teacher' who refused to give the electric shocks? •

continued on next page

Why people don't obey – *continued from previous page*

Factor	Question
Questioning motives	Which of Milgram's variations gave participants more reason to question the authority of the researchers? •
Time for discussion	What were the significant features of the study by Gamson and colleagues that contributed to the participants' disobedience? •
Reactance	What is meant by the term 'reactance'? •
Individual differences	What does Kohlberg mean by: "One can reason in terms of principles and not live up to those principles"? •

AO1 questions

- Outline one reason why people obey, and one way in which people might resist obedience. (3 + 3 marks)
- Outline two ways in which people might resist obedience.* (3 + 3 marks)
- Outline two reasons why people might resist obedience.* (3 + 3 marks)

**These are essentially the same question. The second version emphasizes the psychological processes that might underlie resistance (e.g. feeling responsible or questioning motives).*

AO1+AO2 QUESTIONS ON OBEDIENCE TO AUTHORITY

Two answers to the first question in the panel on the right are provided in the textbook (pp. 260–1). Answer 2 has been written in the classic three-paragraphs format, with AO1 provided in the first paragraph and AO2 in the subsequent two paragraphs.

There are two main ways to tackle this question. The first way is to describe specific aspects of obedience research for the AO1, and then criticize this research in terms of its validity (or lack of validity) for the AO2 content. The alternative approach, and the one taken in Answer 2, is to describe validity criticisms for the AO1, and then take issue with those criticisms for AO2. This has worked very effectively in this answer, as it has given the opportunity to cover both experimental and ecological validity in the same answer, and has avoided the trap of being overly descriptive in the AO2 component. Notice how the second two paragraphs are littered with 'AO2 words' ('However', 'Milgram defended...', 'In contrast...').

AO1+AO2 questions

- "The unacceptability of research into obedience is that it tells us very little about obedience in the real world."

  To what extent have studies of obedience been shown to lack validity? (18 marks)
- Consider whether the findings from social influence research can justify the methods used to obtain such findings. (18 marks)
- Outline and evaluate research into obedience to authority. (18 marks)
- To what extent does social influence research (theories and/or studies) display ecological validity? (18 marks)

ACTIVITY

One for you to try ...

Consider whether the findings from social influence research can justify the methods used to obtain such findings. (18 marks)

In a sense this is a question you might not attempt before completing the next topic (ethical issues in psychological research), but it does no harm to consider these issues here. This question asks you to take a reflective look at social influence research (this can include any or all of majority influence, minority influence and obedience). You do not have to cover all of these, and may be happier to restrict your answer to just a consideration of obedience. There is no one best way to answer this question, although the following approach is a possibility:

- AO1 = description of those procedures used in social influence research that you feel able to take issue with, together with a brief statement of main findings only.
- AO2 = evaluation of the procedures used, including commentary on the ethical issues involved.
- AO2 = evaluation of the importance of the findings (e.g. their validity) in the light of these ethical issues.

You have the whole social influence chapter (textbook pp. 154–90) to resource your answer, but you will find some excellent commentary provided in the Expert interviews with David Mandel (p. 174) and Elliot Aronson (p. 190).

CHECK YOUR UNDERSTANDING

When you have finished working through this topic, try the questions in 'Check your understanding' on p. 180 of the textbook. You can check your answers by looking at the relevant parts of the textbook, listed below.

1 textbook pp. 170, 175
2 textbook p. 170
3 textbook p. 172
4 textbook p. 173
5 textbook p. 175
6 textbook p. 175
7 textbook pp. 175–6
8 textbook pp. 177–8
9 textbook pp. 179–80
10 textbook pp. 174–6

ANSWERS TO ACTIVITIES

Understanding the specification, p. 128

1 The specification mentions the work of Milgram, Hofling, and Meeus and Raaijmakers. The 'e.g.' tells us that these are examples only, although Milgram's work is hard to ignore!
- Milgram's work is covered on pp. 171–5.
- The research of Hofling and colleagues is described on pp. 175–6.
- Meeus and Raaijmakers are not covered in this topic, but other research studies into obedience are, specifically Rank and Jacobson (1977) and Bickman (1974).

2 Experimental validity and ecological validity

3 The specification specifically mentions research studies into obedience, so you need to know at least one Key study: Milgram's original study is given as a Key study on p. 172.

True or false, p. 134

1 True
2 False – it was 65%
3 False – 'foot in the door' effect
4 True
5 False
6 True
7 False
8 False
9 True
10 True

Topic 3 >> Critical issue: ethical issues in psychological research

Already in Topics 1 and 2, we have met the question of how psychologists carry out research into difficult areas, such as social influence. For example, there was the question of whether participants in Milgram's studies might have been harmed psychologically after realizing they were willing to inflict pain on another person when ordered to do so.

In this topic we look more closely at the nature of these ethical issues, and examine how (and how successfully) psychologists have dealt with them in their research. Social influence research and ethical issues have been linked in the specification because some of the most famous studies in this area (e.g. Milgram, Zimbardo) have acquired their notoriety because of the ethical issues they have raised. These studies are also significant because they focused psychologists more closely on the need to preserve the wellbeing of research participants at all times.

UNDERSTANDING THE SPECIFICATION

Here is what the AQA (A) specification says about this topic. It forms part of AS Module 3, Social Psychology and Research Methods.

Read it and then try the activity on the right. You'll find answers to the activity on p. 144.

Social influence

Critical issue: ethical issues in psychological research

Ethical issues surrounding the use of deception, informed consent and the protection of participants from psychological harm, including the relevance of these issues in the context of social influence research. Ways in which psychologists deal with these issues (e.g. through the use of ethical guidelines).

ACTIVITY

Understanding the specification

1 What are the three main ethical issues that you need to know about?

- ________
- ________
- ________

2 In the exam, might you be asked a question specifically about the use of ethical guidelines in social influence research? Give reasons for your answer.

- ________

3 Does this topic involve Key studies (APFCCs)?

- ________

The specification details *three ethical issues* – deception, informed consent and protection from psychological harm. An ethical *issue* is not the same as an ethical *guideline* (the latter is a way of dealing with the former). These particular ethical issues have been chosen because they are important in social influence research, especially in the work of Milgram and Zimbardo. You should, therefore, be aware of how these issues have arisen in social influence research and whether such research can be justified.

Psychologists deal with ethical issues in various ways, but the most obvious way is through the development of *ethical guidelines*. You should know in general terms how ethical guidelines are constructed and applied, and specifically how each of these three ethical issues is dealt with by these guidelines. Remember to treat this area critically, as you may be asked to give criticisms of the particular way of dealing with ethical issues (as AO1), or deal more extensively with the value of ethical guidelines in AO1+AO2 questions.

TOPIC MAP

ACTIVITY

Topic map

Look through pp. 181–91 of the textbook and fill in all the blank boxes in the topic map below.

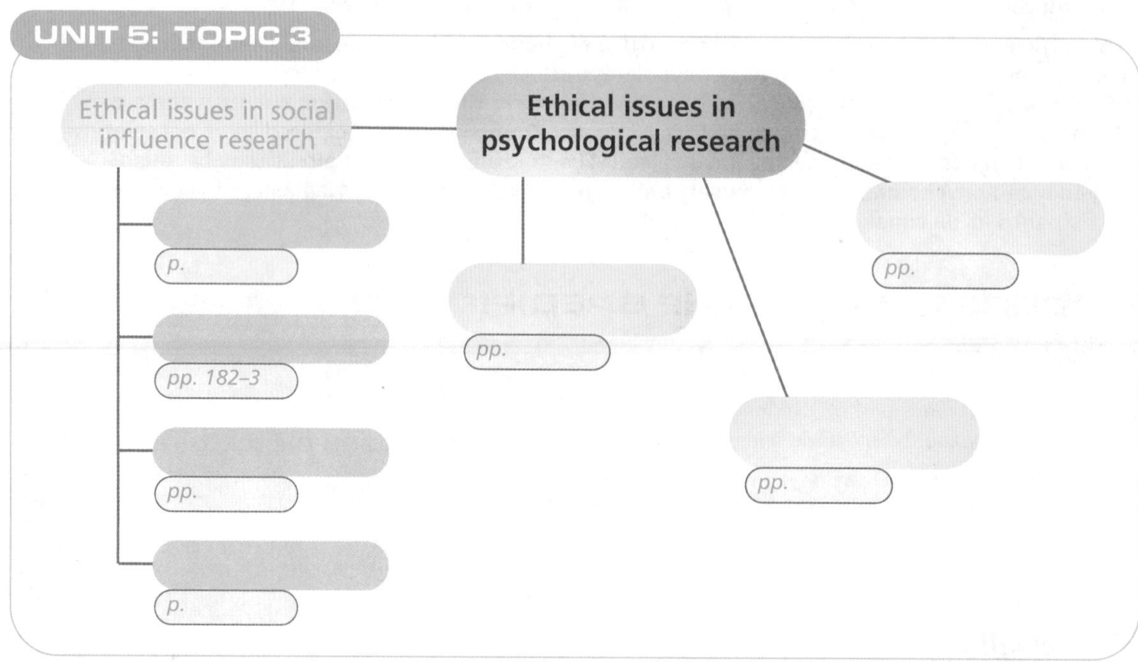

KEEPING TRACK

Use the table below to keep track of your work on this topic and plan your revision.

What I need to learn	Where is it?	Tick if you ... could make a basic attempt	could make a good attempt	have complete mastery of this
Ethical issues in social influence research				
Definition of 'ethical issue'				
Definition of 'deception'				
Definition of 'informed consent'				
Definition of 'protection from psychological harm'				
Description of key ethical issues associated with research on social influence				
Evaluation of key ethical issues associated with research on social influence				
Discussion of whether social influence research is justified in terms of the ethical issues that it raises.				
Ways in which psychologists deal with ethical issues				
Description of use of ethical guidelines				
Evaluation of use of ethical guidelines				
Description of other ways in which psychologists deal with ethical issues, e.g. debriefing, alternatives to deception				
Evaluation of other ways in which psychologists deal with ethical issues				

ETHICAL ISSUES IN SOCIAL INFLUENCE RESEARCH

Ethics is concerned with the rules or principles used to distinguish between right and wrong. Ethical issues are important in social influence research because of the need to preserve the dignity and rights of people taking part in it. The textbook discusses four particular issues:

1 informed consent
2 deception
3 debriefing*
4 protection from harm.

**Debriefing* is not strictly an ethical issue in its own right, but is more a way of dealing with deception and other issues. You are advised not to use debriefing as an ethical issue in this context, although it would be relevant in more general discussion of ethical issues and how to resolve them.

According to the AQA specification, you need to discuss these issues as they apply to psychological research. To help you do this, the textbook includes separate sections on Milgram's and Zimbardo's research and the ethical issues raised by each.

The next few activities give you the chance to think about each issue and how it applies to Milgram's and Zimbardo's studies.

AO1 questions

- What is meant by the terms deception, informed consent and protection of participants from psychological harm? (2 + 2 + 2 marks)
- Explain what is meant by the terms deception and informed consent. (3 + 3 marks)
- Outline **two** ethical issues in social influence research. (3 + 3 marks)
- Outline **one** ethical issue and give an example of how this has arisen in social influence research. (3+ 3 marks)

ACTIVITY

Informed consent

1 What is 'informed consent'?

-

2 Why is it important to gain the informed consent of participants in social influence research?

-

3 What are the two alternatives to fully informed consent? Summarize them below, with advantages and disadvantages of using these alternatives:

Alternative	Advantage	Disadvantage
(a)	•	•
(b)	•	•

4 What issues surrounding consent were raised in Milgram's and Zimbardo's research?

	Criticism	Response to criticism
Milgram's research (textbook pp. 172, 184–5)	•	•
	•	•
Zimbardo's research (textbook pp. 163, 186–7)	•	•
	•	•

ACTIVITY

Deception

1 What is 'deception'?

-

2 Why is deception undesirable?

-

3 Psychologists disagree about the use of deception. When, if ever, is deception acceptable?

-

4 What do the BPS Guidelines say about when deception is acceptable or unacceptable (see textbook p. 188)?

-

5 What are the two alternatives to using deception? Summarize them below, with advantages and disadvantages of using these alternatives:

Alternative	Advantage	Disadvantage
(a)	•	•
(b)	•	•

6 What issues surrounding deception were raised in Milgram's and Zimbardo's research?

	Criticism	Response to criticism
Milgram's research (textbook pp. 172, 184–5)	•	•
	•	•
Zimbardo's research (textbook pp. 163, 186–7)	•	•
	•	•

ACTIVITY

Debriefing

1 What is debriefing?

-

2 Why is it important to debrief participants after social influence research?

-

continued on next page

Debriefing – *continued from previous page*

3 What are the aims of debriefing?

-

4 What issues surrounding debriefing were raised in Milgram's and Zimbardo's research?

	Criticism	Response to criticism
Milgram's research (textbook pp. 172, 184–5)	•	•
	•	•
Zimbardo's research (textbook pp. 163, 186–7)	•	•
	•	•

ACTIVITY

Protection from harm

1 What kinds of risks should participants be protected from in social influence research?

-

2 Why is it important to protect participants from harm during research?

-

3 Psychologists disagree about whether the benefits of research ever outweigh the costs of potential harm to participants. When, if ever, is risk of harm acceptable?

-

4 What issues concerning protection from harm were raised in Milgram's and Zimbardo's research?

	Criticism	Response to criticism
Milgram's research (textbook pp. 172, 184–6)	•	•
	•	•
Zimbardo's research (textbook pp. 163, 186–7)	•	•
	•	•

HOW PSYCHOLOGISTS DEAL WITH ETHICAL ISSUES

To cover the last part of the AQA specification for this topic (see p. 137), you need to be able to discuss ways in which psychologists have tried to deal with ethical issues. You have already thought about several possible approaches:

- through debriefing – as a way of protecting participants from harm, especially when deception has taken place (textbook pp. 183–4)
- by devising alternatives to fully informed consent when it is not possible to gain consent without undermining the research (textbook p. 182)
- by devising alternatives to deception (textbook p. 183).

You could include these in your answers to exam questions about how psychologists deal with ethical issues (such as the ones shown on the right). Perhaps more important, though, is the use of ethical guidelines, discussed below.

AO1 questions

- Outline two ways in which psychologists deal with ethical issues. (3 + 3 marks)
- Outline one way in which psychologists deal with ethical issues and give one criticism of this way. (3 + 3 marks)
- Explain what is meant by protection of participants from psychological harm, and give one way that psychologists deal with this ethical issue. (3 + 3 marks)

Use of ethical guidelines

Ethical guidelines are important because they provide systematic and comprehensive guidance to psychologists about potentially difficult aspects of research. In the UK, the British Psychological Society published and updates a set of guidelines, which are summarized in Table 5.3 on pp. 188–9. In other countries guidelines are drawn up by the relevant professional body.

Although ethical guidelines are not *required* by the specification (i.e. questions cannot be set specifically on ethical guidelines), they are the main 'way' in which psychologists deal with ethical issues. You should, therefore, make sure you know enough about the BPS guidelines to be able write about their purpose, their specific advice on how to deal with the three ethical issues mentioned earlier (deception, etc.) and their strengths and limitations.

ACTIVITY

Use of ethical guidelines

Among the issues covered by the BPS Guidelines are the three discussed earlier in this topic. The Guidelines repeat many of the points already made in the textbook, but also include additional ones. In the space below, note down any additional points made (e.g. about research with children).

1 Consent

- ______
- ______

2 Deception

- ______
- ______

3 Protection of participants

- ______
- ______

The BPS Guidelines also include guidance on two other important ethical issues: the right to withdraw from investigations and respect for confidentiality. What are the important principles outlined in the Guidelines?

4 Right to withdraw

- ______
- ______

5 Confidentiality

- ______
- ______

ACTIVITY

Evaluation of ethical guidelines

In the space below summarize the criticisms of ethical guidelines and their use. Divide your comments into positive and negative aspects. The textbook lists several points.

Positive aspects	Negative aspects
•	•
•	•
•	•
•	•

AO1 + AO2 QUESTIONS ON ETHICAL ISSUES IN PSYCHOLOGICAL RESEARCH

On the right are two sample AO1+AO2 questions on ethical issues in psychological research. A sample answer to the second one is shown on the next page.

You could answer this simply by outlining and evaluating the use of ethical guidelines in research, but it is a good idea to think more widely about other 'ways' in which psychologists meet their ethical responsibilities. The use of the word 'ways' in the question would probably be satisfied by addressing more than one guideline, but this gives us a chance to consider other 'ways' and put their use in the context of actual research.

You should keep referring back to the question to remind yourself of its specific requirements. This one asks for a consideration of how 'successful' these ways have been, so make sure that is what you are discussing.

The following answer deals with prior general consent (pp. 182–3) and debriefing (p. 183–5) in the first part of the AO1 paragraph, and ethical guidelines in the second half (pp. 188–9). This gives us the opportunity to have the second paragraph as AO2 for prior general consent and debriefing, and the third paragraph as AO2 for ethical guidelines.

AO1+AO2 questions

- "Some of the procedures used by social psychologists such as Asch, Zimbardo and Milgram are ethically questionable."

  Briefly outline some of the procedures used in social influence research (theories and/or studies) and evaluate whether these are ethical.

  (18 marks)

- Outline ways in which psychologists have dealt with ethical issues in their research, and consider whether these have been successful.

  (18 marks)

ACTIVITY

One for you to try ...

"Some of the procedures used by social psychologists such as Asch, Zimbardo and Milgram are ethically questionable."

Briefly outline some of the procedures used in social influence research (theories and/or studies) and evaluate whether these are ethical. (18 marks)

Using material from p. 159 (Asch), p. 163 (Zimbardo) and p. 172 (Milgram), as well as material on pp. 184–7, construct an answer to the above question. For your AO2 material, you will find the Expert interview with Elliot Aronson on p. 190 especially valuable.

Sample answer

Outline ways in which psychologists have dealt with ethical issues in their research, and consider whether these have been successful. (18 marks)

Psychologists have used a variety of ways to deal with ethical issues in their research, particularly the ethical concerns surrounding the use of deception. Prior general consent involves telling participants about the general nature of the study and asking them to role-play the experimental procedures as though they were naïve participants. An important aspect of any research design, especially where deception has taken place, is the process of debriefing. This provides post-experimental information to participants and gives them the opportunity to discuss their experience of the research. Debriefing is part of a much wider set of ethical guidelines used in research. Ethical guidelines are necessary to clarify the conditions under which psychological research is acceptable, and give advice about specific ethical issues such as obtaining informed consent and maintaining confidentiality.

Prior general consent has been successfully used in some research. Mixon (1972) found that in a Milgram-type obedience study, role-playing participants behaved much as Milgram's participants did when deceived into thinking they were giving real shocks. However, studies using role-play procedures tend to result in different findings from those where investigators have concealed their true purpose from participants. In such situations, although the ethical issue has been successfully dealt with (the participants have no negative feelings due to having been deceived), the results lack validity and so are less scientifically valuable. Although debriefing does not provide a justification for any unethical aspects of an investigation, it can be effective in preventing undesirable after-effects. Milgram (1964) claimed that the debriefing process was instrumental in helping to protect and reassure his participants.

The existence of ethical guidelines does not, by itself, ensure that all research is carried out in an ethically correct manner. Guidelines, such as those published by the BPS, are sometimes accused of being vague and difficult to enforce. The BPS imposes penalties on members if they infringe ethical codes in their research, but a great deal of the research carried out by psychology students is not directly overseen by the BPS, and so there is potential for ethical guidelines to be breached. The consequence is that this puts participants at risk of the potential damage associated with ethical issues such as deception and lack of informed consent. Ethical guidelines must also be revised constantly to reflect social change and emerging ethical issues (e.g. Internet-based research).

CHECK YOUR UNDERSTANDING

When you have finished working through this topic, try the questions in 'Check your understanding' on p. 191 of the textbook. You can check your answers by looking at the relevant parts of the textbook or this workbook, listed below.

1 textbook p. 181
2 textbook p. 182
3 textbook pp. 182–3
4 textbook p. 183
5 textbook pp. 183–4
6 textbook p. 184
7 textbook pp. 184–5
8 textbook pp. 185–6
9 textbook pp. 184–7, 190
10 workbook pp. 143–4; this question is similar to the second question in the panel on p. 143 – the advice on answering it and sample answer above are therefore relevant.

ANSWERS TO ACTIVITIES

Understanding the specification, p. 144

1 The three ethical issues you need to consider are the use of deception, informed consent and the protection of participants from psychological harm. The textbook discusses these issues on pp. 182–4, along with a fourth important issue, the need to debrief participants after research has finished.

2 No, the use of ethical guidelines is given only as an example, so exam questions can't ask you specifically about this issue. However, in answering questions about how psychologists deal with ethical issues, you can definitely bring in the use of ethical guidelines (textbook pp. 187–9).

3 No, there are no Key studies in this topic.

QUANTITATIVE & QUALITATIVE Research Methods

PREVIEW

There are two topics in this unit. You should read them alongside the following pages in the Collins *Psychology for AS-level* textbook:

Topic		Textbook pages
1	**Experimental investigations in psychology**	**pp. 195–201**
2	**Non-experimental investigations in psychology**	**pp. 202–212**

INTRODUCTION

This unit covers the first part of Research Methods in AS Module 3 (AQA Specification A). The diagram below shows where it fits in to the overall AS qualification.

Read the Preview and Introduction on p. 194 of the textbook now. This will give you an overview of what's in the unit.

Where this unit fits in to the AS qualification

Module 1
- Cognitive Psychology: Human memory
- Developmental Psychology: Attachments in development

Module 2
- Physiological Psychology: Stress
- Individual Differences: Abnormality

Module 3
- Social Psychology: Social influence
- **Research Methods**
  - **Quantitative and qualitative research methods**
  - Research design and implementation
  - Data analysis

In the AS Module 3 exam, there will be one short-answer question on **Research Methods** which you will have to answer.

Topic 1 >> Experimental investigations in psychology

Experimental investigations are one of the main research tools that psychologists use to develop and test their theories. This topic looks at the different types of experiments that psychologists carry out, what the strengths and weaknesses of these are, and what ethical issues they raise. Laboratory experiments are 'true' experiments because they contain the three most important characteristics of experimental research – manipulation of an independent variable, random allocation of participants to conditions and a control group. Quasi-experiments may also involve the manipulation of an independent variable (although this may not be by the researcher), but lack at least one of the other two properties that characterize true experiments.

UNDERSTANDING THE SPECIFICATION

Here is what the AQA (A) specification says about this topic. It forms part of AS Module 3, Social Psychology and Research Methods. You will see that the specification lists five types of research method. This topic concentrates on the first of these, i.e. experiments (shown in bold below). The remaining four (labelled b. to e.) are covered in Topic 2.

Read the specification and then try the activity on the right. You'll find answers to the activity on p. 154.

Research Methods

Quantitative and qualitative research methods

The nature and usage of the following research methods and their advantages and weaknesses and how they relate to the scientific nature of Psychology. The nature and usage of ethical guidelines in Psychology.

a. **Experiments (including laboratory, field and natural experiments).**
b. Investigations using correlational analysis.
c. Naturalistic observations.
d. Questionnaire surveys.
e. Interviews.

ACTIVITY

Understanding the specification

1 The specification mentions three types of experiment. What are they and do you have to know about them all?

- ______________________

____

____

____

____

2 Which of the following do you have to know about with regard to experiments?

- ☐ what they are and how they can be used
- ☐ what the pros and cons of using them are
- ☐ why they are useful to the science of Psychology
- ☐ what ethical issues they raise

3 Does this topic involve Key studies (APFCCs)?

- ______________________

____

For this part of the specification, you must be able to describe briefly the experimental method, and demonstrate an understanding of each of the variations of this method as listed above (i.e. laboratory, field and natural experiments). You may be asked to demonstrate how each of these methods is used in psychological research (for example, you might be asked to design a study using one of these methods). For each method, you should know at least two advantages and two weaknesses. Experimental research methods 'relate to the scientific nature of psychology' in that they are *systematic* (i.e. investigations are designed in such a way that cause-and-effect conclusions can be drawn) and *objective* (i.e. free from bias). This distinguishes psychological knowledge from common sense or subjective opinion. Finally, you should know about the nature of ethical guidelines in psychological research and how to apply these appropriately in hypothetical scenarios.

TOPIC MAP

ACTIVITY

Look through pp. 195–201 of the textbook and fill in the blank spaces on the topic map on p. 147.

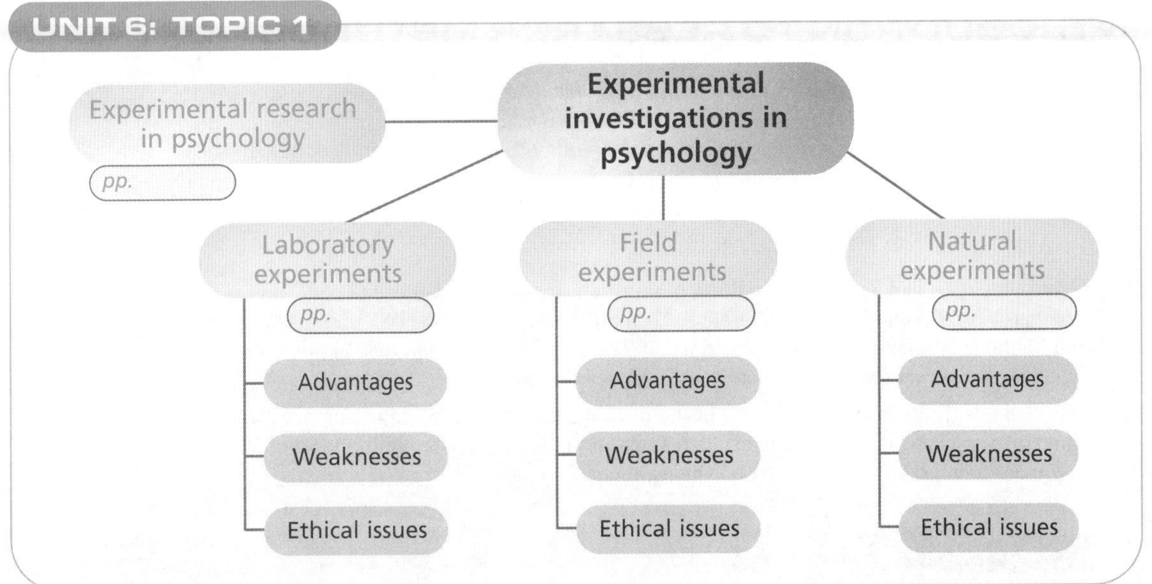

KEEPING TRACK

Use the table below to keep track of your work on this topic and plan your revision. See p. iv (Introduction) for guidance on filling it in.

What I need to learn	Where is it?	Tick if you ... could make a basic attempt	could make a good attempt	have complete mastery of this
Experimental research in psychology				
Definition of 'quantitative data'				
Definition of 'qualitative data'				
Definition of 'experiment'				
Difference between quantitative and qualitative data				
Description of the three main types of experiment: laboratory, field and natural, and the differences between them				
Laboratory experiments				
Definition of 'laboratory experiment'				
Description of key features of a laboratory experiment				
Description of main advantages of laboratory experiments				
Description of main weaknesses of laboratory experiments				
Description of ethical issues associated with laboratory experiments				
Field experiments				
Definition of 'field experiment'				
Description of key features of a field experiment				
Description of main advantages of field experiments				
Description of main weaknesses of field experiments				
Description of ethical issues associated with field experiments				
Natural experiments				
Definition of 'natural experiment'				
Description of key features of a natural experiment				
Description of main advantages of natural experiments				
Description of main weaknesses of natural experiments				
Description of ethical issues associated with natural experiments				

INTRODUCTION TO RESEARCH METHODS

Unit 6, Research Methods, is different from the first five units you have studied. Units 1 to 5 are the 'core' areas designed to give you an introduction to different areas of psychology. They contain the main content of the AS Psychology specification. Unit 6, on the other hand, is all about how psychologists carry out research. In other words, this unit is about the process of research, rather than the content.

Exam questions for research methods

By now you should be familiar with the pattern of questions for Units 1 to 5 – each question is divided into three parts, (a), (b) and (c), with different AO1 and AO2 components. The exam questions in Research Methods are quite different. For a start, in Research Methods there will be just one question which you have to answer. There is no choice as in the earlier units.

Research Methods questions will usually be based on stimulus material – that is, you are given a description of a psychological study, usually with some of the findings, often in the form of a table of results. You are then asked a set of short questions about the study.

ACTIVITY

Research Methods exam questions

To see an example of a possible Research Methods question, turn to p. 262 of the textbook. The stimulus material is all contained in the panel at the top of the page. It is a description of an experiment investigating the therapeutic effects of gardening on adults suffering from stress-related symptoms.

1 Scan through pp. 262–5. How many parts are there to this question?

- ______

2 What is the total number of marks available?

- ______

3 How long do you have to complete the entire question?

- ______

4 So, how long should you spend answering a '3 + 3 marks' question?

- ______

Check your answers by looking at p. 154.

Here are some important points to remember about Research Methods questions:

- The number of parts per question is not fixed.
- The number of marks per part will vary too, so you have to divide your time up to match the number of marks.
- Questions may be asked about anything mentioned in the Research Methods parts of the specification, such as:
  - the type of research method used (covered in Unit 6 of the textbook)
  - advantages and weaknesses of the research method (Unit 6)
  - ethical issues raised by the research (Unit 6)
  - how the research was designed and carried out (Unit 7)
  - how the data were analysed (Unit 7).

Units 6 and 7 in the textbook contain a lot of background information about how psychologists carry out research. Study this carefully because in the Research Methods question, you may be asked anything about any aspect of the research study described in the stimulus material. So, for example, if the study described is a field experiment, you may have to spot that fact. That should then prompt you to think of typical advantages and problems of field experiments – for example, validity is improved because it's a real-life setting, but controls are hard to establish (as described on pp. 199–200 of the textbook).

Bear all this in mind as you read through this material on Research Methods. By really taking in the main points regarding advantages, weaknesses, ethical issues, and so on, you should be able to recall them quickly for top marks in the exam.

EXPERIMENTAL RESEARCH IN PSYCHOLOGY

Throughout your work on Units 1 to 5 of AS Psychology, you will read about all kinds of experiments carried out by psychologists throughout the world – into memory, attachments, stress, and so on. But what exactly is an experiment? What are the features that make a good experiment?

ACTIVITY

Experimental research

Read p. 196 of the textbook and then answer the following questions.

1 Why is the experimental method regarded by psychologists as the most powerful research method?

- __________

2 What are the three key features of a true experiment?

- __________
- __________
- __________

3 What is meant by the following terms?

(a) independent variable __________

(d) dependent variable __________

(c) confounding variable __________

(d) quasi-experiment __________

Check your answers by looking at p. 154.

ACTIVITY

Identifying variables

You need to be absolutely sure of the difference between different types of variable because that is a classic exam question. First, carry out the activity on p. 197 of the textbook. Take time to work out the correct answers before checking the answers given on p. 211 of the textbook.

Then, turn to p. 262 of the textbook and read though the stimulus material at the top of the page. Now answer the following question:

1 What is the independent variable in this study? (1 mark)

- __________

Compare your answer to question 1 with the sample answers given at the top of p. 263.

If you need more practice at spotting variables, look at the Key studies in Units 1 to 5 of the textbook and for those that are experiments, work out what the IV and DVs are. For example:

2 In Brady's 'executive monkey' study (textbook p. 84), what is:

(a) the IV __________

(b) the DV __________

Compare your answer to question 2 with the one given on p.154.

ACTIVITY

Pros and cons of experimental research

Summarize the main advantages and disadvantages of using the experimental method of research. As well as the points listed on p. 196 of the textbook, think about the practical issues of setting up experiments.

Advantages	Disadvantages
•	•
•	•
•	•
•	•
•	•

LABORATORY EXPERIMENTS

This topic looks at three different types of experiment. The first of these is laboratory experiments. As the textbook explains (pp. 197–8), laboratory experiments give researchers high levels of control and so are effective in trying to establish cause-and-effect relationships.

ACTIVITY

Use of laboratory experiments

Read p. 196 of the textbook and then answer the following questions.

1 The textbook says that: "Researchers interested in memory and cognitive processes often carry out laboratory experiments." This is shown in the types of study described in the textbook. Read the 'Procedures' for the nine Key studies in Unit 1, Human memory. These are described on pp. 6, 7, 9, 11, 12, 26, 27, 31 and 35 of the textbook. How many of these were laboratory experiments?

•

2 Now look at the five Key studies in Unit 3, Stress (pp. 84, 85, 90, 94 and 95) and the four in Unit 4, Abnormality (pp. 143, 144, 147 and 149). How many of these were laboratory experiments?

•

3 Comment on your answers to questions 1 and 2. Why do some areas of research lend themselves better to investigation by laboratory experiment than others?

•

Compare your answers with those given on pp. 154–5.

On p. 198 of the textbook, the major advantages and weaknesses are clearly described, together with some of the ethical issues that often arise in laboratory experiments. Read through the bulleted points listed and then carry out the following activities.

ACTIVITY

Advantages of lab experiments

1 **Replicability** – Two of the Key studies described in Unit 1 of the textbook were later replicated, with varying results. Read through the studies on p. 27 (Levinger and Clark's study of repression) and p. 35 (Loftus' study of eyewitness testimony). Note carefully what is said under 'Criticisms'. In what way did the later studies throw important light on the findings of the first experiments?

(a) Levinger and Clark

(b) Loftus

2 **Control over variables** – Good control means that we can have confidence in the findings of a study. Poor control undermines the findings. Look at the description of Brady's 'executive monkey' study (textbook p. 84). In what way was this experiment poorly controlled?

-

Compare your answers with those on p. 155.

ACTIVITY

Weaknesses of lab experiments

1 **Loss of validity** – Many of the Key studies into memory (Unit 1) have been criticized for lack of validity. Name two studies and describe how each one could be criticized for lack of ecological validity.

-
-

2 **Demand characteristics** – Milgram's research into obedience was criticized by Orne and Holland, who claimed that participants showed demand characteristics. How did they do this, according to Orne and Holland (see textbook p. 175)?

-

Compare your answers with those on p. 155.

ACTIVITY

Ethical issues in laboratory experiments

1 **Consent** – What issues of consent were raised by Zimbardo's prison simulation study (textbook p. 163)?

-

2 **Deception** – In Milgram's study of obedience (textbook p. 172), in what way were participants deceived? What experiment did they think they were taking part in?

-

3 **Use of animals** – What ethical issues regarding use of animals were raised by the following studies?

- Harlow and Harlow's study of attachment in monkeys (textbook p. 53)
- Brady's 'executive monkey' study (textbook p. 84)

Compare your answers with those given on p. 155.

FIELD EXPERIMENTS

Field experiments share many of the same characteristics as laboratory experiments, with the major difference that the setting is a natural one, i.e. where those being studied normally live or work. This affects many of the issues regarding strengths, weaknesses and ethical questions.

ACTIVITY

Advantages and weaknesses of field experiments

Read through the descriptions of the two experiments on p. 199 of the textbook. Then summarize how these studies demonstrated the advantages and weaknesses described on pp. 199–200.

Advantages	Andersson (1982)	Klaus and Kennell (1976)
Improved ecological validity	•	•
Reduction of demand characteristics	•	•
Weaknesses		
Establishing controls	•	•
Generalizing to other situations	•	•

Compare your answers with those given on p. 155.

ACTIVITY

Ethical issues in field experiments

In both the field experiments described on p. 199, researchers intervened in the natural environment of those being studied. What ethical objections could be raised to:

1 Andersson's study of long-tailed widow birds?

•

2 Klaus and Kennell's study of bonding between mothers and infants?

•

Compare your answers with those given on p. 155.

NATURAL EXPERIMENTS

Natural experiments differ from laboratory and field experiments in that the researchers don't control the IV and don't allocate participants to conditions. In other words, the researchers have much less control over the experiment, but make use of naturally occurring situations.

Examples of natural experiments described in the textbook are:

- the study by Hodges and Tizard (1989) into the effects of privation – see p. 63
- the study by Kiecolt-Glaser *et al.* (1984) into stress and the immune system – see p. 85
- the study by Johansson *et al.* (1978) into stress in a Swedish sawmill – see p. 94.

ACTIVITY

Natural experiments

On pp. 200–1 of the textbook is a list of advantages, weaknesses and ethical issues relating to natural experiments. Read through them, along with the three Key studies listed above. In the space below, give an example of how each advantage, weakness and ethical issue is illustrated by one or more of the studies described.

Advantages	Example(s) from Key studies
Reduction of demand characteristics	•
Lack of direct intervention	•
Weaknesses	
Loss of control	•
Likelihood of desired behaviour being displayed	•
Ethical issues	
Consent	•
Protection of participants	•
Confidentiality	•

ANSWERING RESEARCH METHODS EXAM QUESTIONS

Dependent on whether a particular question is assessing AO1, AO2 or AO3, you may be asked to describe a particular method (AO1), give strengths and weaknesses of that method (AO2), or comment on its suitability within a particular context (AO3). The final part of each Research Methods question often asks you to design a study using a particular type of experimental design. You would then need to think about the specific nature of that design, how it could be put into practice in that context, together with any ethical issues that are or might be raised. The following activity gives some examples of questions in this area.

ACTIVITY

Research Methods exam questions

Read through the description of the study investigating the therapeutic effects of gardening on adults suffering from stress-related symptoms (textbook p. 262).

1 What sort of experiment is this? (1 mark)

-

2 Give two advantages of this type of experiment that are demonstrated in the study. (3 + 3 marks)

-
-

3 Give two weaknesses of this type of experiment that are demonstrated in the study. (3 + 3 marks)

-
-

4 Identify one ethical issue that the researchers do not appear to have considered and explain how this ethical issue could have been dealt with. (1 + 2 marks)

-

Compare your answers with those given opposite.

CHECK YOUR UNDERSTANDING

When you have finished working through this topic, try the questions in 'Check your understanding' on p. 201 of the textbook. Check your answers by looking at the relevant parts of the textbook or this workbook, listed below.

1 textbook p. 195
2 textbook pp. 198, 200, 201
3 textbook p. 196
4 textbook p. 198
5 textbook p. 198; workbook p. 151
6 textbook p. 199
7 textbook pp. 199–200; workbook p. 152
8 textbook p. 200
9 textbook pp. 200–1; workbook p. 153
10 textbook p. 196; workbook p. 149

ANSWERS TO ACTIVITIES

Understanding the specification, p. 146

1 The three types of experiment you need to know about are laboratory, field and natural experiments. The textbook covers these in order on pp. 197–201.
2 To meet the requirements of the specification, you need to know about all these aspects of experiments.
3 There are no Key studies in this topic, nor for any part of Research Methods.

Research Methods exam questions, p. 148

1 Eight parts in total, labelled (a) to (h)
2 30 marks
3 30 minutes (half of the AS Module 3 exam, which is 1 hour long)
4 Six minutes, or in other words, a mark a minute.

Experimental research, p. 149

1 Because of its potential to investigate the causes of events, and thus to identify cause-and-effect relationships.
2 See the first three bullet points on p. 196.
3 (a) The variable manipulated by the researcher to see what effect this has on the DV.
(b) The variable that is assumed to be affected by changes in the IV.
(c) Uncontrolled variable that produces an unwanted effect on the DV, thus obscuring the effect of the IV.
(d) An experiment where the investigator lacks complete control over the IV and/or the allocation of participants to a group.

Identifying variables, p. 149

3 (a) IV = whether or not the monkeys could press the lever to postpone the electric shocks.
(b) DV = levels of stress, measured in terms of gastric ulceration and subsequent death.

Use of laboratory experiments, p. 150

1 All except one of the nine Key studies in Unit 1 were laboratory experiments. The only non-experimental investigation was the research by McCloskey and colleagues into flashbulb memory, carried out by interviews.
2 Only one of the Key studies in Units 3 and 4 was a laboratory experiment: Brady's 'executive monkey' experiment (see textbook p. 84). The others used a mixture of types of research.

3 The areas of research of Units 3 and 4 (stress and abnormality) do not lend themselves easily to laboratory experiments. For example, it is hard to think of any experiment that could be set up to investigate eating disorders.

Advantages of laboratory experiments, p. 151

1 (a) Levinger and Clark's findings were not replicated in later research. For example, Bradley and Baddeley's experiments found that emotional associations improved memory, rather than making it worse! Holmes' review of studies of repression and forgetting found no convincing experimental support for Levinger and Clark's conclusions.

(b) The findings of the Loftus study, on the other hand, were replicated in later studies, e.g. Loftus and Loftus (1980).

2 The experiment was poorly controlled because Brady allotted the monkeys to the different groups according to whether they were active bar-pressers or not.

Weaknesses of lab experiments, p. 151

1 For example, Baddeley *et al.* (1975), textbook p. 6, and Peterson and Peterson (1959), textbook p. 7. Both of these studies used artificial stimuli (lists of unconnected words and letters), which do not reflect the everyday use of short-term memory.

2 According to Orne and Holland, Milgram's participants showed demand characteristics by 'going along with the experiment'; they knew they weren't really giving shocks and just pretended to be distressed. Note that Milgram refuted these claims (see textbook p. 175).

Ethical issues in laboratory experiments, p. 151

1 Those participants in Zimbardo's study who were given the role of 'prisoner' did not know the full details of how they would be treated and so could not have given their fully informed consent. For example, they did not they would be arrested at home and they could not have known how harshly the 'guards' were going to treat them.

2 Participants in Milgram's studies were told that they were taking part in an experiment about the role of punishment in learning. In other words, they believed the experiment was focusing on the 'learner' to whom they were giving shocks and how that person responded to punishment. They were deceived about the true purpose of the study, which was to investigate their own response to orders.

3 Harlow and Harlow's experiment was unethical because it deprived monkeys of the opportunity to form 'healthy' attachments. The monkeys grew up indifferent or abusive to other monkeys.

Brady's executive study subjected monkeys to suffering and many of the animals died as a direct result of the experiment. Such an experiment would not be allowed today.

Advantages and weaknesses of field experiments, p. 152

- Improved ecological validity – Both studies took place in 'real-life' settings (the birds' natural habitat and a maternity hospital). They reflected real-life behaviour and so had good ecological validity.
- Reduction of demand characteristics – Neither the birds nor the women knew they were being observed and so should not have become aware of the study. Demand characteristics (where participants try to make sense of the situation they are in) would therefore have been avoided.
- Establishing controls – In neither experiment could the researchers exercise control over all variables. For example, what if some of the birds became ill and died, or were killed? Or what if some of the mothers in the group allowed less contact had demanded more contact and become distressed?
- Generalizing to other situations – Andersson's study only tells us about the mating behaviour of long-tailed widow birds. We could generalize to other long-tailed birds, such as peacocks, but that would have to be demonstrated in a separate study of those birds.

Ethical issues in field experiments, p. 152

1 Andersson altered the tail length of the birds, some having their tails lengthened and others shortened. Given the fact that tail length was found to be a determining factor in mating success, Andersson was effectively choosing which birds would be successful in mating. Did the researcher have the right to do this? Could they be sure that their intervention wouldn't have an effect on the overall population of long-tailed widow birds?

2 Here again, the researchers were determining who, in the end, would be likely to have the more positive reaction to their babies. You might want to ask whether the women had given consent to being allocated to one of the groups. Were there any women who wanted more contact with their babies, but were 'not allowed' it because they were in the wrong group?

Research Methods exam questions, p. 154

1 Despite the fact that this involves digging a garden (so you might think it was a 'field' experiment), it is actually a laboratory experiment. The researcher controls the IV and can randomly allocate participants to the two conditions.

2 An advantage of this method as used in this context is that the researchers are able to match participants fairly precisely in terms of those factors (such as age and severity of stress-related symptoms) that might otherwise confound the relationship between the IV (the gardening therapy) and the DV (changes in stress-related symptoms after 10 weeks).

A second advantage is that this method allows greater replicability of procedures. As the researchers can control all aspects of the experiment (e.g. the type of counselling received, the nature of the counsellor, the time spent gardening and the nature of the gardening), it is easier to recreate the exact conditions and so increase confidence in the results.

3 A weakness of the laboratory experiment that is evident in this research is the possibility of demand characteristics. As some patients are being given extra therapy, they may feel pressure to report that it is having a beneficial effect. In this way they are behaving in a manner that they feel is helpful to the researcher, rather than giving a true indication of the therapeutic value of gardening.

A second weakness is that this method may lack ecological validity and present an artificial view of the value of gardening therapy. Although patients are engaging in light gardening at the clinic, it cannot be assumed that these therapeutic gains would apply to other forms of gardening, which may be far more stressful than the stressful situations that caused the patient to seek help in the first place!

4 Two possible answers to this question with a commentary on each are given at the top of p. 264 of the textbook.

Topic 2 >> Non-experimental investigations in psychology

Non-experimental methods have become more and more popular for use in psychological investigations. As the textbook explains (p. 194), this is partly as a reaction to highly controlled experimental methods that often lack relevance to real life. This topic looks at the different types of non-experimental investigations that psychologists use and the situations where they are most appropriate. Don't assume that because these methods are 'non' experimental, they are 'unscientific' and therefore relatively worthless. The weaknesses of one method (e.g. the artificiality of the laboratory experiment) are often the strengths of another (e.g. the real-life nature of natural observation) and vice versa.

UNDERSTANDING THE SPECIFICATION

Here is what the AQA (A) specification says about this topic. It forms part of AS Module 3, Social Psychology and Research Methods. You will see that the specification lists five types of research method. You have already looked at the first of these, i.e. experiments, in Topic 1. The remaining four (labelled b. to e.) are the focus of this topic.

Read the specification and then try the activity on the right. You'll find answers to the activity on p. 163.

Research Methods

Quantitative and qualitative research methods

The nature and usage of the following research methods and their advantages and weaknesses and how they relate to the scientific nature of Psychology. The nature and usage of ethical guidelines in Psychology.

a. Experiments (including laboratory, field and natural experiments).

b. Investigations using correlational analysis.

c. Naturalistic observations.

d. Questionnaire surveys.

e. Interviews.

ACTIVITY

Understanding the specification

1 The specification mentions four types of non-experimental method. What are they and do you have to know about them all?

- ______________________________

____

____

____

____

2 Which of the following do you have to know about with regard to each of these non-experimental methods?

- ☐ what they are and how they can be used
- ☐ what the pros and cons of using them are
- ☐ why they are useful to the science of Psychology
- ☐ what ethical issues they raise

3 Does this topic involve Key studies (APFCCs)?

- ______________________________

____

You must be able to describe briefly each of the four non-experimental methods listed above and know how they are used in psychological research. For each method, you should know at least two advantages and two weaknesses in sufficient detail for a 3-mark question – that's four methods × two advantages and two disadvantages. You may be asked to demonstrate how each of these methods is used in psychological research (for example, you might be asked to design a study using one of these methods). Finally, you should know about the nature of ethical guidelines in these methods and how to apply them appropriately in hypothetical scenarios.

TOPIC MAP

ACTIVITY

Look through pp. 202–12 of the textbook and fill in the blank spaces on the topic map on p. 157.

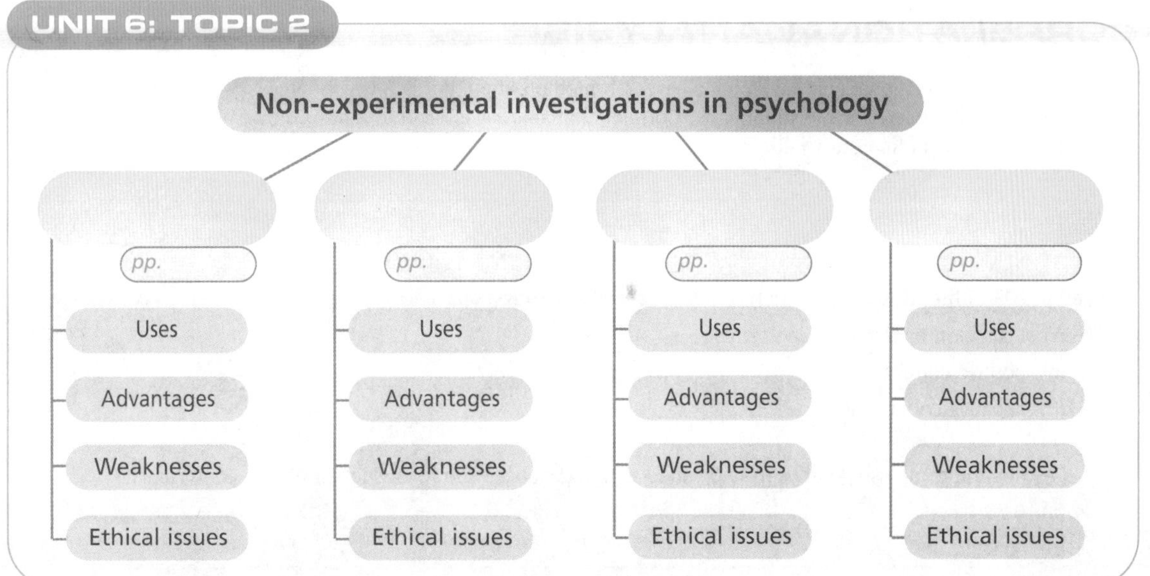

KEEPING TRACK

Use the table below to keep track of your work on this topic and plan your revision.

What I need to learn	Where is it?	*Tick if you ...* could make a basic attempt	could make a good attempt	have complete mastery of this
Correlational analysis				
Definition of 'correlational analysis'				
Description of the key features of investigations using correlational analysis				
Description of the main uses of correlational analysis				
Description of main advantages of using correlational analysis				
Description of main weaknesses of using correlational analysis				
Description of ethical issues associated with investigations using correlational analysis				
Naturalistic observation				
Definition of 'naturalistic observation'				
Description of the key features of naturalistic observation				
Description of the main uses of naturalistic observation				
Description of main advantages of naturalistic observation				
Description of main weaknesses of naturalistic observation				
Description of ethical issues associated with naturalistic observation				
Questionnaire surveys				
Definition of 'questionnaire surveys'				
Description of key features of questionnaire surveys				
Description of the main uses of questionnaire surveys				
Description of main advantages of questionnaire surveys				
Description of main weaknesses of questionnaire surveys				
Description of ethical issues associated with questionnaire surveys				
Interviews				
Definition of 'interviews'				
Description of key features and main uses of interviews				
Description of main advantages of interviews				
Description of main weaknesses of interviews				
Description of ethical issues associated with interviews				

CORRELATIONAL ANALYSIS

Strictly speaking, correlational analysis is not a research method at all, but is a way of analysing data gathered, for example, from interviews or questionnaires. Correlational analysis is used to measure the relationships between variables, or to find out whether there is a relationship at all.

ACTIVITY

Correlational analysis

Read p. 203 of the textbook and then answer the following questions.

1 What is meant by the following terms?

(a) positive correlation

(b) negative correlation

2 Describe the relationship between two variables that produced the following correlation coefficients:

(a) 0.78

(b) –0.01

(c) –0.92

3 What are the main uses of correlational analysis?

-
-
-

Compare your answers with those given on p. 164.

Several of the Key studies described in the textbook have used correlational analysis. As well as the study by Murstein described on p. 203, look at:

- p. 60 – Bowlby's study into the effects of deprivation, the so-called '44 thieves' study
- p. 85 – the study by Kiecolt-Glaser *et al.* into stress and the immune system
- p. 90 – the study by Rahe *et al.* of life changes and stress, using the SRRS scale.

The activity at the top of p. 204 of the textbook will help you to understand how Bowlby used correlational analysis to investigate the link between frequent, early separations and emotional maladjustment. The next activity gives you a chance to analyse the approach of the other studies.

ACTIVITY

Studies that have used correlational analysis

For the two studies listed below, identify what the variables being investigated were, what method of research was used and what correlation, if any, was found.

	Kiecolt-Glaser *et al.* (1984)	Rahe *et al.* (1970)
Variables investigated	•	•
Method of research used	•	•
Correlation found	•	•

Compare your answers with those given on p. 164.

NATURALISTIC OBSERVATION

Naturalistic observation is a very useful method for studying how people or animals behave in their natural environment. The obvious benefits of this are that those being studied should be behaving naturally (as long as they don't know they are being observed), so what is observed is 'real-life' behaviour.

ACTIVITY

Use of naturalistic observation

Read pp. 200–1 of the textbook and then answer the following questions.

1 Read the following statement and then decide whether or not you agree with it. Give clear reasons for your answer, based on the characteristics of naturalistic observation described on p. 205 of the textbook.

"The Channel 4 TV series *Big Brother* is a form of laboratory-based naturalistic observation."

-

2 Read the description of the Robertsons' research into separation on pp. 59 and 61 of the textbook.

(a) What are features of this research that make it naturalistic observation?

-

(b) Why was naturalistic observation the appropriate method for this research into separation?

-

3 Read the description of Schaffer and Emerson's research into the development of attachments on pp. 44–5 of the textbook.

(a) What are features of this research that make it naturalistic observation?

-

(b) In what ways does this research demonstrate the advantages described on pp. 205–6, i.e. value as a preliminary research tool and validity.

-

Compare your answers with those given on p. 164.

On p. 206 of the textbook, the main weaknesses of naturalistic observation are described, together with some of the ethical issues it raises. Read through the bulleted points listed and then carry out the following two activities.

ACTIVITY

Weaknesses of naturalistic observation

In the space on the next page, summarize the weaknesses of naturalistic observation. Give examples of how any of the research described might have been affected by these – think, for example, of the animal observation studies, or the studies of children by the Robertsons and by Schaffer and Emerson.

Weaknesses of naturalistic observation

Weakness	Key issue	Example from actual research
Control	•	•
Observer effects	•	•
Costs	•	•
Categorizing data	•	•
Replicability	•	•

ACTIVITY

Ethical issues of naturalistic observation

Read through the list of ethical issues described on p. 206 of the textbook. What particular factors would researchers have to consider when carrying out an observation of children?

-
-
-

Compare your answers with those given on p. 164.

QUESTIONNAIRE SURVEYS

Questionnaires enable researchers to survey large numbers of people about their behaviours, beliefs or attitudes. They are therefore an efficient and cost-effective way of getting information from a large sample of people, provided that they are well-written and that they are filled in accurately (and truthfully).

In the Research Methods part of the AS exam, the stimulus material could include an example of a questionnaire. You might be asked to comment on the types of question asked and how appropriate they are. Knowing the advantages and drawbacks of different types of question will help you to answer such questions.

ACTIVITY

Open and closed questions

Summarize the main advantages and drawbacks of different types of question in the space below.

	Advantages	Disadvantages
Closed questions	•	•
Open questions	•	•

HINT

Closed questions

Closed questions are not only those that require a 'Yes/No' answer; they include any question where the researcher limits the range of answers, as illustrated in the examples on p. 207 of the textbook.

ACTIVITY

Advantages and weaknesses of questionnaire surveys

In the space below summarize the three main advantages and weaknesses of questionnaire surveys.

Advantages	Weaknesses
•	•
•	•
•	•

ACTIVITY

Questionnaire surveys and ethical issues

Ethical issues relating to questionnaire surveys are described on pp. 208–9 of the textbook. In their investigation of self-esteem and eating disorders, to which ethical issues would Button *et al.* (textbook p. 149) have had to pay particular attention? Give reasons for your answer.

•

•

Compare your answers with those given on p. 164.

INTERVIEWS

Many of the Key studies described in the textbook have used interviews as a way of gathering information. These include the following:

- the study of flashbulb memory by McCloskey *et al.* (1988) – textbook p. 26
- Bowlby's (1944) '44 thieves' study – p. 60
- Friedman and Rosenman's (1974) study of stress and cardiovascular disorders – p. 95
- the study into bulimia nervosa by Kendler *et al.* (1991) – p. 144
- the study of childhood abuse and bulimia by Wonderlich *et al.* (1996) – p. 147.

As this list shows, interviews can be suitable for investigating a range of aspects of psychology, from memory to eating disorders. Interviews may be structured, unstructured or a mixture of both.

ACTIVITY

Structured and unstructured interviews

1 Summarize the main advantages and weaknesses of different types of interview in the space below.

	Advantages	Disadvantages
Structured	•	•
	•	•
Unstructured	•	•
	•	•

2 In their study of Type A behaviour pattern and cardiovascular disease, Friedman and Rosenman used structured interviews to gather data. Why was a structured approach particularly suitable for this investigation? *Hint*: think about the size of the sample and the way interviewees were categorized.

•

Check your answer to question 2 by looking at p. 164.

ACTIVITY

Advantages and weaknesses of using interviews

Complete the following table summarizing the advantages and weaknesses of using interviews. Include all the points listed on pp. 209–10, but add any others you can think of. To help you, re-read the five Key studies listed on p. 161 and think about how the interview approach was used in them.

Advantages	Weaknesses
•	•
•	•
•	•

ANSWERING RESEARCH METHODS EXAM QUESTIONS

Dependent on whether a particular question is assessing AO1, AO2 or AO3, you may be asked to describe a particular method (AO1), give strengths and weaknesses of that method (AO2), or comment on its suitability within a particular context (AO3). The final part of each Research Methods question often asks you to design a study using a particular type of non-experimental design. You would then need to think about the specific nature of that design, how it could be put into practice in that context, together with any ethical issues that might be raised. The following activity gives some examples of questions in this area.

ACTIVITY

Research Methods exam questions

Read through the description on p. 262 of the textbook of the study investigating the therapeutic effects of gardening on adults suffering from stress-related symptoms. As an extension to this investigation, the researchers wanted to find out what it was about the gardening that the patients found so beneficial.

1 Suggest an appropriate non-experimental method that would give them this information, and explain your choice. (1 + 2 marks)

-

2 Using the method identified above, outline the procedures that would be used for this investigation. (6 marks)

-

3 Identify one ethical issue that might arise in this investigation and explain how you would overcome it. (1 + 2 marks)

-

Compare your answers with those given on p. 164.

CHECK YOUR UNDERSTANDING

When you have finished working through this topic, try the questions in 'Check your understanding' on p. 211 of the textbook. Check your answers by looking at the relevant parts of the textbook or this workbook, listed below.

1 textbook p. 203
2 textbook p. 204
3 textbook p. 205
4 textbook p. 205
5 textbook pp. 205–6
6 textbook pp. 207–8
7 textbook p. 207
8 textbook p. 208; workbook p. 161
9 textbook p. 209
10 textbook p. 209
11 textbook p. 210; workbook p. 162

ANSWERS TO ACTIVITIES

Understanding the specification, p. 156

1 The four types of non-experimental method you need to know about are investigations using correlational analysis, naturalistic observations, questionnaire surveys and interviews. The textbook covers these in order on pp. 203–11.

2 To meet the requirements of the specification, you need to know about all these aspects of non-experimental methods.

3 There are no Key studies in this topic.

Correlational analysis, p. 158

1 (a) Positive correlation – a relationship between two variables where high scores on one variable are associated with high scores on the other

(b) Negative correlation – a relationship between two variables where high scores on one variable are associated with low scores on the other

2 (a) a strong positive correlation

(b) no correlation

(c) very strong (near perfect) negative correlation

3
- to investigate the extent of variables thought likely to co-vary
- in the early stages of research, to isolate relationships from a complex web of variables
- to establish the reliability and validity of psychological measuring instruments

Studies that have used correlational analysis, p. 158

Kiecolt-Glaser *et al.* (1984)

- Variables investigated:
  - levels of stress
  - functioning of the immune system.
- Method of research used – Natural experiment, involving measurement of immune function and using questionnaires to assess psychological variables
- Correlation found – Negative correlation between levels of stress and functioning of the immune system

Rahe *et al.* (1970)

- Variables investigated:
  - number of 'life events' experienced, measured in Life Change Units
  - incidence of illness.
- Method of research used – Natural experiment, involving measurement of health and using questionnaires to measure life changes.
- Correlation found – Positive correlation (+0.118) between Life Change scores and incidence of illness

Use of naturalistic observation, p. 159

1 You will have your own views about *Big Brother*, but you may have raised the following points:

- The housemates' behaviour is certainly observed (by millions!) and recorded (on TV), but you might question whether the *Big Brother* house is a natural setting.
- Although supposedly a house, the *Big Brother* set can be compared to a giant laboratory, to which the inmates gradually become accustomed and where they behave naturally.
- It is not naturalistic in that attempts are made to influence the behaviour being investigated, through artificial tasks and use of rewards.
- The housemates are aware that they are being observed, but it is arguable whether or not the main observer ('big brother') is participating. 'He' certainly makes his presence felt and his voice heard.

2 (a) The research was naturalistic because the environment was not artificial and the variables were not controlled.

(b) Researching infant deprivation through laboratory experiments would be unethical.

3 (a) Because the research was conducted in the children's homes in everyday situations.

(b) The use of parental observation reduced demand characteristics (validity). Such research could provide the basis for further study, for example into phases of developments in attachments (value).

Ethical issues of naturalistic observation, p. 160

All the ethical issues described apply to children as much as to adults. For example, they have a right to privacy and confidentiality. A particular issue is consent. Children may not always fully understand the implications of issues such as confidentiality or use of findings, and consent would need to be sought from their parents or guardians.

Questionnaire surveys and ethical issues, p. 161

Button and colleagues. would have had to pay particular attention to the following issues:

- Privacy – The girls taking part would have to be assured of complete privacy and confidentiality of information they provided.
- Consent – Button and colleagues had to gain consent both from the girls and from responsible adults. In fact, some head teachers did not give consent, so the sample was incomplete.
- Risk of harm – Discussing such issues as eating disorders and self-esteem can be distressing, so measures would be needed to protect the girls from any psychological harm, e.g. through debriefing and support.

Structured and unstructured interviews, p. 162

2 The number of men interviewed (3,200) meant that several interviewers would have been used. Using a structured interview would ensure that all the interviewers asked the same questions and found out the same kind of information.

The researchers categorized men according to their responses. Having structured interviews would ensure that interviewers used the same criteria when categorizing them.

Research methods exam questions, p. 163

1 A suitable method would be the semi-structured interview. This would enable the researchers to ask some prepared questions about gardening (to gain the information they wanted), but would also give opportunities for the interviewee to expand on their answers.

2 Each person who underwent the gardening therapy would be interviewed by one of the researchers. A number of prepared questions such as 'On a scale of 1 to 10, how relaxed did you feel when gardening?' or 'Which aspect of the gardening did you find most relaxing?' would be put to the interviewee and the interviewer could then probe further as necessary to obtain more complete information. The interview could be tape-recorded so that the researchers could analyse it later, looking for particular themes concerning the therapeutic effectiveness of gardening. For example, they may discover that it was being out in the fresh air that people found most beneficial in reducing stress rather than the gardening itself.

3 A potential ethical issue is maintaining confidentiality. As interviews are to be recorded, permission must be obtained from each person being interviewed, and steps taken to ensure that recordings are made anonymously.

7 RESEARCH DESIGN & IMPLEMENTATION & Data Analysis

PREVIEW

There are two topics in this unit. You should read them alongside the following pages in the Collins *Psychology for AS-level* textbook:

INTRODUCTION

This unit covers the first part of Research Methods in AS Module 3 (AQA Specification A). The diagram below shows where it fits in to the overall AS qualification.

Read the Preview and Introduction on p. 214 of the textbook now. This will give you an overview of what's in the unit.

Where this unit fits in to the AS qualification

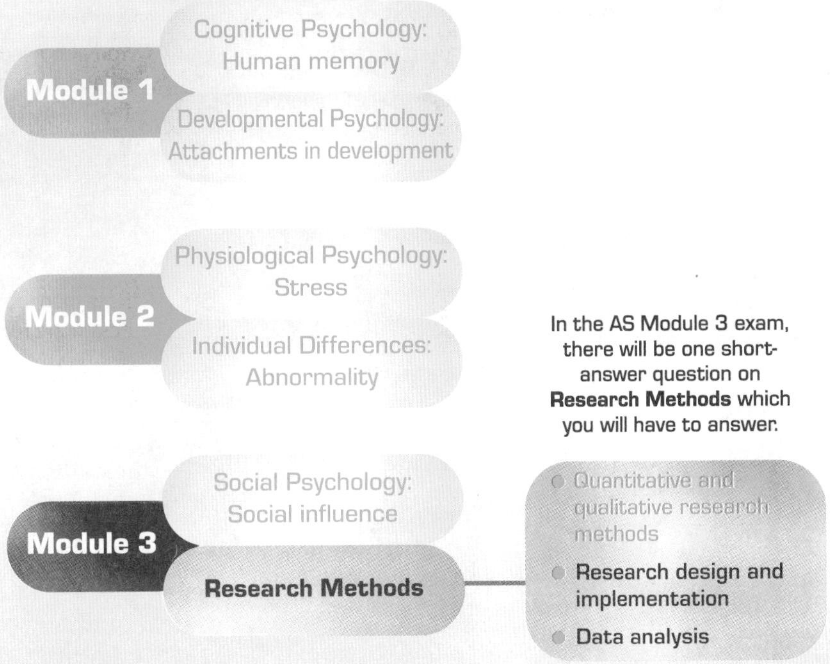

In the AS Module 3 exam, there will be one short-answer question on **Research Methods** which you will have to answer.

Topic 1 >> Research design and implementation

This topic covers a wide range of issues to do with the design of research investigations, both experimental and non-experimental studies. This is a long topic and there is a lot to take in, so you may need to spend a bit of time going over some areas. Most of the 30 marks awarded for the research methods question are for AO3 (Assessment Objective 3), which means that you will be asked to use your knowledge in hypothetical research scenarios, rather than just demonstrate your understanding of what the different concepts mean.

UNDERSTANDING THE SPECIFICATION

Here is what the AQA (A) specification says about this topic. It forms part of AS Module 3, Social Psychology and Research Methods. You will see that the specification lists five types of research method.

Read it and then try the activity below. You'll find answers to the activity on p. 178.

Research Methods

Research design and implementation

a. Aims and hypotheses (including the generation of appropriate aims; the formulation of different types of the experimental/alternative hypothesis (directional/non-directional), and the null hypothesis).

b. Research designs: experimental (including independent groups, repeated measures and matched participants) and the design of naturalistic observations, questionnaire surveys and interviews.

c. Factors associated with research design, including the operationalisation of the IV/DV; conducting pilot studies; control of variables; techniques for assessing and improving reliability and validity (internal and external (ecological) validity); ethics.

d. The selection of participants (including random sampling).

e. The relationship between researchers and participants (including demand characteristics and investigator effects).

ACTIVITY

Understanding the specification

1 Under 'Aims and hypotheses', what three things do you have to study (indicated by the 'including')?

-
-
-

2 How many types of experimental research design will you study in this topic, and what are they?

-
-
-

3 You also need to study the design of three types of non-experimental investigation. What are they?

-
-
-

4 How many factors associated with research design are listed?

-

5 What two aspects of the relationship between researchers and participants do you have to study?

-
-

Compare your answers with those on p. 178.

In this part of the specification you are required to know how to word the aims of an investigation and different kinds of hypothesis. You should be clear on the difference between directional and non-directional hypotheses and their relationship with the null hypothesis. You will need to know the key features of each of the research designs listed, explain why certain designs are chosen over others and be able to demonstrate how you would avoid the pitfalls which lead to poor design. You should be able to name types of reliability and validity and know how to assess and improve them in investigations. You will have learned many important aspects of ethics in the previous section – now you must demonstrate your competence in dealing with ethical issues and applying ethical guidelines. You must know what 'random sampling' means and show a working knowledge of at least two other ways of selecting research participants. You should also be able to explain how researchers and participants can affect each other's behaviour and demonstrate how you can minimize the problems this could cause.

TOPIC MAP

ACTIVITY

Below is a skeleton topic map – most of the boxes have been left blank. Look through pp. 215–29 of the textbook and fill in all the blank boxes.

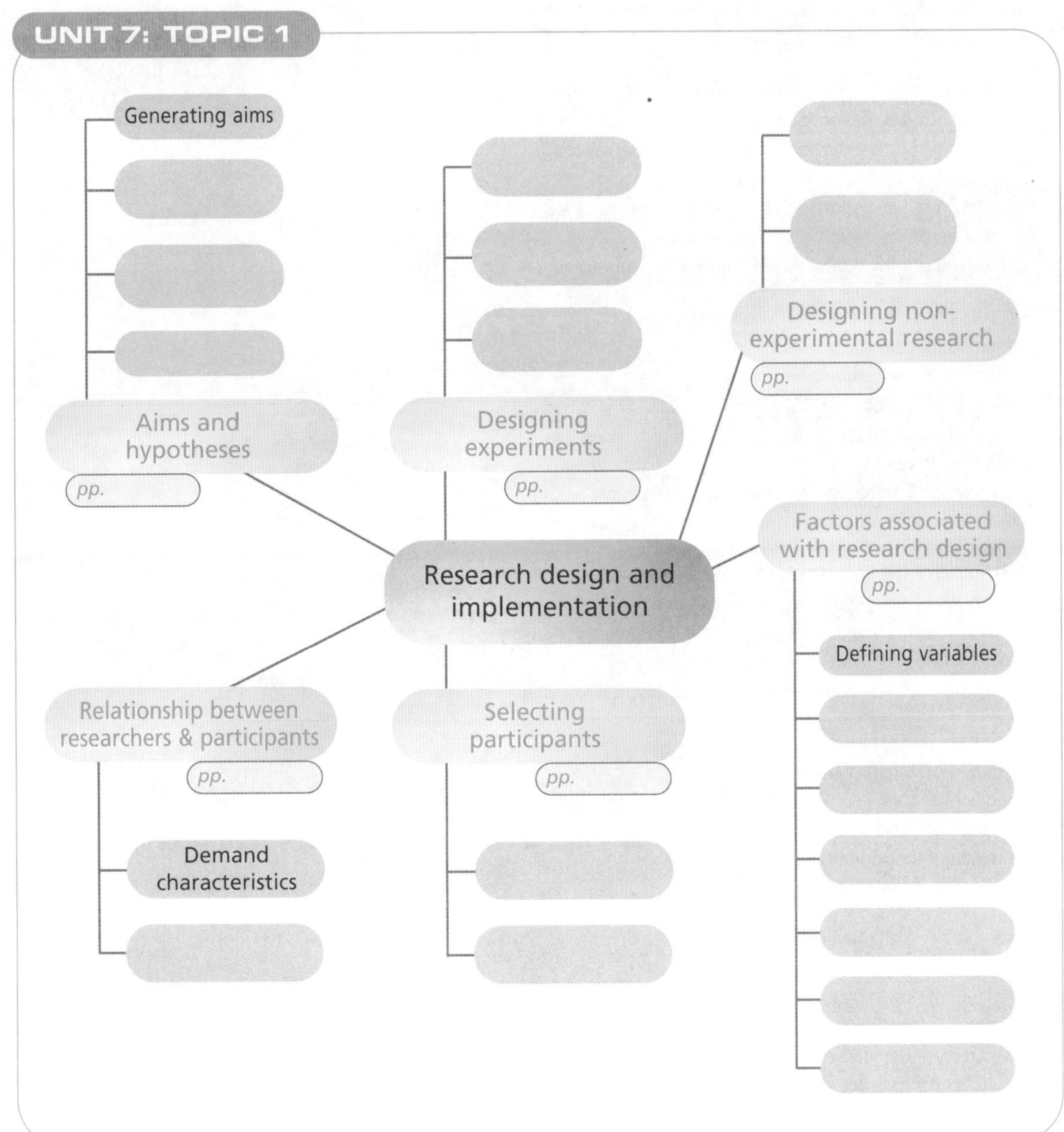

KEEPING TRACK

Use the table below to keep track of your work on this topic and plan your revision. See p. iv (Introduction) for guidance on how to fill it in.

What I need to learn		Tick if you ...		
Aims and hypotheses	Where is it?	could make a basic attempt	could make a good attempt	have complete mastery of this
Definition of 'aim'				
Definition of 'hypothesis'				
Definition of 'null hypothesis' and 'alternative hypothesis'				
Definition of 'directional' and 'non-directional hypothesis'				
Experimental research designs				
Definition of 'independent groups design'				
Definition of 'repeated measures design'				
Definition of 'matched participants design'				
Description of the main features of these experimental designs				
Evaluation of the strengths and weaknesses of these designs				
Non-experimental research designs				
Description of key design issues in naturalistic observations				
Description of how behaviour is sampled in observations				
Description of how data are recorded				
Description of key design issues in questionnaire surveys				
Description of key design issues in interviews				
Description of how questions are phrased and organized				
Factors associated with research design				
Definition of 'operationalization'				
Definition of 'pilot study'				
Definition of 'ethics'				
Definition of 'reliability'				
Definition of 'validity'				
Definition of 'internal validity' and 'external validity'				
Explanation of why independent variables and dependent variables need to be operationalized				
Description of the importance of controlling variables				
Description of the importance of pilot studies				
Description of techniques for assessing and improving reliability				
Description of techniques for improving validity				
Discussion of ethical issues relating to psychological research				
Selecting participants				
Definition of 'target population'				
Definition of 'sample'				
Definition of 'random sample'				
Definition of 'opportunity sample'				
Description of sampling techniques				
The relationship between researchers and participants				
Definition of 'demand characteristics'				
Definition of 'investigator effects'				
Description of the relationship between researchers and participants				
Description of demand characteristics				
Description of investigator effects				

AIMS AND HYPOTHESES

Aims

The aim of any research study describes the intended purpose of the investigation, that is what the investigation is actually going to investigate. As the textbook explains, aims are sometimes quite broad, especially in non-experimental studies based on, say, interviews. In experimental research, aims may be stated quite precisely.

ACTIVITY

Aims

Look at the aims of Key studies contained in this workbook. Note down one example of an aim that is fairly precise and one that is fairly broad. *Hint:* try looking in Unit 1 for a specific aim and in Unit 4 for a broader aim.

- Specific aim: ______
- Broad aim: ______

Compare your answers with those on p. 178.

Hypotheses

A research hypothesis is a testable statement that makes a general prediction at the start of the experiment about what the researcher expects to happen. Hypotheses are used in both experimental and non-experimental research:

- In experimental research, hypotheses propose the existence of a cause-and-effect relationship between two variables.
- In non-experimental research, hypotheses may propose a link or correlation between variables, or may predict a pattern of responses (for example, in the way people behave in particular situations).

Now do the activity on the right.

ACTIVITY

Writing hypotheses

Read the text describing hypotheses on pp. 216–17 of the textbook. What are the qualities of a well-phrased hypothesis?

- ______

Compare your answers with those on p. 178.

ACTIVITY

Understanding hypotheses

Complete the following chart to summarize what the different types of hypothesis are.

When analysing data, researchers test the null hypothesis

Null hypothesis = ______

If the null hypothesis is rejected, researchers may accept the alternative hypothesis

Alternative hypothesis = ______

The alternative hypothesis may be either directional or non-directional

Directional hypothesis: ______

Non-directional hypothesis: ______

ACTIVITY

Directional or non-directional?

State whether the following hypotheses are directional or non-directional:

	Directional	Non-directional
1 There is a link between personality type (A, B or X) and levels of cardiovascular (heart) disease.	____	____
2 Type A behaviour pattern increases levels of cardiovascular (heart) disease.	____	____
3 Childhood sexual abuse is a risk factor for eating disorders.	____	____
4 There is a correlation between marital status of parents and the development of eating disorders.	____	____
5 Features of the work environment such as type of work and levels of responsibility influence the levels of stress suffered by employees.	____	____
6 Repetitive, machine-based work contributes to higher levels of stress among workers than more varied work where employees have control over pacing.	____	____

Compare your answers with those on p. 178.

The activity at the bottom of p. 217 of the textbook will also give you the chance to try writing hypotheses for some research studies. This is something you may be asked to do for the Research Methods question in the exam. The following activity contains an example of the type of question you might be asked.

ACTIVITY

Describing hypotheses

Turn to p. 262 of the textbook and read though the stimulus material at the top of the page.
Now answer the following questions:

1 Give an appropriate experimental/alternative hypothesis for this study. (2 marks)

- ____________________

2 State whether the hypothesis given in response to question 1 is directional or non-directional, and justify your choice. (3 marks)

- ____________________

Compare your answers with those given on p. 262 of the textbook.

DESIGNING EXPERIMENTS

When designing any kind of research, researchers have to make several key decisions. These are summarized on p. 218 of the textbook. If the research is experimental, one of the main decisions is how participants will be used in the experiment. The three options are outlined in the textbook on pp. 219–21.

These experimental designs are known by several different names, but the textbook uses the ones referred to in the AQA AS Psychology specification.

To remember the various names, simply remember the key words:, shown in bold

- **independent** groups (measures, participants) or **between** groups (participants, etc.)
- **repeated** measures (or **related** measures or **within** participants)
- **matched** participants (subjects, pairs).

Independent groups design

In an independent groups design, participants should be allocated randomly. Read what the textbook says about this and the reasons for random allocation (see pp. 219–20).

ACTIVITY

Independent groups design

1 What is the major disadvantage of an independent groups design?

-

2 Read the details of Brady's 'executive monkey' study on p. 84 of the textbook. What were the two 'conditions' in this study?

-
-

In what way did Brady's study demonstrate the need for random allocation of participants in an independent groups design?

-

3 Read what the textbook says about natural experiments (p. 220 second paragraph). Then read the details of Hodges and Tizard's study of children who had spent their early years in an institution (textbook p. 63). What were the two 'conditions' in this study?

-
-

In what way was the children's temperament a possible confounding variable?

-

Compare your answers with those given on p. 178.

Repeated measures design

In a repeated measures design, every participant is exposed to each condition. One danger of this method is so-called 'order effect', mentioned in Table 7.3 on p. 221 of the textbook.

ACTIVITY

Repeated measures design

1 In a repeated measures design, in what way are participants used as their own controls?

-

2 What is meant by the term 'order effect'?

-

3 Order effects can be minimized by either counterbalancing or randomization. Briefly, explain what is meant by these terms:

- counterbalancing:
- randomization:

Compare your answers with those given on p. 178.

Matched participants design

In the matched participants design, participants are paired up on relevant variables (e.g. age, intelligence), with the two people being allocated to different conditions. This should avoid the main problems of the other two designs, i.e. individual differences and order effects.

ACTIVITY

Matched participants design

Read through the stimulus material at the top of p. 262 of the textbook. This describes an experiment with a matched participants design.

1 What were the variables on which the participants were matched up?

-

2 Suggest one advantage and one disadvantage of using a matched participants design in this study. (2 + 2 marks)

- Advantage =
- Disadvantage =

Compare your answers with those on p. 178 of this workbook and p. 263 of the textbook.

The advantages and disadvantages of different experimental designs are explained in Table 7.3 (textbook p. 221). You might find it useful to create your own version, summarizing the main points in a few key words or phrases. The activity below suggests one or two more strengths and weaknesses you could add to your table.

ACTIVITY

Which design?

Which of the three experimental designs described ...

1 is generally most time-consuming and expensive to organize?

2 is generally the easiest to organize?

3 has the danger of demand characteristics, because participants have more opportunity to guess the purpose of the study?

4 requires fewest participants?

5 involves 'rejecting' some possible participants because they don't fit?

6 is most prone to order effects?

7 is most prone to problems of participants' individual differences?

Compare your answers with those on p. 179.

DESIGNING NON-EXPERIMENTAL RESEARCH

This section of the topic covers the three types of non-experimental research covered in Unit 6, namely naturalistic observations, questionnaire surveys and interviews.

ACTIVITY

Designing naturalistic observations

1 Read through the description of sampling given on p. 222 of the textbook and then decide what type of sampling is being described below. The study is a naturalistic observation of children in a playgroup.

(a) Every instance of aggressive behaviour is recorded.

(b) Observations are made every 15 minutes and the child's mood recorded.

(c) Observations are made and recorded about behaviour during the first ten minutes of each hour.

2 Why is sampling necessary in many naturalistic observations?

-

Compare your answers with those on p. 179.

Questionnaire surveys and interviews

In the Research Methods part of the AS exam, the stimulus material could include the description of a questionnaire survey or interview. It might also include an example of relevant 'paperwork', such as the questionnaire itself or an interview schedule. Your task may be to assess the strengths and weaknesses of the material provided. For example, if it is a questionnaire, aspects of the questionnaire you could focus on include the following:

- *Purpose* – How well does the questionnaire serve the overall purpose of the research?
- *Question form* – Are the questions in a suitable form, e.g. open/closed (see textbook p. 207)? Is the number of questions about right?
- *Question wording* – Are the questions well phrased and easy to understand? Is it clear how to answer the questions? Are the questions free from bias or emotiveness (see Table 7.4, textbook p. 223)?
- *Data* – What sort of data are the questions designed to gather – qualitative or quantitative? Is that the most appropriate type of data for the area being investigated?
- *Ethical issues* – What ethical issues are raised (see textbook pp. 208–9) and how are they dealt with?

ACTIVITY

Assessing an interview schedule

Figure 7.3 in the textbook (p. 224) is an example of an interview schedule used in a study of the development of gender identity.

1 What sort of interview would this schedule be used in: structured, semi-structured or unstructured? See textbook p. 209 to remind yourself about different types of interview.

- ______

2 Give one advantage and one disadvantage of using this type of interview for this investigation.

- Advantage = ______
- Disadvantage = ______

3 How appropriate is the form and number of questions for this research?

- ______

4 The following questions in the interview schedule could be criticized for one or more of the reasons listed in Table 7.4 (textbook p. 223). What are these criticisms?

(a) Question 4 ______

(b) Question 5 ______

(c) Question 8 ______

Compare your answers with those given on p. 179.

FACTORS ASSOCIATED WITH RESEARCH DESIGN

Defining and operationalizing variables

You looked in detail at variables in Unit 6 (see textbook pp. 196–7, workbook p. 149), in particular at the difference between dependent and independent variables (DV and IV). Here, the textbook explains what is meant by 'operational' definitions of variables and how operationalizing variables allows researchers to measure them more accurately.

ACTIVITY

Defining and operationalizing variables

Look at the study into duration of long-term memory carried out by Bahrick *et al.* (1975) (textbook p. 11). Here, the dependent variable concerns the measurement of very long-term memory. Operationalizing this variable means finding a way of measuring it accurately.

1 Suggest an operational definition of very long-term memory for this study.

- ______________________________

2 Suggest an operational definition of the IV for this study.

- ______________________________

Compare your answers with those given on p. 179.

Controlling variables

The main point of experimental research is to investigate the relationship between two variables (the IV and the DV). However, in most areas of psychology, as in life generally, things are rarely very simple. Other variables may come into play and have an effect on the relationship being investigated. These unwanted or extraneous variables are said to be confounding when they obscure the findings of the research.

Read what the textbook says on p. 225 about confounding variables and types of error. Then try the activity below.

ACTIVITY

Types of error

1 (a) In the study of stress in the workplace by Johansson *et al.* (textbook p. 94), what unwanted variable might have confounded the results?

- ______________________________

(b) Was this a random or constant error?

- ______________________________

(c) What other unwanted variables might have had an effect on this natural experiment (think about other differences between those studied)?

- ______________________________

____

____

2 (a) In Peterson and Peterson's study of short-term memory (textbook p. 7), what unwanted variable might have confounded the results?

- ______________________________

(b) Was this a random or constant error?

- ______________________________

Compare your answers with those given on p. 179.

In the Research Methods question in the AS exam, you may be given the description of a research study and asked to identify one or more confounding variables affecting it. Typical things to look for include:

- differences between participants, such as age, gender, social class, personality type
- inadequate controls in the experiment, such as when participants are not allocated to conditions appropriately (e.g. not randomly)
- differences in the tasks that participants are asked to perform, or the conditions in which they perform them, or in the way that their performance is measured.

Conducting pilot studies

Read the text on conducting pilot studies on p. 226 of the textbook and then do the activity below.

ACTIVITY

Pilot studies

Summarize the key features of pilot studies, including what they are used for and how they should be designed.

-

Assessing and improving reliability

For a definition of 'reliability', see textbook p. 216. This topic looks at two aspects of reliability: observer reliability and test reliability.

ACTIVITY

Improving observer reliability

Read 'Assessing and improving observer reliability' on p. 226 of the textbook. Then answer the following questions:

1 Why is it important to use more than one observer?

-

2 Describe two ways in which observer reliability can be improved.

-
-

Compare your answers with those given on p. 179.

HINT

Inter-rater reliability

'Inter-rater' means 'between people doing the rating'. 'Inter-rater reliability' is sometimes referred to as 'inter-observer reliability'.

ACTIVITY

Research Methods exam

Turn to p. 262 of the textbook and read though the stimulus material at the top of the page. Answer the following question:

Why was it necessary for both psychologists to interview participants before allocating them to Group A or Group B? (3 marks)

-

Compare your answers with the sample answers given on p. 263 of the textbook.

ACTIVITY

Improving test reliability

1 Read 'Assessing and improving test reliability' on p. 227 of the textbook. Then complete the table to summarize the key points about the two methods of improving test reliability described.

Test method	What it aims to assess	How it does it
Split–half method	●	●
Test–retest method	●	●

2 Read the Key study on p. 47 of the textbook – Ainsworth and Bell's study of attachment using the Strange Situation. Then read the second paragraph on p. 48. Which of the two tests above does this paragraph describe and what did the test demonstrate?

●

Check your answer to question 2 by looking at p. 179.

Assessing and improving validity

The question of validity is considered in detail in Unit 5 Topic 2 (see workbook p. 132), where the question is raised of how valid lab-based research into obedience can be. Look again at that material and check that you understand the difference between experimental validity and ecological validity.

ACTIVITY

Improving test validity

Read the text about 'Test validity' on pp. 227–8 of the textbook. Then complete the table to summarize the key points about the techniques described of assessing test validity.

Technique	How it works	Example of use
Face validity	●	●
Content validity	●	●
Concurrent validity	●	●
Predictive validity	●	●

SELECTING PARTICIPANTS

ACTIVITY

Selecting participants

1 Pages 228–9 of the textbook describe issues involved in selecting participants. Read the text and then without looking back, define the following terms:

- Target population
- Representative sample

2 Complete the following table to summarize the main features of different types of sampling.

Method	How it works	Evaluation (criticism)
Random sampling	•	+ –
Self-selected sample	•	+ –
Opportunity sample	•	+ –

RELATIONSHIP BETWEEN RESEARCHER AND PARTICIPANTS

Problems may arise in research because of the way participants and researchers behave and interact. These problems are described on p. 229 of the textbook. Demand characteristics – where participants try to make sense of the research situation – were mentioned in Unit 6 (see textbook p. 198, workbook p. 151).

ACTIVITY

Participant and researcher behaviour

In the table below summarize the ways in which the behaviour and interaction of participants and researchers can influence research.

Participant behaviour (demand characteristics)	Researcher behaviour (investigator effects)
•	•
•	•
•	•

CHECK YOUR UNDERSTANDING

When you have finished working through this topic, try the questions in 'Check your understanding' on p. 230 of the textbook. Check your answers by looking at the relevant parts of the textbook or this workbook, listed below.

1 textbook p. 216
2 textbook p. 217
3 repeated measures, textbook p. 220
4 textbook p. 221, workbook p. 171
5 textbook p. 222
6 textbook p. 226
7 textbook p. 226
8 textbook p. 226
9 textbook p. 227
10 textbook p. 227
11 textbook pp. 227–8
12 textbook p. 228
13 textbook p. 228
14 textbook p. 229
15 textbook p. 229

ANSWERS TO ACTIVITIES

Understanding the specification, p. 166

1 (a) The generation of appropriate aims
(b) The formulation of different types of the experimental/alternative hypothesis (directional/non-directional)
(c) An accurate statement of the null hypothesis appropriate to each type of experimental/alternative hypothesis

2 There are three types of experimental research design you will look at:
(a) independent groups design
(b) repeated measures design
(c) matched participants design

3 (a) Design of naturalistic observations
(b) Design of questionnaire surveys
(c) Design of interviews

4 Five

5 (a) Demand characteristics
(b) Investigator effects

Aims, p. 169

An example of a precisely stated aim is the Key study on p. 6, Baddeley's study of the capacity of STM.

An example of a broader aim is in the Key study on p. 149.

Writing hypotheses, p. 169

Hypotheses need to be clear and testable.

They need to be stated precisely, but not so precise that they lack more general application.

They should clearly describe the variables being investigated and the type of relationship being predicted (cause-and-effect, correlational).

Directional or non-directional?, p. 170

1 Non-directional
2 Directional
3 Directional
4 Non-directional
5 Non-directional
6 Directional

Independent groups design, p. 171

1 Individual differences in the participants affecting the results.

2 'Yoked' monkeys: received all the shocks and had no control over them.
'Executive' monkeys: were able to press a lever to postpone shocks for 20 seconds.
Brady didn't allocate monkeys randomly to the two conditions, but chose monkeys that were the most active bar-pressers to be 'executives'. This difference between the two groups may have affected the way they responded and so undermined Brady's findings.

3 The two conditions were: (a) children who were adopted and (b) children who were restored to their natural homes.
The children's temperaments may have influenced whether or not they were adopted or restored. For example, children may have been selected for adoption because they were more attractive and socially able. Such children would be more likely to form closer attachments because of their temperament. This factor would then confound the results of the study.

Repeated measures design, p. 171

1 All participants are exposed to each experimental condition. One of the conditions may be the control condition, and so participants' responses to this condition can be compared with their responses to the other condition(s).

2 Order effects are positive or negative influences that occur when participants take part in two or more conditions in a particular order. There may be improvement (because the participant gets better at a particular test through practice) or worsening (because of fatigue or boredom).

3 (a) Counterbalancing involves presenting tasks so that equal numbers of participants do them in different orders.
(b) Randomization involves presenting experimental conditions in a random order.

Matched participants design, p. 172

1 Age and severity of stress-related symptoms.

2 Compare your answers with the sample answers given on p. 263 of the textbook.

Which design?, p. 172

1 Matched participants
2 Independent groups
3 Repeated measures
4 Repeated measures
5 Matched participants
6 Repeated measures
7 Independent groups

Designing naturalistic observations, p. 172

1 (a) Event sampling
(b) Time point sampling
(c) Time interval sampling

2 It may not be practical to observe and record all the participants' behaviour displayed over a period of time, e.g. because that would involve one or more full-time observers.

Assessing an interview schedule, p. 173

1 This is semi-structured. There is a schedule of nine questions, but the questions are fairly open-ended, so interviewees have the chance to expand on their answers.

2 An advantage of this is that the interview has good validity: interviewees can give full, honest answers, rather than being restricted to 'closed' options which may not reflect their true experiences.

A disadvantage is that it may be more difficult to compare interviewees' answers, as different people may respond in different ways to the same question (e.g. with much more detail).

3 The number of questions is appropriate, with a mixture of 'factual' questions about the school's policies and more personal questions about the person's response to them.

The form of questions is interesting: most of the questions are actually phrased as 'closed' questions (e.g. 'Can you ...' to which the answer could be simply 'no'!), but they are open-ended in meaning, asking the interviewee to give examples. It might have been better to phrase them as direct questions, e.g. Question 7: 'What kind of thing would have happened if ...'. The interviewer could then ask for further examples, if the interviewee dries up.

4 (a) Question 4 is rather vague: 'How was children's behaviour dealt with?' – What sort of behaviour is being referred to? Good? Bad? Gender-stereotyped?
(b) Question 5: 'reinforce or challenge stereotyped gender definitions' is rather jargon-laden and might be met with a response of 'What do you mean?'
(c) Question 8 is a double-barrelled question: the first half asks for factual information (examples of ways in which rules were enforced), while the second half asks for a personal response. It's also not clear what is meant by 'them' in the second part. Does it refer to the rules, or the ways in which the rules were enforced?

Defining and operationalizing variables, p. 174

1 An operational definition might be the number of names correctly identified from participant's own high-school yearbook.

2 The IV is whether participants were given a list of names to choose from (recognition) or had to name the photos with no prompt (recall).

Types of error, p. 174

1 (a) Individual differences – people attracted to high-risk demanding jobs may have the type of personality that also makes them vulnerable to stress.
(b) Constant error
(c) There may have been differences in age, gender or social class between the two groups that had an influence on individuals' responses to stress.

2 (a) The counting task was intended to stop participants thinking about the trigrams they had to remember, but may have caused interference, rather than just delay.
(b) Constant error

Improving observer reliability, p. 175

1 In order to get a more consistent or reliable assessment of participants. Observers' independent assessments/scores can be compared (e.g. using correlational analysis) and if there is strong positive correlation, we can be confident that the observations are reliable.

2 Training of observers in the techniques being used.

Reaching agreement about the operational definitions of key terms used in the research.

Improving test reliability, p. 176

2 Test–retest method. The test demonstrated that the Strange Situation Classification is reliable because the classification for individual children is usually the same at different ages.

Topic 2 >> Data analysis

Psychological investigations produce data in a variety of forms. A major distinction is between quantitative (numerical) and qualitative (non-numerical) data. This topic looks at the various ways in which researchers analyse, interpret and present these forms of data.

Whereas quantitative data reflect the traditional 'number-crunching' approach to psychological investigations, qualitative data are generally non-numerical, and may involve what participants said, rather than what they did. These two types of data now co-exist in psychology, so you will find many examples of each technique throughout the textbook. Familiarity with how researchers have used quantitative and qualitative analysis in their research will help you to answer examination questions on this topic.

UNDERSTANDING THE SPECIFICATION

Here is what the AQA (A) specification says about this topic. It forms part of AS Module 3, Social Psychology and Research Methods. You will see that the specification lists four types of data analysis.

Read it and then try the activity below. You'll find answers to the activity on p. 188.

Research Methods

Data analysis

a. Analysis of qualitative data that could be derived from naturalistic observations, questionnaire surveys and interviews.

b. Measures of central tendency and dispersion (including the appropriate use and interpretation of medians, means, modes, ranges and standard deviations).

c. The nature of positive and negative correlations and the interpretation of correlation coefficients.

d. Graphs and charts (including the appropriate use and interpretation of histograms, bar charts, frequency polygons and scattergraphs).

ACTIVITY

Understanding the specification

1 The specification lists three types of non-experimental investigation that produce qualitative data. What are they?

-
-
-

2 How many different types of graphs and charts do you need to know about and what are they?

-
-
-
-

3 What three aspects of correlational analysis do you need to study?

-
-
-

4 According to the specification you need to know about three measures of central tendency. What are they? (You may need to look further ahead in this topic to answer this question.)

-
-
-

5 What two measures of dispersion do you need to know about?

-
-

Compare your answers with those on p. 188.

You will need to demonstrate that you can choose and utilize appropriate techniques of analysis for the qualitative data that might be obtained from the different types of investigation named in the specification.

must know each of the descriptive statistics of central tendency and dispersion listed, and must be able to demonstrate how to apply them correctly (you will not be required to calculate the standard deviation in an exam, but you might be asked to work out a simpler measure, such as a median or range).

You should be able to recognize and interpret positive and negative correlations (e.g. on a scattergraph) and correlation coefficients.

Finally, you must know about each of the 'visual' forms of descriptive data presentation mentioned in the specification, as well as knowing how to interpret them.

TOPIC MAP

ACTIVITY

Below is a skeleton topic map – several of the boxes have been left blank. Look through pp. 231–43 of the textbook and fill in all the blank boxes.

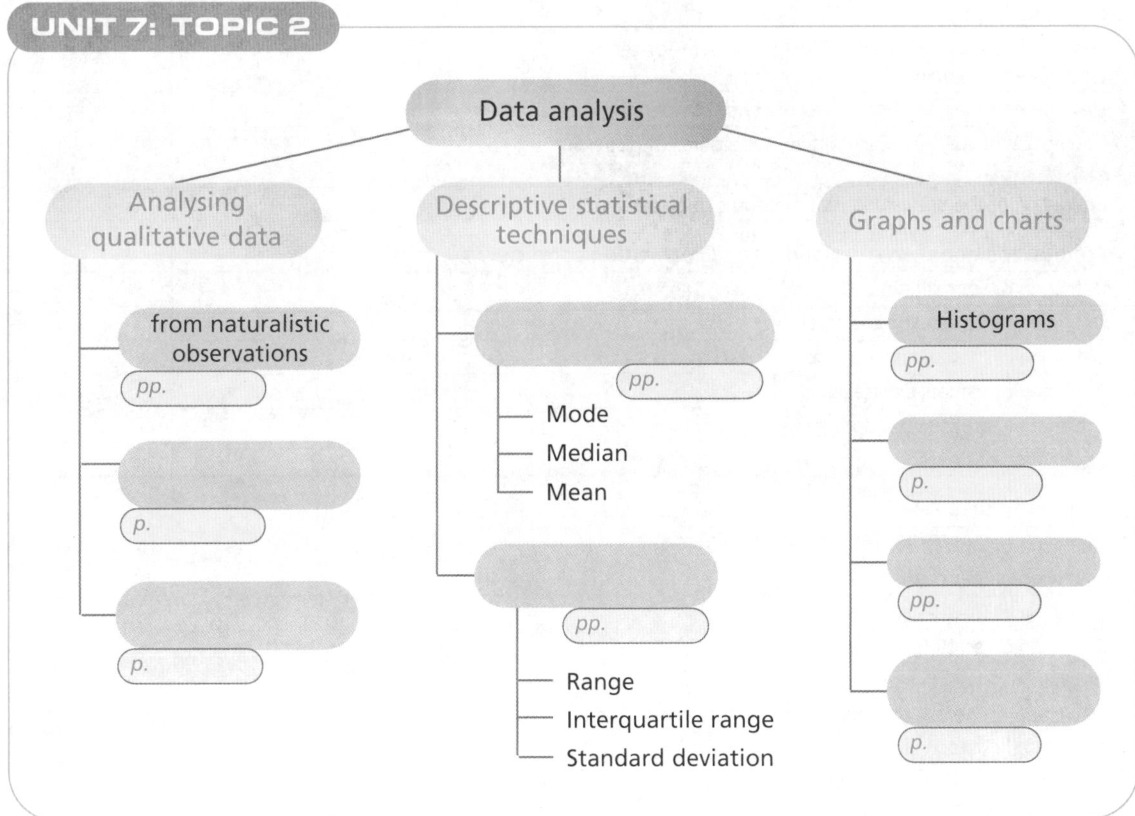

KEEPING TRACK

Use the table below to keep track of your work on this topic and plan your revision. See p. iv (Introduction) for guidance on how to fill it in.

What I need to learn	Where is it?	Tick if you ... could make a basic attempt	could make a good attempt	have complete mastery of this
Analysis of qualitative data				
Description of ways in which data from naturalistic observations may be analysed				
Description of ways in which data from questionnaire surveys may be analysed				
Description of ways in which data from interviews may be analysed				
Measures of central tendency and dispersion				
Definition of 'measures of central tendency'				
Definition of 'mode', 'median' and 'mean'				
Definition of 'measures of dispersion'				
Definition of 'range', 'interquartile range' and 'standard deviation'				
Description of ways in which different measures of central tendency may be used				
Evaluation of the use of measures of central tendency				
Description of ways in which different measures of dispersion may be used				
Evaluation of the use of different measures of dispersion				
Positive and negative correlations, and correlation coefficients				
Definition of 'correlation'				
Definition of 'correlation coefficient'				
Definition of 'positive correlation'				
Definition of 'negative correlation'				
Explanation of positive and negative correlations				
Explanation of how to interpret correlation coefficients				
Graphs and charts				
Definition of 'histogram'				
Definition of 'bar chart'				
Definition of 'frequency polygon'				
Definition of 'scattergraph (scattergram)'				
Description of how different types of chart and graph may be used				
Evaluation of the use of different types of chart and graph				

ANALYSING QUALITATIVE DATA

The techniques used to analyse qualititative data are different from those used to analyse quantitative data. The main difference lies in the nature of the data being analysed. Quantitative data are numerical, which means that they can be analysed mathematically. Qualitative data can exist in all sorts of forms – from transcripts of interviews to hours of videotape recordings of naturalistic observations. Data gathered in these forms need the interpretive skills of the researcher to make sense of them.

ACTIVITY

Analysing qualitative data

Read the text on p. 232 of the textbook and then answer the following questions:

1 When analysing qualititative data, what are researchers usually looking for?

- ____
- ____

2 Broadly, what techniques do researchers use to analyse qualitative data?

- ____

Data from naturalistic observations

Naturalistic observations can produce either qualitative or quantitative data. The diary extract on p. 233 shows an example of qualititative data.

ACTIVITY

Data from naturalistic observations

1 Look at figures 7.1 and 7.2 on p. 222. What kind of data would be gathered by researchers using these recording methods?

- ____

2 Naturalistic observations have good ecological validity, but the textbook mentions three possible 'threats' from the way data are gathered and analysed. What are these?

- ____
- ____
- ____

Compare your answers with those on p. 188.

Data from questionnaire surveys

Questionnaire surveys can also provide either qualitative or quantitative data, depending largely on the types of question asked. Closed questions generally provide quantitative data as the answer options are restricted and so can be analysed mathematically. Open questions will lead to qualitative data, as there is no restriction on what the person answering might say.

ACTIVITY

Data from questionnaire surveys

Read the text under this heading on p. 233 of the textbook, as well as the text on open and closed questions on p. 207.

1 The panel at the bottom of p. 207 gives examples of closed questions. For each of the five examples (checklists, placing items in rank order, etc.), how would you analyse the responses?

(a) Checklist of GCSE subjects studied ____

(b) Placing GCSE subjects in rank order ____

(c) Attitude scales ____

(d) Likert scales ____

(e) Semantic differential scale ____

2 Rewrite the question under 'Likert scales' about factors in relationships as an open question.

- ____

3 Give one advantage and one disadvantage of using an open question instead of a closed one to find out people's views on relationships.

- Advantage: ____
- Disadvantage: ____

Compare your answers with those on p. 188.

Data from interviews

Read the text under this heading on p. 234 of the textbook, as well as the 'Bristol riots' panel on p. 235. As the textbook explains, analysing data from interviews is a complex procedure and there are many pitfalls to avoid. Some of the main issues involve:

- choosing the best way of presenting the data
- distinguishing between facts, researcher's interpretations and participants' interpretations
- remaining objective when selecting participants and presenting data.

ACTIVITY

Data from interviews

Briefly describe one way in which the qualitative data from these interviews might be analysed. (3 marks)

-

Compare your answers with those on p. 188.

ACTIVITY

Analysing qualitative data

Having read about different ways of analysing qualitative data, what do you think are the main strengths and weaknesses of this kind of analysis?

Advantages	Weaknesses
•	•
•	•
•	•

DESCRIPTIVE STATISTICAL TECHNIQUES

Because quantitative data are numerical in form, they can be analysed mathematically. The techniques for summarizing quantitative data are known as descriptive statistics. The two most commonly used techniques are:

- *measures of central tendency* – giving us a typical or 'average' value for a set of data
- *measures of dispersion* – telling us how the data are spread across the range of values.

Measures of central tendency

Statisticians use measures of central tendency as a way of describing the typical or average value in a set of data. The mode, median and mean are three measures of central tendency. They are calculated in different ways and hence can tell us different things about a set of data.

ACTIVITY

Measures of central tendency

Read through the text describing how to calculate and use the mode, median and mean (textbook pp. 235–8). Each of these measures has advantages and weaknesses. Summarize these in the table below.

Measure	Advantages	Weaknesses
Mode	•	•
Median	•	•
Mean	•	•

ACTIVITY

Using measures of central tendency

1 To check that you can calculate each of the three measures of central tendency described, work out the mode, median and mean for each of the following sets of data:

	Mode	Median	Mean
(a) 2 3 3 4 4 6 7 7 7 9 12 13 14			
(b) 12 16 16 22 26 30 32 34 36 40 56 56			
(c) 2.4 2.5 3.0 3.2 3.3 4.2 5.2 7.3 9.0 14.8			

2 For each of these sets of data, how suitable do you think it is to use the mode, median or mean as an indication of the 'typical' value?

(a)

(b)

(c)

Compare your answers with those given on p. 188.

Measures of dispersion

The two main measures of dispersion are the range and the standard deviation. Start by reading the description of the range (and interquartile range) on p. 238 of the textbook, including the panels describing how to calculate them.

ACTIVITY

The range

1 What does the range tell you about a set of data?

•

2 What are the two major disadvantages of the range?

•

•

3 How does the interquartile range overcome one of these disadvantages?

•

4 For each of the three sets of data given in the last activity, work out both the range and the interquartile range.

	Range	Interquartile range
(a)		
(b)		
(c)		

5 Comment on your answers to question 4(c).

•

Compare your answers with those on p. 188.

The standard deviation (SD) provides a measure of how values are spread around the mean in a set of data. The SD is quite complex to calculate (its main disadvantage), but you don't need to know how to calculate it for AS psychology. However, you do need to know what it is and what it tells us. It is also worth remembering the fixed properties described on p. 239 of the textbook and illustrated in Fig. 7.4.

ACTIVITY

The standard deviation

1 Why is the standard deviation the most powerful measure of dispersion?

- ____________________

2 In order for the standard deviation to be meaningful, what two conditions should be met?

- ____________________
- ____________________

3 When data are normally distributed, what percentage of scores lie within two standard deviations either side of the mean?

- ____________________

Compare your answers with those on p. 188.

USING AND INTERPRETING GRAPHS AND CHARTS

Pages 240–2 of the textbook describe several different kinds of graphs and charts, with examples.

ACTIVITY

Graphs and charts

Read pp. 240–1, up to the heading 'Scattergraphs and the interpretation of correlation coefficients'.

1 What is the main advantage of using graphs and charts to present data?

- ____________________

2 What is the main disadvantage?

- ____________________

3 Look at the graph on p. 14 of the textbook. What sort of graph is this and why is that suitable for presenting Glanzer and Cunitz's data?

- ____________________

4 Look at Table 5.2 on p. 173. What kind of graph or chart would be most suitable to present Milgram's findings? Give reasons for your answer.

- ____________________

5 Look at Fig. 7.8 on p. 242. What do the two lines between 0 and 50 on the y-axis mean and why are they there?

- ____________________

Compare your answers with those on p. 188.

HINT

Ordinal and nominal data

Bar charts are used to present data for ordinal or nominal levels of measurement:

- 'Ordinal' refers to items placed **in order**, e.g. 1st, 2nd, 3rd, and so on.
- 'Nominal' refers to items given **names** or labels, as in Fig. 7.6 where the bars are labelled with the terms 'Aggression', 'Autonomy', etc.

Scattergraphs and correlation coefficients

Scattergraphs are used to display correlational relationships. In Unit 6 you looked in some detail at what these are (see textbook pp. 203–5, workbook p. 158). Figure 7.8 (textbook p. 242) shows how correlational relationships appear when plotted on scattergraphs. Note the difference between a strong correlation (where all the crosses fall nearly on a straight line) and a weak correlation (where they are more widely scattered).

The activities on pp. 242 and 243 of the textbook will give you plenty of practice at interpreting correlational relationships and scattergraphs.

ANSWERING EXAM QUESTIONS

Each exam question is worth 30 marks, although there is no set rule that says that this topic must be worth one-third of the marks (i.e. 10 marks). There will, however, certainly be some questions on data analysis to answer. Of the overall 30 marks, 3 are given for AO1 (knowledge and understanding), 6 for AO2 (analysis and evaluation) and by far the most (21) for AO3 (designing, conducting and reporting).

AO1 questions ask you to demonstrate your knowledge of data analysis, but not in the context of the stimulus material. An example of an AO1-type question for data analysis is the following:

- Describe one way in which qualitative data from questionnaire surveys could be analysed. (3 marks)

AO2 questions ask you to demonstrate your ability to evaluate methods of data analysis, but not in the context of the stimulus material. Examples of AO2-type questions for data analysis would include:

- Give one advantage and one disadvantage of the use of the mean as a measure of central tendency. (2 + 2 marks)
- Give two advantages of using a scattergraph to demonstrate correlation. (2 + 2 marks)

AO3 questions ask you to apply your knowledge of data analysis, in the context of the stimulus material. Examples of AO3-type questions for data analysis would include:

- How might the researcher have constructed the interview to obtain data suitable for qualitative analysis? (3 marks)
- Which method of central tendency would be most suitable to use with the data presented in Table 1? Explain your answer. (1 + 2 marks)
- Using the data in Table 2, outline two conclusions that could be drawn from this investigation. (3 + 3 marks)
- Suggest a suitable method of representing these data graphically. Give reasons for your choice. (1 + 2 marks)

CHECK YOUR UNDERSTANDING

When you have finished working through this topic, try the questions in 'Check your understanding' on p. 244 of the textbook. Check your answers by looking at the relevant parts of the textbook or this workbook, listed below.

1. mode, median and mean – textbook p. 235
2. median – textbook p. 236
3. textbook p. 237
4. textbook p. 238
5. range and standard deviation – textbook pp. 238–9; workbook p. 185
6. textbook p. 238
7. textbook pp. 240–1
8. textbook p. 241
9. negative – textbook pp. 241–2
10. textbook pp. 241–2

ANSWERS TO ACTIVITIES

Understanding the specification, p. 180

1
- naturalistic observations
- questionnaire surveys
- interviews

2 There are four types of graphs and charts you need to know about:
- histograms
- bar charts
- frequency polygons
- scattergraphs

3
- nature of positive correlations
- nature of negative correlations
- interpretation of correlation coefficients

4 Measures of cental tendency: mode, median, mean

5 Measures of dispersion: range, standard deviation

Data from naturalistic observations, p. 183

1 Quantitative data

2 The three threats are:
- the way behaviours are categorized, e.g. the operational definitions used
- inadequate sampling
- mishandling or inadequate handling of the system used.

Data from questionnaire surveys, p. 183

1 (a) Checklist of GCSE subjects studied – you could add up the totals for each subject and either rank them in order or work out the percentage of people studying each subject.

(b) Placing GCSE subjects in rank order – you could calculate an average score for each subject based on the rankings totals.

(c) Attitude scales – you could work out the percentages of people responding to each answer on the scale.

(d) Likert scales – you could calculate an average rating for each subject based on the ratings given by all the respondents.

(e) Semantic differential scale – you could assign a value to each position on the scale and work out the average value based on the responses of all the people answering.

2 Which do you think are the most important factors in the relationship between you and your partner?

3 The advantage of an open question is that the factors respondents mention should be the ones that really are important in their relationship. There should be good validity. When prompts are given, respondents may simply 'coast' through questions or may give answers they think they ought to give (demand characteristics).

The disadvantage of an open question is that it is harder to analyse. The quantitative data gained from the closed question can be analysed mathematically and so different factors can be compared.

Data from interviews, p. 184

One way of analysing the data from these interviews is through categorization. This would involve the grouping of common items together (such as statements referring to the police) in order to identify themes within the data.

Measures of central tendency, p. 185

1 (a) Mode = 7, Median = 7, Mean = 7

(b) Modes = 16 and 56, Median = 31, Mean = 31.3

(c) No mode, Median = 3.75, Mean = 5.49

2 (a) All three measures give identical values, so all appear suitable.

(b) The modes are unsuitable as they are both extreme values. The median and mean are very close, so would appear suitable.

(c) There is no mode here. The median is more suitable than the mean, which is affected by the outlying high scores – only three values are above the mean, while seven are below it.

The range, p. 185

1 The range describes the difference between the highest and lowest scores in a set of data.

2 The range gives no indication of the distribution of values and is badly affected by outlying scores.

3 The interquartile range excludes any outlying values by ignoring the top 25 per cent and bottom 25 per cent of values.

4 (a) Range = 13, interquartile range = 10.5 – 3.5 = 7

(b) Range = 45, interquartile range = 38 – 19 = 19

(c) Range = 12.5, interquartile range = 6.25 – 3.1 = 3.15

5 The range is very wide (12.5, where the highest value is 14.8), whereas the interquartile range is much smaller (3.15). This suggests, correctly, that most of the values are grouped relatively closely together, once you exclude the outlying high scores.

The standard deviation, p. 186

1 Because it uses all the scores in a data set.

2 Data should be approximately normally distributed.

Data should be measured in fixed units, with points of measurement an equal distance apart.

3 95.44 per cent.

Graphs and charts, p. 186

1 They act as visual aids, giving us an at-a-glance summary of data and any patterns within the data.

2 They can be misleading when poorly presented or can be manipulated to exaggerate certain features of the data.

3 Frequency polygon. Suitable because it allows us to compare two sets of results on the same graph.

4 Bar chart. The variables shown on the *x*-axis are non-continuous, i.e. separate, so a histogram would not be suitable.

5 They indicate that the *y*-axis has been broken. This is because all the values on the *y*-axis fall between 50 and 80; if the *y*-axis went from 0 to 80, there would be lots of empty space on each graph.